Y0-ABC-406

Publisher
Jim Scheikofer
The Family Handyman®

Director, Publication Services
Sue Baalman-Pohlman
HDA, Inc. (Home Design Alternatives)

Editor
Kimberly King
HDA, Inc. (Home Design Alternatives)

Newsstand Sales
David Algire
Reader's Digest Association, Inc.

Marketing Manager
Andrea Vecchio
The Family Handyman®

Production Manager
Judy Rodriguez
The Family Handyman®

Plans Administrator
Curtis Cadenhead
HDA, Inc. (Home Design Alternatives)

Copyright 2004 by
Home Service Publications, Inc.,
publishers of
The Family Handyman Magazine,
2915 Commers Drive, Suite 700,
Eagan, MN 55121.
Plan copyrights held by home
designer/architect.

The Family Handyman Contents

Vol. 18, No. 8

Featured Homes

Plan #711-065D-0013 is featured on page 67.
Photo courtesy of Studer Residential Designs

Plan #711-001D-0003 is featured on page 113.
Photo courtesy of HDA, Inc., St. Louis, MO

Sections

The Family Handyman magazine and HDA, Inc. (Home Design Alternatives) are pleased to join together to bring you this collection of relaxed living home plans featuring many different styles for many different budgets from some of the nation's leading designers and architects.

Technical Specifications - At the time the construction drawings were prepared, every effort was made to ensure that these plans and speci- fications meet nationally recognized building codes (BOCA, Southern Building Code Congress and others). Because national building codes change or vary from area to area some drawing modifications and/or the assistance of a professional designer or architect may be necessary to comply with your local codes or to accommodate specific building conditions. We advise you to consult with your local building official for information regarding codes governing your area.

On The Cover...

See page 9 for more information on the cover home

Plan #711-011D-0046 is featured on page 9.
Photo courtesy of Alan Mascord Design Associates, Inc., photographer; Bob Greenspan

Reader's Digest

COVERED FRONT PORCH

Plan #711-025D-0018

1,970 total square feet of living area

Price Code C

Special features

- Striking corner fireplace is a stylish addition to the great room
- Open dining room allows the area to flow into the great room for added spaciousness
- Large pantry in the kitchen
- 3 bedrooms, 2 baths, 2-car side entry garage
- Slab foundation

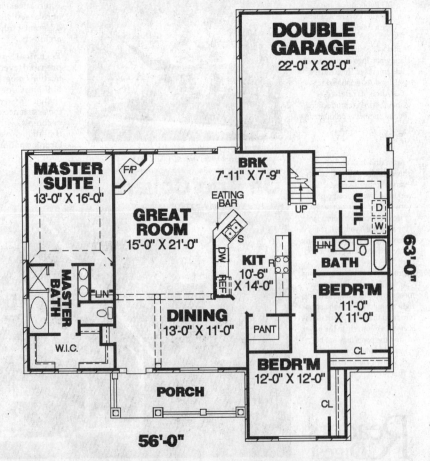

DON'T EXPECT PAINT TO DO A PRIMER'S JOB!

ZINSSER Primers Improve Your Paint's Performance!

Paint is formulated to provide rich, beautiful colors. ZINSSER primers are formulated to provide the ideal surface for paint. Whether it's a new house or an old apartment, your paint job will look better and last longer if you prime with ZINSSER first. Here's why:

- **ZINSSER primers hide previous colors.** They completely block even the darkest colors and prevent them from showing through your new paint job.

- **ZINSSER primers stick to glossy surfaces without tedious sanding.** Prime over glossy paint, clear finishes, metal, Formica® and other slick surfaces – even tile – without sanding.

- **ZINSSER primers seal the surface so you get a more uniform color and sheen.** They seal new drywall, builder's flat paint, new wood – any surface – so your paint job looks better and you use less paint.

- **ZINSSER primers permanently block knots and stains and prevent them from bleeding through the paint.** Water stains, graffiti, ink, grease – even knots in new wood – are no match for ZINSSER primers.

Since 1849, ZINSSER has been the leader for paint primer-sealers and other innovative products for surface sealing and preparation. Get professional results the next time you paint. Prime with ZINSSER first.

Before you paint, prime with...

Practical Two-Story

Plan #711-003D-0001

2,058 total square feet of living area

Price Code C

Special features

- Handsome two-story foyer with balcony creates a spacious entrance area
- Vaulted ceiling in the master bedroom with private dressing area and large walk-in closet
- Skylights furnish natural lighting in the hall and master bath
- Conveniently located second floor laundry closet near bedrooms
- 3 bedrooms, 2 1/2 baths, 2-car garage
- Basement foundation, drawings also include slab and crawl space foundations

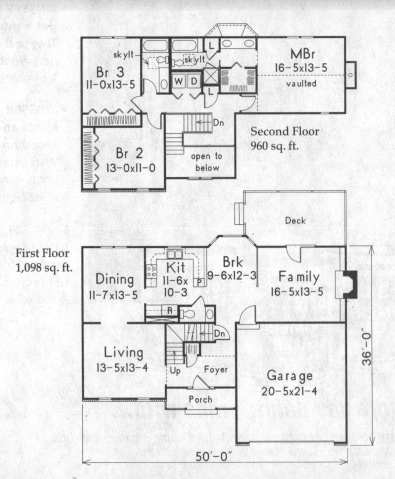

Br 3
11-0x13-5

MBr
16-5x13-5
vaulted

Br 2
13-0x11-0

open to below

Second Floor
960 sq. ft.

First Floor
1,098 sq. ft.

Deck

Dining
11-7x13-5

Kit
11-6x
10-3

Brk
9-6x12-3

Family
16-5x13-5

Living
13-5x13-4

Foyer

Porch

Garage
20-5x21-4

36'-0"

50'-0"

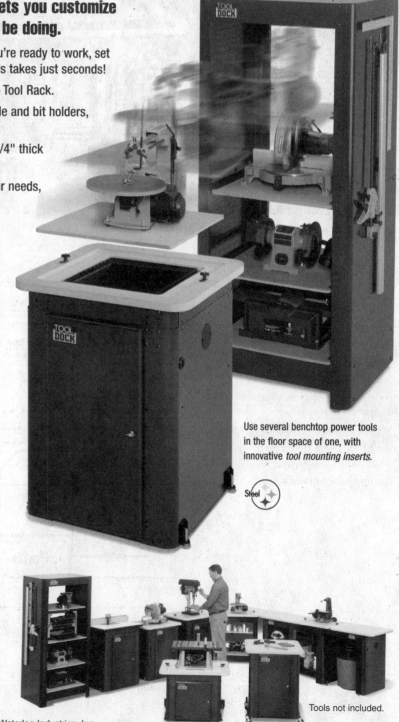

Corner Fireplace In Great Room   Plan #711-038D-0040

1,642 total square feet of living area   Price Code B

Special features

- Built-in cabinet in dining room adds a custom feel
- Secondary bedrooms share an oversized bath
- Master bedroom includes private bath with dressing table
- 3 bedrooms, 2 baths, 2-car garage
- Crawl space foundation

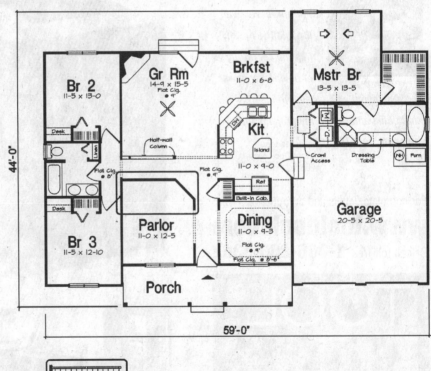

Br 2
11-5 x 13-0

Gr Rm
14-9 x 15-5
Flat Clg.
● 9'

Brkfst
11-0 x 6-8

Mstr Br
13-5 x 13-5

Desk

Linen

Kit.

Island

Flat Clg.
● 8'

Half-wall Column

Flat Clg.
● 9'

11-0 x 9-0

Crawl Access

Dressing Table

Furn.

Desk

Ref.

Built-In Cab.

Garage
20-5 x 20-5

Parlor
11-0 x 12-5

Dining
11-0 x 9-3

Flat Clg.
● 9'

Br 3
11-5 x 12-10

Flat Clg. ● 8'-6"

44'-0"

Porch

59'-0"

DN 14R

Optional Basement Stairs

The Family Handyman

Enhances Any Neighborhood
Plan #711-008D-0010

1,440 total square feet of living area   **Price Code A**

48'-0"

Dining
12-10x11-10
vaulted clg

Kit
8-7x
11-7

Br 3
11-1x11-7

Br 2
11-7x10-1

Great Room
21-8x17-5
vaulted clg

MBr
11-4x14-1

W D

Dn

Porch depth 5-0

Garage
21-4x23-8

54'-0"

Special features

- Kitchen connects to dining room
- Master bedroom enjoys private bath and two closets
- An oversized two-car side entry garage offers plenty of storage for bicycles, lawn equipment, etc.
- 3 bedrooms, 2 baths, 2-car side entry garage
- Basement foundation, drawings also include crawl space and slab foundations

TO ORDER BLUEPRINTS USE THE FORM ON PAGE 15
OR CALL TOLL-FREE 1-877-671-6036
View thousands more home plans online at
www.familyhandyman.com/homeplans

Charming Country Farmhouse

Plan #711-067D-0015

2,571 total square feet of living area

Price Code D

Special features

- 9' ceilings throughout the first floor
- Office/guest bedroom #5 can easily be converted to either an office or bedroom depending on what is needed
- Elegant French doors lead from the kitchen into the formal dining area
- 4 bedrooms, 2 1/2 baths, 2-car side entry garage
- Basement, crawl space or slab foundation, please specify when ordering

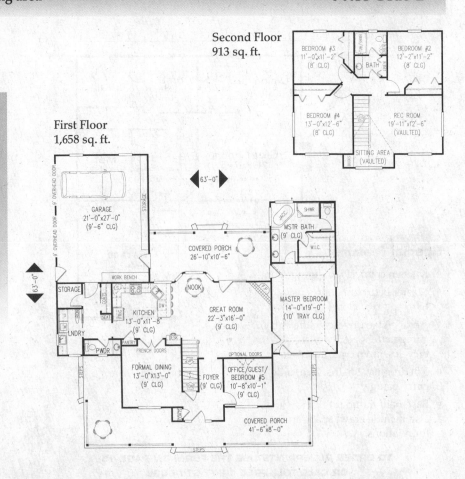

Second Floor
913 sq. ft.

BEDROOM #3
11'-0"x11'-2"
(8' CLG)

BEDROOM #2
12'-2"x11'-2"
(8' CLG)

BATH

BEDROOM #4
13'-0"x12'-6"
(8' CLG)

REC ROOM
19'-11"x12'-6"
(VAULTED)

SITTING AREA
(VAULTED)

First Floor
1,658 sq. ft.

63'-0"

63'-0"

GARAGE
21'-0"x27'-0"
(9'-6" CLG)

STORAGE

COVERED PORCH
26'-10"x10'-6"

MSTR BATH
(9' CLG)

JACC

SHWR

W.I.C.

WORK BENCH

STORAGE

NOOK

KITCHEN
13'-0"x11'-8"
(9' CLG)

GREAT ROOM
22'-3"x16'-0"
(9' CLG)

MASTER BEDROOM
14'-0"x19'-0"
(10' TRAY CLG)

LNDRY

PANTRY

PWDR

FRENCH DOORS

FORMAL DINING
13'-0"x13'-0"
(9' CLG)

FOYER
(9' CLG)

OPTIONAL DOORS

OFFICE/GUEST/
BEDROOM #5
10'-8"x10'-1"
(9' CLG)

COVERED PORCH
41'-6"x8'-0"

STEPS

Wood Beams Create A Tudor Feel   Plan #711-011D-0046

2,277 total square feet of living area

Price Code E

Special features

- Lots of windows in the great room create an inviting feeling
- First floor den/bedroom #4 would make an ideal home office
- Enormous dining area and kitchen combine to create a large gathering area overlooking into great room
- 4 bedrooms, 3 baths, 2-car garage
- Crawl space foundation

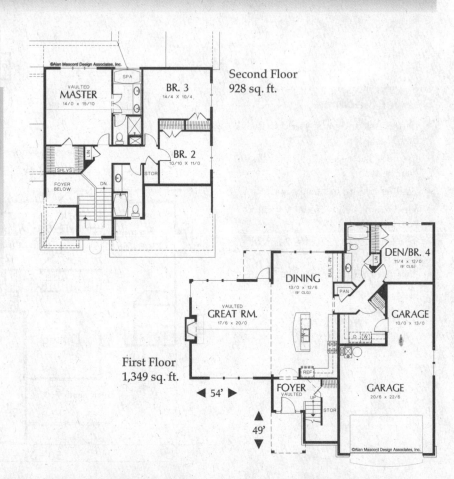

©Alan Mascord Design Associates, Inc.

Second Floor
928 sq. ft.

VAULTED
MASTER
14/0 x 15/10

SPA

BR. 3
14/4 X 10/4

BR. 2
10/10 x 11/0

SHLVS

FOYER
BELOW

DN.

STOR

First Floor
1,349 sq. ft.

VAULTED
GREAT RM.
17/6 x 20/0

DINING
13/0 x 12/6
(9' CLG)

DEN/BR. 4
11/4 x 12/0
(9' CLG)

BUILT-IN

PAN

GARAGE
10/0 x 13/0

REF

FOYER
VAULTED

UP

STOR

GARAGE
20/6 x 22/6

◄ 54' ►

49'

©Alan Mascord Design Associates, Inc.

TO ORDER BLUEPRINTS USE THE FORM ON PAGE 15 OR CALL TOLL-FREE 1-877-671-6036
View thousands more home plans online at www.familyhandyman.com/homeplans

9

The Family Handyman

Angled Porch Greets Guests
Plan #711-058D-0002

2,059 total square feet of living area

Price Code C

Special features

- Large desk and pantry add to the breakfast room
- Laundry is located on second floor near bedrooms
- Vaulted ceiling in master bedroom
- Mud room is conveniently located near garage
- 3 bedrooms, 2 1/2 baths, 2-car garage
- Basement foundation

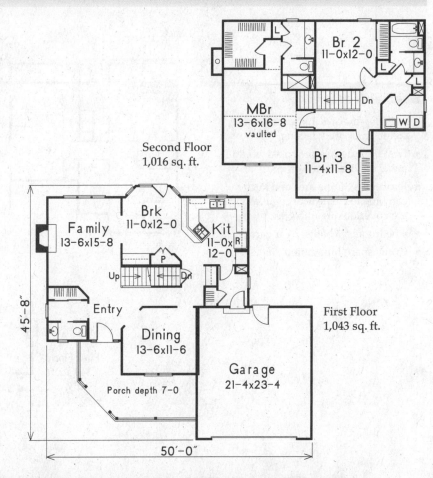

Second Floor
1,016 sq. ft.

First Floor
1,043 sq. ft.

TO ORDER BLUEPRINTS USE THE FORM ON PAGE 15 OR CALL TOLL-FREE 1-877-671-6036
View thousands more home plans online at www.familyhandyman.com/homeplans

Spacious And Functional Home

Plan #711-004D-0001

2,505 total square feet of living area

Price Code D

Special features

- The garage features extra storage area and ample workspace
- Laundry room is accessible from the garage and the outdoors
- Deluxe raised tub and immense walk-in closet grace master bath
- 3 bedrooms, 2 1/2 baths, 2-car side entry garage
- Basement foundation, drawings also include crawl space foundation

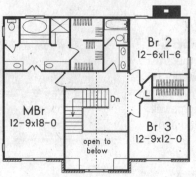

**Second Floor
1,069 sq. ft.**

Br 2
12-6x11-6

MBr
12-9x18-0

Dn

open to
below

Br 3
12-9x12-0

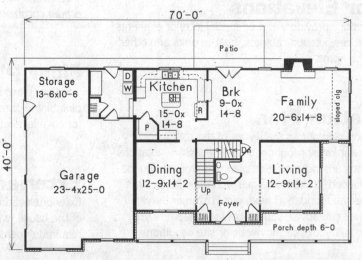

70'-0"

Patio

40'-0"

Storage
13-6x10-6

D
W

Kitchen
15-0x
14-8

Brk
9-0x
14-8

R

Family
20-6x14-8

sloped clg

P

Garage
23-4x25-0

Dining
12-9x14-2

Up

Living
12-9x14-2

Foyer

Porch depth 6-0

**First Floor
1,436 sq. ft.**

TO ORDER BLUEPRINTS USE THE FORM ON PAGE 15 OR CALL TOLL-FREE 1-877-671-6036
View thousands more home plans online at www.familyhandyman.com/homeplans

11

Our Blueprint Packages Offer...

Quality plans for building your future, with extras that provide unsurpassed value, ensure good construction and long-term enjoyment.

A quality home - one that looks good, functions well, and provides years of enjoyment - is a product of many things - design, materials, craftsmanship.

But it's also the result of outstanding blueprints - the actual plans and specifications that tell the builder exactly how to build your home.

And with our BLUEPRINT PACKAGES you get the absolute best. A complete set of blueprints is available for every design in this book. These "working drawings" are highly detailed, resulting in two key benefits:

☐ Better understanding by the contractor of how to build your home and...

☐ More accurate construction estimates.

When you purchase one of our designs, you'll receive all of the BLUEPRINT components shown here - elevations, foundation plan, floor plans, sections, and/or details. Other helpful building aids are also available to help make your dream home a reality.

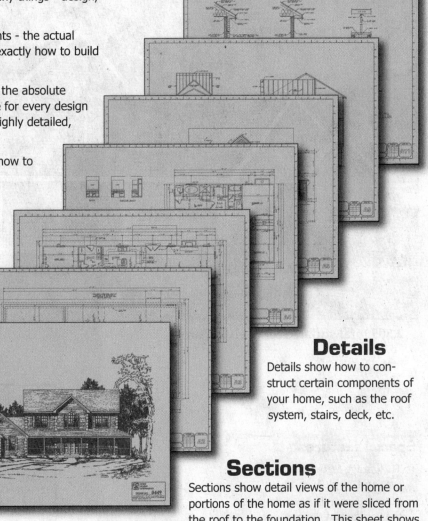

Details

Details show how to construct certain components of your home, such as the roof system, stairs, deck, etc.

Cover Sheet

The cover sheet is the artist's rendering of the exterior of the home. It will give you an idea of how your home will look when completed and landscaped.

Sections

Sections show detail views of the home or portions of the home as if it were sliced from the roof to the foundation. This sheet shows important areas such as load-bearing walls, stairs, joists, trusses and other structural elements, which are critical for proper construction.

Interior Elevations

Interior elevations provide views of special interior elements such as fireplaces, kitchen cabinets, built-in units and other features of the home.

Floor Plans

The floor plans show the placement of walls, doors, closets, plumbing fixtures, electrical outlets, columns, and beams for each level of the home.

Foundation Plan

The foundation plan shows the layout of the basement, crawl space, slab or pier foundation. All necessary notations and dimensions are included. See plan page for the foundation types included. If the home plan you choose does not have your desired foundation type, our Customer Service Representatives can advise you on how to customize your foundation to suit your specific needs or site conditions.

Exterior Elevations

Exterior elevations illustrate the front, rear and both sides of the house, with all details of exterior materials and the required dimensions.

What Kind Of Plan Package Do You Need?

Now that you've found the home you've been looking for, here are some suggestions on how to make your Dream Home a reality. To get started, order the type of plans that fit your particular situation.

YOUR CHOICES

☐ **The 1-Set Study Package -** We offer a 1-set plan package so you can study your home in detail. This one set is considered a study set and is marked "not for construction." It is a copyright violation to reproduce blueprints.

☐ **The Minimum 5-Set Package -** If you're ready to start the construction process, this 5-set package is the minimum number of blueprint sets you will need. It will require keeping close track of each set so they can be used by multiple subcontractors and tradespeople.

☐ **The Standard 8-Set Package -** For best results in terms of cost, schedule and quality of construction, we recommend you order eight (or more) sets of blueprints. Besides one set for yourself, additional sets of blueprints will be required by your mortgage lender, local building department, general contractor and all subcontractors working on foundation, electrical, plumbing, heating/air conditioning, carpentry work, etc.

☐ **Reproducible Masters -** If you wish to make some minor design changes, you'll want to order reproducible masters. These drawings contain the same information as the blueprints but are printed on erasable and reproducible paper which clearly indicates your right to copy or reproduce. This will allow your builder or a local design professional to make the necessary drawing changes without the major expense of redrawing the plans. This package also allows you to print copies of the modified plans as needed. The right of building only one structure from these plans is licensed exclusively to the buyer. You may not use this design to build a second or multiple dwelling(s) without purchasing another blueprint. Each violation of the Copyright Law is punishable in a fine.

☐ **Mirror Reverse Sets -** Plans can be printed in mirror reverse. These plans are useful when the house would fit your site better if all the rooms were on the opposite side than shown. They are simply a mirror image of the original drawings causing the lettering and dimensions to read backwards. Therefore, when ordering mirror reverse drawings, you must purchase at least one set of right-reading plans. Some of our plans are offered mirror reverse right-reading. This means the plan, lettering and dimensions are flipped but read correctly. See the Home Plans Index on page 14 for availability and pricing.

Other Helpful Building Aids...

Your Blueprint Package will contain the necessary construction information to build your home. We also offer the following products and services to save you time and money in the building process.

Material List

Material lists are available for many of the plans in this book. Each list gives you the quantity, dimensions and description of the building materials necessary to construct your home. You'll get faster and more accurate bids from your contractor while saving money by paying for only the materials you need. See the Home Plans Index on page 14 for availability and pricing.

Detail Plan Packages

Framing, Plumbing & Electrical Plan Packages: Three separate packages offer homebuilders details for constructing various foundations; numerous floor, wall and roof framing techniques; simple to complex residential wiring; sump and water softener hookups; plumbing connection methods; installation of septic systems and more. Each package includes three-dimensional illustrations and a glossary of terms. Purchase one or all three. **Cost: $20.00 each or all three for $40.00.**

Note: These drawings do not pertain to a specific home plan.

The Legal Kit™

Our Legal Kit provides contracts and legal forms to help protect you from the potential pitfalls inherent in the building process. The Kit supplies commonly used forms and contracts suitable for homeowners and builders. It can save you a considerable amount of time and help protect you and your assets during and after construction. **Cost: $35.00**

Express Delivery

Most orders are processed within 24 hours of receipt. Please allow 7-10 business days for delivery. If you need to place a rush order, please call us by 11:00 a.m. Monday-Friday CST and ask for express service (allow 1-2 business days).

Technical Assistance

If you have questions, call our technical support line at 1-314-770-2228 between 8:00 a.m. and 5:00 p.m. Monday-Friday CST. Whether it involves design modifications or field assistance, our designers are extremely familiar with all of our designs and will be happy to help you. We want your home to be everything you expect it to be.

HD | HOME DESIGN ALTERNATIVES, INC.

Important Information To Know Before You Order

■ **Exchange Policies -** Since blueprints are printed in response to your order, we cannot honor requests for refunds. However, if for some reason you find that the plan you have purchased does not meet your requirements, you may exchange that plan for another plan in our collection within 90 days of purchase. At the time of the exchange, you will be charged a processing fee of 25% of your original plan package price, plus the difference in price between the plan packages (if applicable) and the cost to ship the new plans to you.

Please note: Reproducible drawings can only be exchanged if the package is unopened.

■ **Building Codes & Requirements -** At the time the construction drawings were prepared, every effort was made to ensure that these plans and specifications meet nationally recognized codes. Our plans conform to most national building codes. Because building codes vary from area to area, some drawing modifications and/or the assistance of a professional designer or architect may be necessary to comply with your local codes or to accommodate specific building site conditions. We advise you to consult with your local building official for information regarding codes governing your area.

Questions? Call Our Customer Service Number
1-877-671-6036

BLUEPRINT PRICE SCHEDULE — BEST VALUE

Price Code	1-Set*	SAVE $110 5-Sets	SAVE $200 8-Sets	Reproducible Masters
AAA	$225	$295	$340	$440
AA	$275	$345	$390	$490
A	$325	$395	$440	$540
B	$375	$445	$490	$590
C	$425	$495	$540	$640
D	$475	$545	$590	$690
E	$525	$595	$640	$740
F	$575	$645	$690	$790
G	$650	$720	$765	$865
H	$755	$825	$870	$970

Plan prices guaranteed through March 31, 2005.
Please note that plans are not refundable.

■ **Additional Sets** -** Additional sets of the plan ordered are available for $45.00 each. Five-set, eight-set, and reproducible packages offer considerable savings.

■ **Mirror Reverse Plans** -** Available for an additional $15.00 per set, these plans are simply a mirror image of the original drawings causing the dimensions and lettering to read backwards. Therefore, when ordering mirror reverse plans, you must purchase at least one set of right-reading plans. Some of our plans are offered mirror reverse right-reading. This means the plan, lettering and dimensions are flipped but read correctly. See the Home Plans Index on page 14 for availability and pricing.

■ **One-Set Study Package* -** We offer a one-set plan package so you can study your home in detail. This one set is considered a study set and is marked "not for construction." It is a copyright violation to reproduce blueprints.

*1-Set Study Packages are not available for all plans.
**Available only within 90 days after purchase of plan package or reproducible masters of same plan.

SHIPPING & HANDLING CHARGES

U.S. SHIPPING	1-4 Sets	5-7 Sets	8 Sets or Reproducibles
Regular (allow 7-10 business days)	$15.00	$17.50	$25.00
Priority (allow 3-5 business days)	$25.00	$30.00	$35.00
Express* (allow 1-2 business days)	$35.00	$40.00	$45.00

CANADA SHIPPING (to/from) - Plans with suffix 032D or 62D

	1-4 Sets	5-7 Sets	8 Sets or Reproducibles
Standard (allow 8-12 business days)	$25.00	$30.00	$35.00
Express* (allow 3-5 business days)	$40.00	$40.00	$45.00

Overseas Shipping/International - Call, fax, or e-mail (plans@hdainc.com) for shipping costs.

* For express delivery please call us by 11:00 a.m. Monday-Friday CST

HOW TO ORDER

For fastest service, Call Toll-Free
1-877-671-6036
24 HOURS A DAY

Three Easy Ways To Order

1. CALL toll-free 1-877-671-6036 for credit card orders. MasterCard, Visa, Discover and American Express are accepted.

2. FAX your order to 1-314-770-2226.

3. MAIL the Order Form to:

HDA, Inc.
4390 Green Ash Drive
St. Louis, MO 63045

ORDER FORM

Please send me -

PLAN NUMBER 711BT - _____

PRICE CODE _____ (see Plan Index)

Specify Foundation Type - see plan page for availability
☐ Slab   ☐ Crawl space   ☐ Pier
☐ Basement   ☐ Walk-out basement

☐ Reproducible Masters $ _____
☐ Eight-Set Plan Package $ _____
☐ Five-Set Plan Package $ _____
☐ One-Set Study Package (no mirror reverse) $ _____
Additional Plan Sets**
_____ (Qty.) at $45.00 each $ _____
Mirror Reverse**
☐Right-reading $150 one-time charge
(see index on page 14 for availability) $ _____
☐Print in Mirror Reverse *(when right-reading is not available)*
_____ (Qty.) at $15.00 each $ _____
☐ Material List** (see page 14) $ _____
☐ Legal Kit (see page 13) $ _____
Detail Plan Packages: (see page 13)
☐ Framing   ☐ Electrical   ☐ Plumbing $ _____
                                SUBTOTAL $ _____
SALES TAX (MO residents add 6%) $ _____
☐ Shipping / Handling (see chart at left) $ _____
TOTAL ENCLOSED (US funds only) $ _____
(Sorry no CODs)

I hereby authorize HDA, Inc. to charge this purchase to my credit card account (check one):

☐ MasterCard   ☐ VISA   ☐ DISCOVER   ☐

Credit Card number_____

Expiration date_____

Signature _____

Name_____
(Please print or type)

Street Address_____
(Please do not use PO Box)

City _____

State _____   Zip _____

Daytime phone number (_____) - _____

I'm a ☐ Builder/Contractor   I ☐ have
      ☐ Homeowner   ☐ have not
      ☐ Renter   selected my general contractor

Thank you for your order!

15

Quick & Easy Customizing
Make Changes To Your Home Plan In 4 Steps

Plan 2829
BEFORE

Here's an affordable and efficient way to make changes to your plan.

1. **Select the house plan that most closely meets your needs.** Purchase of a reproducible master is necessary in order to make changes to a plan.

2. **Call 1-877-671-6036 to place your order.** Tell the sales representative you're interested in customizing a plan. A $50 nonrefundable consultation fee will be charged. You will then be instructed to complete a customization checklist indicating all the changes you wish to make to your plan. You may attach sketches if necessary. If you proceed with the custom changes the $50 will be credited to the total amount charged.

3. **FAX the completed customization checklist** to our design consultant at 1-866-477-5173 or e-mail customize@hdainc.com. Within 24-48* business hours you will be provided with a written cost estimate to modify your plan. Our design consultant will contact you by phone if you wish to discuss any of your changes in greater detail.

4. **Once you approve the estimate,** a 75% retainer fee is collected and customization work gets underway. Preliminary drawings can usually be completed within 5-10* business days. Following approval of the preliminary drawings your design changes are completed within 5-10* business days. Your remaining 25% balance due is collected prior to shipment of your completed drawings. You will be shipped five sets of revised blueprints or a reproducible master, plus a customized materials list if required.

*Prices and Terms are subject to change without notice.

Plan 2829
AFTER

Sample Modification Pricing Guide

The average prices specified below are provided as examples only. They refer to the most commonly requested changes, and are subject to change without notice. Prices for changes will vary or differ, from the prices below, depending on the number of modifications requested, the plan size, style, quality of original plan, format provided to us (originally drawn by hand or computer), and method of design used by the original designer. To obtain a detailed cost estimate or to get more information, please contact us.

Categories	Average Cost*
Adding or removing living space	Quote required
Adding or removing a garage	Starting at $400
Garage: Front entry to side load or vice versa	Starting at $300
Adding a screened porch	Starting at $280
Adding a bonus room in the attic	Starting at $450
Changing full basement to crawl space or vice versa	Starting at $220
Changing full basement to slab or vice versa	Starting at $260
Changing exterior building material	Starting at $200
Changing roof lines	Starting at $360
Adjusting ceiling height	Starting at $280
Adding, moving or removing an exterior opening	$65 per opening
Adding or removing a fireplace	Starting at $90
Modifying a non-bearing wall or room	$65 per room
Changing exterior walls from 2"x4" to 2"x6"	Starting at $200
Redesigning a bathroom or a kitchen	Starting at $120
Reverse plan right reading	Quote required
Adapting plans for local building code requirements	Quote required
Engineering and Architectural stamping and services	Quote required
Adjust plan for handicapped accessibility	Quote required
Interactive Illustrations (choices of exterior materials)	Quote required
Metric conversion of home plan	Starting at $400

*Prices and Terms are subject to change without notice.

Formal Living And Dining Areas   Plan #711-051D-0015

2,380 total square feet of living area

Price Code D

Special features

- Family room makes a statement with windows flanking a center fireplace
- Large kitchen is ideal for family gathering
- The secluded master bedroom makes a cozy place to relax
- 3 bedrooms, 2 baths, 3-car side entry garage
- Basement foundation

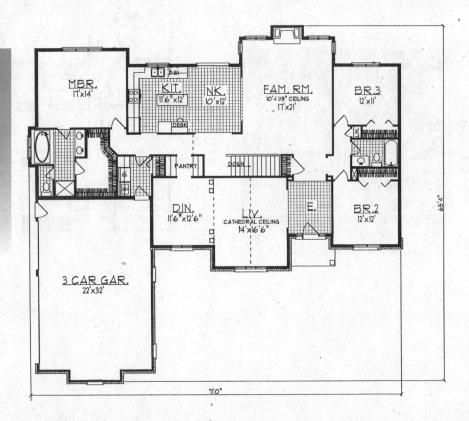

TO ORDER BLUEPRINTS USE THE FORM ON PAGE 15 OR CALL TOLL-FREE 1-877-671-6036
View thousands more home plans online at www.familyhandyman.com/HOMEPLANS

17

Unique L-Shaped Design

Plan #711-011D-0011

2,155 total square feet of living area

Price Code C

Special features

- Great room has 10' tray ceiling, corner fireplace and columns
- Well-appointed master suite features a 10' tray ceiling
- Two secondary bedrooms share a bath
- Secluded den makes an ideal home office
- 3 bedrooms, 2 1/2 baths, 3-car side entry garage
- Crawl space foundation

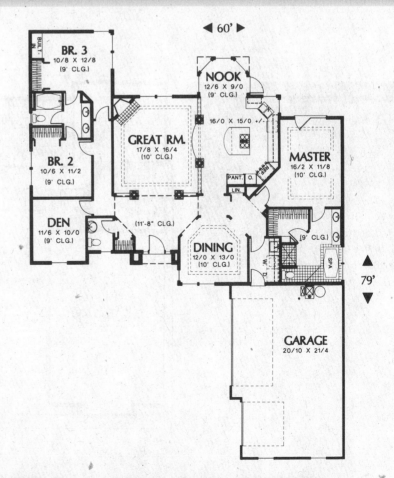

Sculptured Roof Line And Facade   Plan #711-006D-0003

1,674 total square feet of living area   **Price Code B**

Special features

- Vaulted great room, dining area and kitchen all enjoy central fireplace and log bin
- Convenient laundry / mud room located between garage and family area with handy stairs to basement
- Easily expandable screened porch and adjacent patio with access from dining area
- Master bedroom features full bath with tub, separate shower and walk-in closet
- 3 bedrooms, 2 baths, 2-car garage
- Basement foundation, drawings also include crawl space and slab foundations

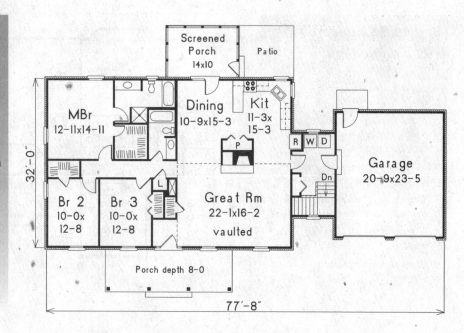

TO ORDER BLUEPRINTS USE THE FORM ON PAGE 15 OR CALL TOLL-FREE 1-877-671-6036
View thousands more home plans online at www.familyhandyman.com/homeplans

19

High Ceilings Create Openness

Plan #711-058D-0027

2,516 total square feet of living area

Price Code D

Special features

- 12' ceilings in living areas
- Plenty of closet space in this open ranch plan
- Large kitchen/breakfast area joins great room via see-through fireplace creating two large entering spaces
- Large three-car garage has extra storage area
- The master bedroom has an eye-catching bay window
- 3 bedrooms, 2 1/2 baths, 3-car garage
- Basement foundation

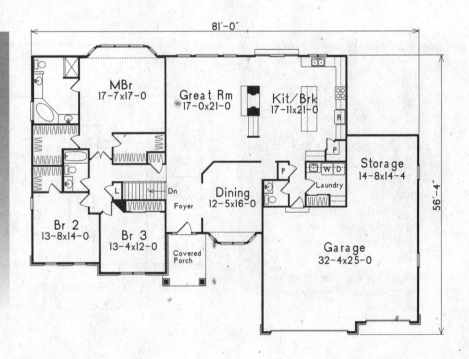

Spectacular View In Great Room   Plan #711-027D-0002

3,796 total square feet of living area   **Price Code F**

Special features

- Entry foyer leads directly to great room with fireplace and wonderful view through wall of windows
- Kitchen and breakfast room feature large island cooktop, pantry and easy access outdoors
- Master bedroom includes vaulted ceiling and pocket door entrance into master bath that features double-bowl vanity and a large tub
- 4 bedrooms, 3 1/2 baths, 2-car garage
- Basement foundation

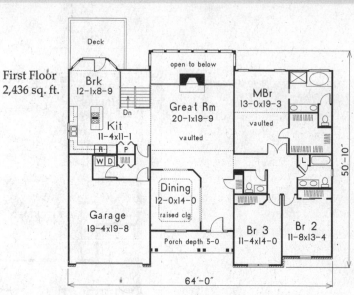

First Floor 2,436 sq. ft.

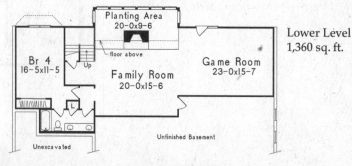

Lower Level 1,360 sq. ft.

Built-In Computer Desk

Plan #711-055D-0017

1,525 total square feet of living area

Price Code B

Special features

- Corner fireplace is highlighted in the great room
- Unique glass block window over whirlpool tub in master bath brightens interior
- Open bar overlooks both the kitchen and great room
- Breakfast room leads to an outdoor grilling and covered porch
- 3 bedrooms, 2 baths, 2-car garage
- Basement, walk-out basement, crawl space or slab foundation, please specify when ordering

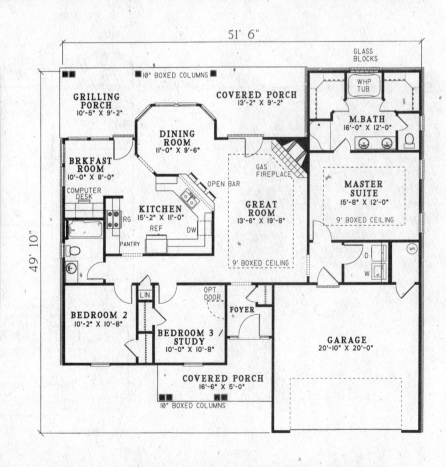

Optimum Style For Family Living   Plan #711-067D-0010

2,431 total square feet of living area   **Price Code D**

Special features

- Second floor includes a wonderful casual family room with corner fireplace and reading nook
- The great room, living and dining areas all combine to create one large space ideal for entertaining or family gatherings
- Built-in pantry in breakfast area
- 4 bedrooms, 2 1/2 baths, 2-car garage with shop/storage area
- Basement, crawl space or slab foundation, please specify when ordering

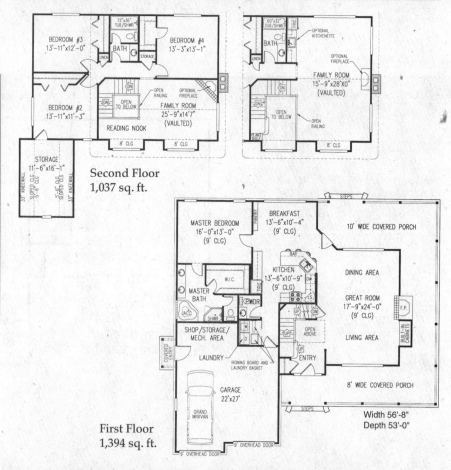

Second Floor
1,037 sq. ft.

BEDROOM #3
13'-11"x12'-0"

BEDROOM #2
13'-11"x11'-3"

BATH

BEDROOM #4
13'-3"x13'-1"

72"x36"
TUB/SHWR

LINEN
STORAGE

OPEN TO BELOW

OPEN RAILING

OPTIONAL FIREPLACE

FAMILY ROOM
25'-9"x14'-7"
(VAULTED)

READING NOOK

8' CLG   8' CLG

STORAGE
11'-6"x16'-1"
SLOPED CLG
5'-6" CLG

33" KNEEWALL

BATH

60"x32"
TUB/SHWR

LINEN

OPTIONAL KITCHENETTE

OPTIONAL FIREPLACE

FAMILY ROOM
15'-9"x28'X0"
(VAULTED)

OPEN TO BELOW

OPEN RAILING

PLANT SHELF

8' CLG

First Floor
1,394 sq. ft.

MASTER BEDROOM
16'-0"x13'-0"
(9' CLG)

BREAKFAST
13'-6"x10'-4"
(9' CLG)

10' WIDE COVERED PORCH

KITCHEN
13'-6"x10'-9"
(9' CLG)

DINING AREA

GREAT ROOM
17'-9"x24'-0"
(9' CLG)

LIVING AREA

BUILT-IN CABINETS

F.P.

W.I.C.

MASTER BATH

WDR

SHOP/STORAGE/
MECH. AREA

LAUNDRY

IRONING BOARD AND
LAUNDRY BASKET

OPEN ABOVE

ENTRY

COVERED ENTRY

GARAGE
22'x27'

GRAND MINIVAN

9' OVERHEAD DOOR   9' OVERHEAD DOOR

STEPS

8' WIDE COVERED PORCH

Width 56'-8"
Depth 53'-0"

TO ORDER BLUEPRINTS USE THE FORM ON PAGE 15 OR CALL TOLL-FREE 1-877-671-6036
View thousands more home plans online at www.familyhandyman.com/homeplans

23

1,253 total square feet of living area   **Price Code A**

Special features

- Sloped ceiling and fireplace in family room add drama
- U-shaped kitchen is efficiently designed
- Large walk-in closets are found in all the bedrooms
- 3 bedrooms, 2 baths, 2-car garage
- Crawl space or slab foundation, please specify when ordering

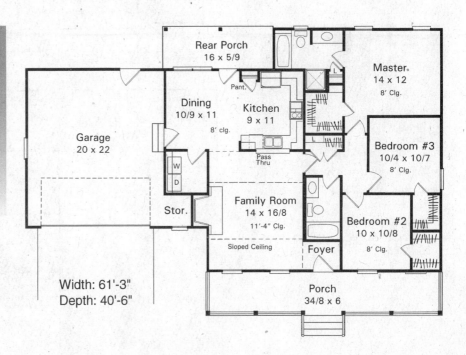

Rear Porch
16 x 5/9

Master
14 x 12
8' Clg.

Pant.

Dining
10/9 x 11
8' clg.

Kitchen
9 x 11

Garage
20 x 22

Bedroom #3
10/4 x 10/7
8' Clg.

Pass
Thru

W
D

Stor.

Family Room
14 x 16/8
11'-4" Clg.

Bedroom #2
10 x 10/8
8' Clg.

Sloped Ceiling

Foyer

Width: 61'-3"
Depth: 40'-6"

Porch
34/8 x 6

First Floor Creates Open Living   Plan #711-056D-0011

2,379 total square feet of living area

Price Code D

Special features

- Second floor laundry room is convenient to all bedrooms
- See-through fireplace enhances the family room and grand room
- Dining room is accented with columns and is open to grand room
- 4 bedrooms, 2 1/2 baths, 2-car garage
- Basement foundation

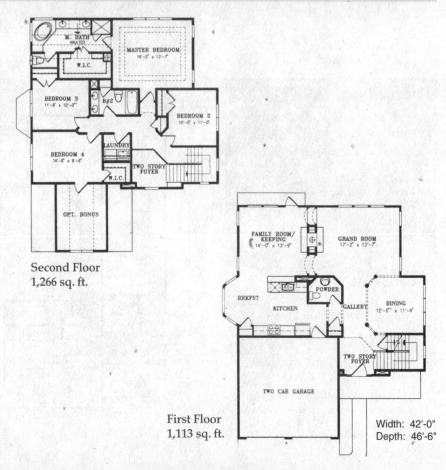

Second Floor
1,266 sq. ft.

M. BATH VAULTED

MASTER BEDROOM
16'-5" x 13'-7"

W.I.C.

BEDROOM 3
11'-9" x 10'-0"

B#2

BEDROOM 2
10'-0" x 11'-0"

BEDROOM 4
14'-6" x 9'-6"

LAUNDRY

TWO STORY FOYER

W.I.C.

OPT. BONUS

FAMILY ROOM/ KEEPING
14'-0" x 13'-9"

GRAND ROOM
17'-2" x 13'-7"

BRKFST

KITCHEN

POWDER

GALLERY

DINING
12'-0" x 11'-4"

TWO STORY FOYER

TWO CAR GARAGE

First Floor
1,113 sq. ft.

Width: 42'-0"
Depth: 46'-6"

TO ORDER BLUEPRINTS USE THE FORM ON PAGE 15 OR CALL TOLL-FREE 1-877-671-6036
View thousands more home plans online at www.familyhandyman.com/homeplans

25

Home With Front Orientation   Plan #711-007D-0055

J.N. HANSEN S.D.G.

2,029 total square feet of living area   **Price Code D**

Special features

- Stonework, gables, roof dormer and double porches create a country flavor
- Kitchen enjoys extravagant cabinetry and counterspace in a bay, island snack bar, built-in pantry and cheery dining area with multiple tall windows
- Angled stair descends from large entry with wood columns and is open to vaulted great room with corner fireplace
- Master bedroom boasts two walk-in closets, double-doors leading to an opulent master bath and a private porch
- 3 bedrooms, 2 baths, 2-car side entry garage
- Basement foundation, drawings also include crawl space and slab foundations

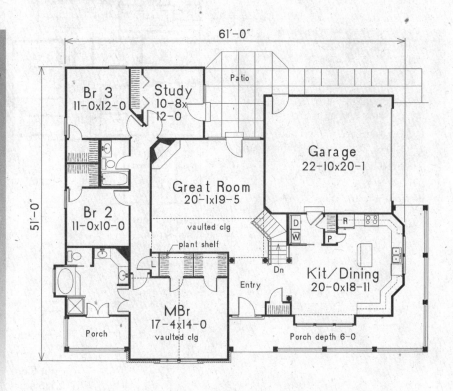

Wrap-Around Country-Style Home   Plan #711-037D-0004

2,449 total square feet of living area

Price Code E

Special features

- Striking living area features fireplace flanked with windows, cathedral ceiling and balcony
- First floor master bedroom has twin walk-in closets and large linen storage
- Dormers add space for desks or seats
- 3 bedrooms, 2 1/2 baths, 2-car detached garage
- Slab foundation, drawings also include crawl space foundation

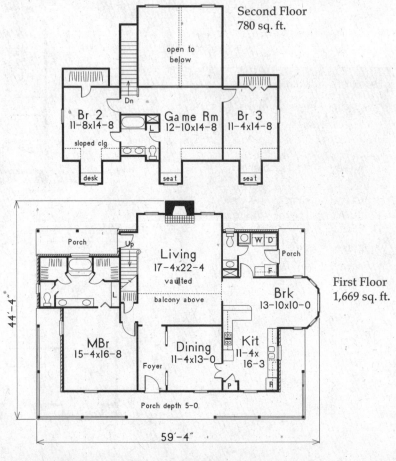

Second Floor
780 sq. ft.

open to below

Br 2
11-8x14-8

Game Rm
12-10x14-8

Br 3
11-4x14-8

sloped clg

desk   seat   seat

Dn

First Floor
1,669 sq. ft.

Porch   Up   Living
17-4x22-4
vaulted

W D
F

Porch

Brk
13-10x10-0

balcony above

MBr
15-4x16-8

Dining
11-4x13-0

Kit
11-4x
16-3

Foyer

P

R

44'-4"

Porch depth 5-0

59'-4"

TO ORDER BLUEPRINTS USE THE FORM ON PAGE 15 OR CALL TOLL-FREE 1-877-671-6036
View thousands more home plans online at www.familyhandyman.com/homeplans

27

Large Two-Story Foyer

Plan #711-033D-0001

2,733 total square feet of living area

Price Code F

Special features

- 9' ceilings throughout first floor
- Master bedroom features double-door entry, large bay window and master bath with walk-in closet and separate tub and shower
- Efficiently designed kitchen adjoins an octagon-shaped breakfast nook, which opens to the outdoors
- 4 bedrooms, 2 1/2 baths, 2-car garage
- Basement foundation

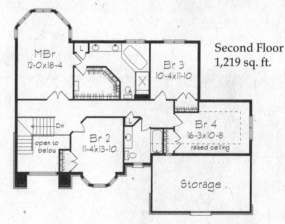

Second Floor 1,219 sq. ft.

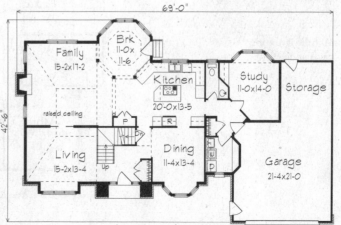

First Floor 1,514 sq. ft.

Circular Stairway Adds To Entry   Plan #711-021D-0020

2,360 total square feet of living area

Price Code D

Special features

- Master bedroom includes sitting area and large bath
- Sloped family room ceiling provides view from second floor balcony
- Kitchen features island bar and walk-in butler's pantry
- 3 bedrooms, 2 1/2 baths, 2-car side entry garage
- Crawl space foundation, drawings also include slab and basement foundations

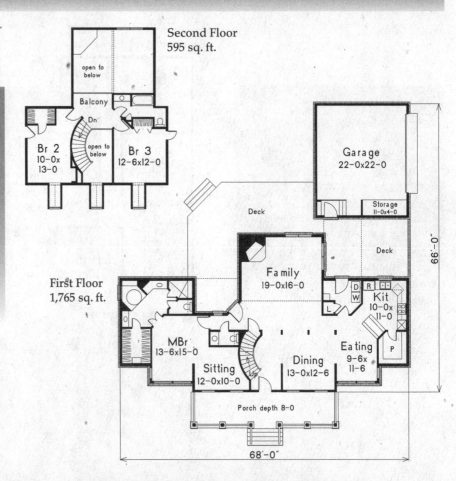

Second Floor
595 sq. ft.

open to below

Balcony
Dn

open to below

Br 2
10-0x
13-0

Br 3
12-6x12-0

First Floor
1,765 sq. ft.

Garage
22-0x22-0

Storage
11-0x4-0

Deck

Deck

Family
19-0x16-0

D W R
Kit
10-0x
11-0

L

MBr
13-6x15-0

Eating
9-6x
11-6

P

Sitting
12-0x10-0

Up

Dining
13-0x12-6

66'-0"

Porch depth 8-0

68'-0"

TO ORDER BLUEPRINTS USE THE FORM ON PAGE 15 OR CALL TOLL-FREE 1-877-671-6036
View thousands more home plans online at www.familyhandyman.com/homeplans

29

Soaring Covered Portico

Plan #711-048D-0009

2,041 total square feet of living area

Price Code C

Special features

- Columned foyer projects past living and dining rooms into family room
- Kitchen conveniently accesses dining room and breakfast area
- Master bedroom features double-doors to patio and pocket door to master bath with walk-in closet, double-bowl vanity and tub
- 4 bedrooms, 2 baths, 2-car garage
- Slab foundation, drawings also include crawl space foundation

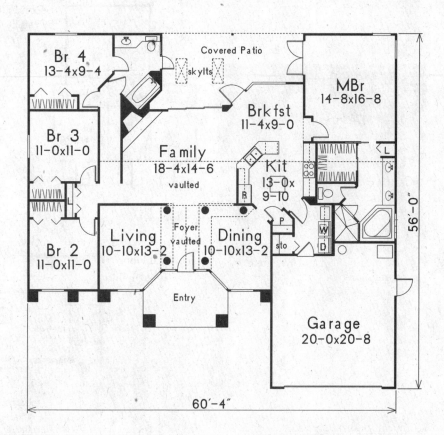

30

TO ORDER BLUEPRINTS USE THE FORM ON PAGE 15 OR CALL TOLL-FREE 1-877-671-6036
View thousands more home plans online at www.familyhandyman.com/homeplans

1,912 total square feet of living area

Price Code D

Special features

- The kitchen enjoys an abundance of counterspace and opens to the dinette with extra seating
- A cozy atmosphere is created in the bayed dinette
- The expansive great room boasts a 10' ceiling
- The entry opens into the formal dining room with a beautiful picture window
- 3 bedrooms, 2 1/2 baths, 3-car garage
- Basement foundation

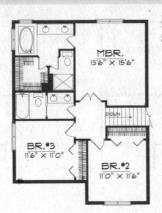

Second Floor
826 sq. ft.

MBR.
13'6" X 15'6"

BR.#3
11'6" X 11'0"

BR.#2
11'0" X 11'6"

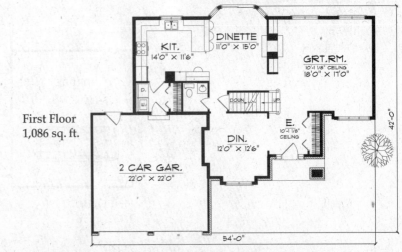

First Floor
1,086 sq. ft.

KIT.
14'0" X 11'6"

DINETTE
11'0" X 15'0"

GRT.RM.
10'-1 1/8" CEILING
18'0" X 17'0"

DIN.
12'0" X 12'6"

2 CAR GAR.
22'0" X 22'0"

54'-0"

42'-0"

TO ORDER BLUEPRINTS USE THE FORM ON PAGE 15 OR CALL TOLL-FREE 1-877-671-6036
View thousands more home plans online at www.familyhandyman.com/HOMEPLANS

31

Dormers Create A Farmhouse Feel   Plan #711-070D-0006

1,841 total square feet of living area   **Price Code C**

Special features

- Sunny bayed breakfast room is cheerful for meals
- The master suite remains separate from the other bedrooms for privacy
- Bonus rooms on the second floor have a total of 295 additional square feet of living area
- 3 bedrooms, 2 1/2 baths, 2-car side entry garage
- Basement foundation

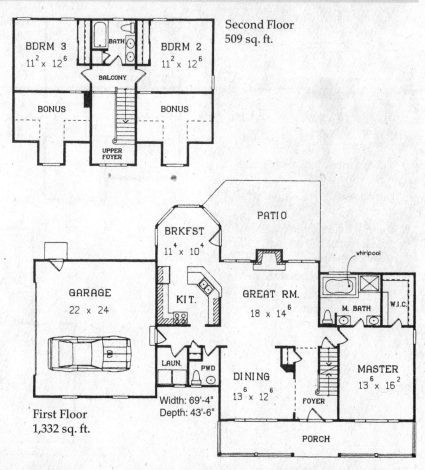

Second Floor
509 sq. ft.

BDRM 3
11² x 12⁶

BATH

BDRM 2
11² x 12⁶

BALCONY

BONUS

BONUS

UPPER FOYER

BRKFST
11⁴ x 10⁴

PATIO

whirlpool

GARAGE
22 x 24

KIT.

GREAT RM.
18 x 14⁶

M. BATH

W.I.C.

LAUN.

PWD

DINING
13⁶ x 12⁶

FOYER

MASTER
13⁶ x 16²

Width: 69'-4"
Depth: 43'-6"

First Floor
1,332 sq. ft.

PORCH

Ranch With Classy Features   Plan #711-001D-0007

2,874 total square feet of living area   **Price Code E**

Special features

- Large family room with sloped ceiling and wood beams adjoins the kitchen and breakfast area with windows on two walls
- Large foyer opens to family room with massive stone fireplace and open stairs to the basement
- Private master bedroom with raised tub under the bay window, dramatic dressing area and a huge walk-in closet
- 4 bedrooms, 2 1/2 baths, 2-car side entry garage
- Basement foundation

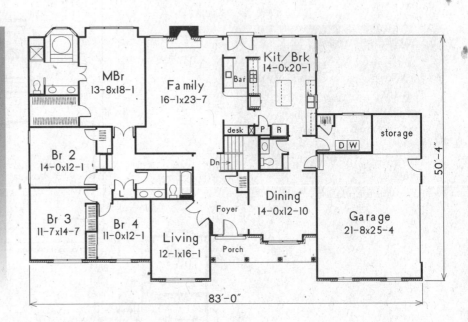

TO ORDER BLUEPRINTS USE THE FORM ON PAGE 15 OR CALL TOLL-FREE 1-877-671-6036
View thousands more home plans online at www.familyhandyman.com/homeplans

33

2,115 total square feet of living area

Price Code C

Special features

- Cathedral ceiling in great room adds spaciousness
- Two-story foyer is a grand entrance
- Efficiently designed kitchen with breakfast area, snack bar and built-in desk
- 4 bedrooms, 2 1/2 baths, 3-car garage
- Basement foundation

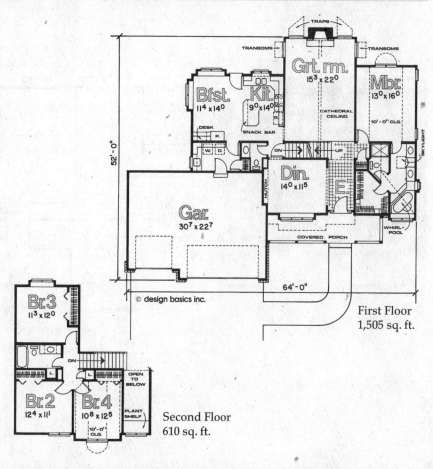

First Floor
1,505 sq. ft.

Second Floor
610 sq. ft.

Stately Home

Plan #711-053D-0025

3,017 total square feet of living area

Price Code E

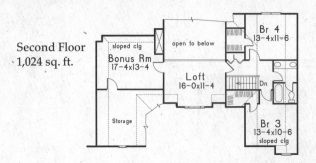

Second Floor
1,024 sq. ft.

sloped clg | open to below

Bonus Rm
17-4x13-4

Br 4
13-4x11-6

Loft
16-0x11-4

Dn

Storage

Br 3
13-4x10-6
sloped clg

Special features

- Convenient L-shaped entry brings formality to this 1 1/2 story plan
- Loft features palladian window overlooking family room
- First floor bedrooms each have a private full bath
- Master bedroom includes bay window and a corner tub in the bath
- Bonus room above the garage is included in the square footage
- 4 bedrooms, 3 1/2 baths, 2-car side entry garage
- Partial basement/crawl space foundation

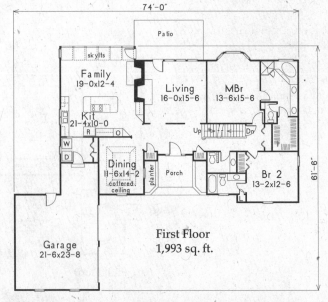

74'-0"

Patio

skylts

Family
19-0x12-4

Living
16-0x15-6

MBr
13-6x15-6

Kit
21-4x10-0

Up

Dn

61'-6"

W
D

Dining
11-6x14-2
coffered ceiling

planter

Porch

Br 2
13-2x12-6

Garage
21-6x23-8

First Floor
1,993 sq. ft.

TO ORDER BLUEPRINTS USE THE FORM ON PAGE 15 OR CALL TOLL-FREE 1-877-671-6036
View thousands more home plans online at www.familyhandyman.com/homeplans

35

Open Family Living

Plan #711-035D-0047

1,818 total square feet of living area

Price Code C

Special features

- Spacious breakfast area extends into family room and kitchen
- Master suite has tray ceiling and a vaulted bath with walk-in closet
- Optional bonus room above the garage has an additional 298 square feet of living area
- 3 bedrooms, 2 1/2 baths, 2-car garage
- Walk-out basement, slab or crawl space foundation, please specify when ordering

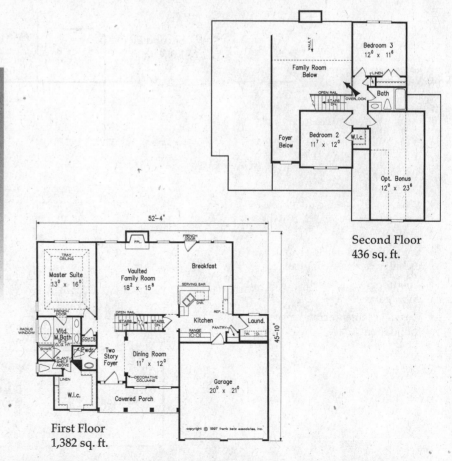

Second Floor
436 sq. ft.

First Floor
1,382 sq. ft.

2,362 total square feet of living area   **Price Code D**

Special features

- Versatile bedroom #4 or den/study is adjacent to master bedroom entry and powder/pool bath
- Island kitchen overlooks breakfast nook and family room
- Foyer opens into formal living room
- 4 bedrooms, 3 baths, 2-car side entry garage
- Slab foundation

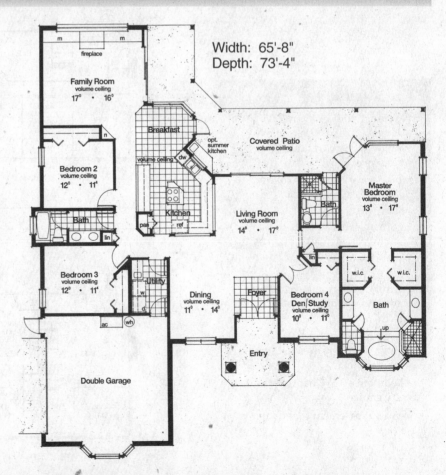

Width: 65'-8"
Depth: 73'-4"

Family Room
volume ceiling
17⁰ • 16⁰

fireplace

Breakfast

opt. summer kitchen

Bedroom 2
volume ceiling
12⁰ • 11⁴

Bath

Kitchen

Covered Patio
volume ceiling

Bath

Master Bedroom
volume ceiling
13⁸ • 17⁰

Living Room
volume ceiling
14⁸ • 17⁰

Bedroom 3
volume ceiling
12⁰ • 11⁴

Utility

w.i.c.   w.i.c.

Dining
volume ceiling
11⁰ • 14⁰

Foyer

Bedroom 4
Den/Study
volume ceiling
10⁰ • 11⁰

Bath

Entry

Double Garage

TO ORDER BLUEPRINTS USE THE FORM ON PAGE 15 OR CALL TOLL-FREE 1-877-671-6036
View thousands more home plans online at www.familyhandyman.com/homeplans

37

Prestigious And Family Oriented

Plan #711-007D-0084

3,420 total square feet of living area

Price Code F

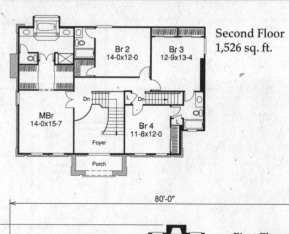

Second Floor
1,526 sq. ft.

Br 2
14-0x12-0

Br 3
12-9x13-4

MBr
14-0x15-7

Br 4
11-8x12-0

Foyer

Porch

Special features

- Hip roofs, elliptical windows and brick facade with quoins emphasize stylish sophisticated living
- Grand foyer has flared staircase in addition to secondary stair from kitchen
- Enormous kitchen features a cooktop island, walk-in pantry, angled breakfast bar and computer desk
- Splendid gallery connects family room and wet bar with vaulted hearth room
- Master bedroom has a coffered ceiling, double walk-in closets and a lavish bath
- 4 bedrooms, 3 1/2 baths, 3-car rear entry garage
- Walk-out basement foundation

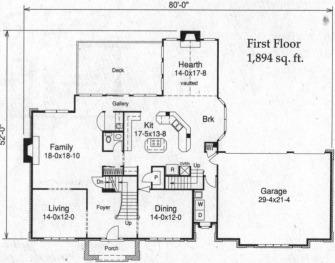

80'-0"

52'-0"

First Floor
1,894 sq. ft.

Deck

Hearth
14-0x17-8
vaulted

Gallery

Kit
17-5x13-8

Brk

Family
18-0x18-10

Garage
29-4x21-4

Living
14-0x12-0

Foyer

Dining
14-0x12-0

Porch

2,544 total square feet of living area

Price Code D

Special features

- Central family room becomes gathering place
- Second floor recreation room is a great game room for children
- First floor master bedroom is secluded from main living areas
- 3 bedrooms, 2 1/2 baths, 2-car side entry garage
- Basement foundation, drawings also include crawl space and slab foundations

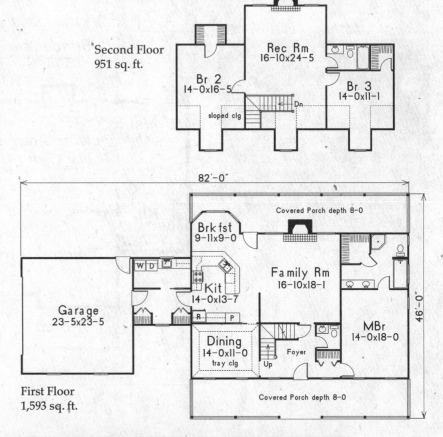

Second Floor
951 sq. ft.

Rec Rm
16-10x24-5

Br 2
14-0x16-5

sloped clg

Dn

Br 3
14-0x11-1

82'-0"

Brk fst
9-11x9-0

Covered Porch depth 8-0

W D

Kit
14-0x13-7

Family Rm
16-10x18-1

Garage
23-5x23-5

R   P

46'-0"

Dining
14-0x11-0
tray clg

Foyer

MBr
14-0x18-0

Up

First Floor
1,593 sq. ft.

Covered Porch depth 8-0

TO ORDER BLUEPRINTS USE THE FORM ON PAGE 15 OR CALL TOLL-FREE 1-877-671-6036
View thousands more home plans online at www.familyhandyman.com/homeplans

39

Scalloped Porch Cornice Adds Flair   **Plan #711-052D-0036**

1,772 total square feet of living area   **Price Code B**

Special features

- Dramatic palladian window and scalloped porch are attention grabbers
- Island kitchen sink allows for easy access and views into the living and breakfast areas
- Washer and dryer closet easily accessible from all bedrooms
- 3 bedrooms, 2 baths, 3-car drive under garage
- Basement foundation

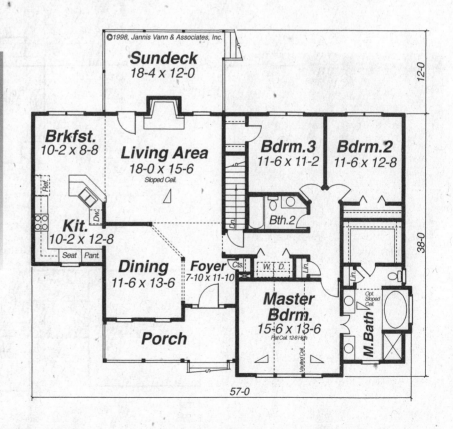

©1998, Jannis Vann & Associates, Inc.

Sundeck 18-4 x 12-0

Brkfst. 10-2 x 8-8

Living Area 18-0 x 15-6 Sloped Ceil.

Bdrm.3 11-6 x 11-2

Bdrm.2 11-6 x 12-8

Kit. 10-2 x 12-8

Seat Pant.

Bth.2

Dining 11-6 x 13-6

Foyer 7-10 x 11-10

W D

Porch

Master Bdrm. 15-6 x 13-6 Flat Ceil. 12-8 High

M.Bath

Opt. Sloped Ceil.

12-0

38-0

57-0

3,204 total square feet of living area

Price Code G

Special features

- The master bedroom highlights a sunny sitting area, tray ceiling, huge walk-in closet and a corner spa tub in the bath
- Decorative columns introduce the expansive great room which features a fireplace, built-in shelves and a serving counter shared with the kitchen
- A handy office just off the entry doubles as a guest room and has private access to a full bath
- A full bath near the rear door from the kitchen is convenient
- 4 bedrooms, 4 baths, 3-car side entry garage
- Basement or crawl space foundation, please specify when ordering

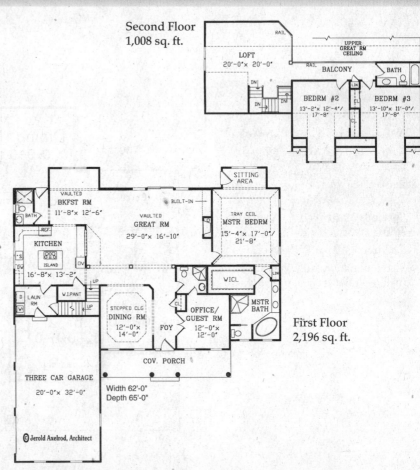

Second Floor 1,008 sq. ft.

First Floor 2,196 sq. ft.

Width 62'-0"
Depth 65'-0"

© Jerold Axelrod, Architect

TO ORDER BLUEPRINTS USE THE FORM ON PAGE 15 OR CALL TOLL-FREE 1-877-671-6036
View thousands more home plans online at www.familyhandyman.com/HOMEPLANS

41

1,442 total square feet of living area

Price Code A

Special features

- Centrally located living room with recessed fireplace and 10' ceiling
- Large U-shaped kitchen offers an eating bar and pantry
- Expanded garage provides extra storage and work area
- Spacious master bedroom with sitting area and large walk-in closet
- 3 bedrooms, 2 baths, 2-car garage
- Slab foundation, drawings also include crawl space foundation

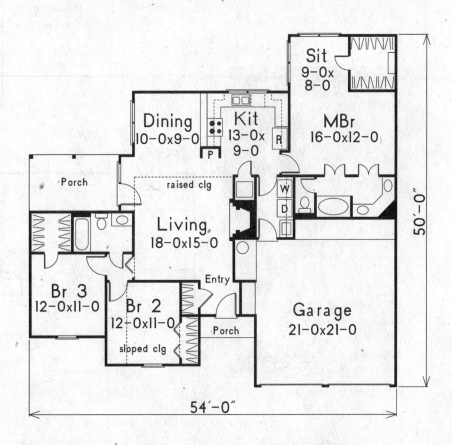

Sit 9-0x 8-0

Dining 10-0x9-0

Kit 13-0x 9-0

MBr 16-0x12-0

Porch

raised clg

Living 18-0x15-0

Br 3 12-0x11-0

Br 2 12-0x11-0

Entry

sloped clg

Porch

Garage 21-0x21-0

50'-0"

54'-0"

Luxurious Master Suite

Plan #711-035D-0006

1,671 total square feet of living area

Price Code B

Special features

- Kitchen is conveniently located between the breakfast and dining rooms
- Vaulted family room is centrally located
- Laundry room is located near the garage for easy access
- 3 bedrooms, 2 baths, 2-car side entry garage
- Slab, crawl space or walk-out basement foundation, please specify when ordering

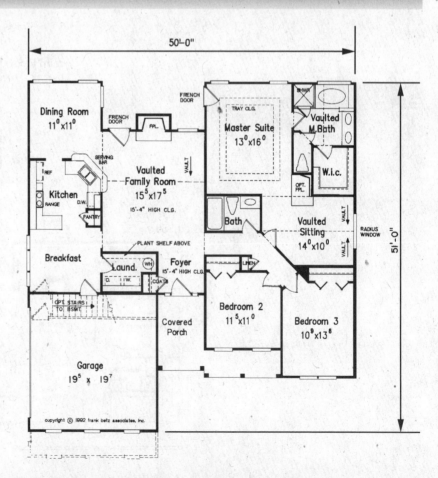

Triple Dormers

Plan #711-024D-0021

2,360 total square feet of living area

Price Code D

Special features

- First floor master bedroom has a private bath with step-up tub
- Living area fireplace is flanked by double French doors that lead to a spacious deck
- Dormers accentuate second floor bedrooms and bath
- 4 bedrooms, 2 1/2 baths, 2-car side entry garage
- Slab foundation

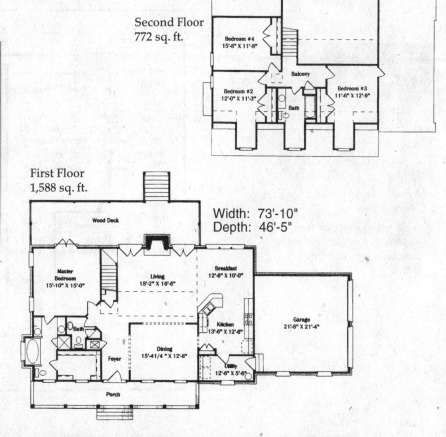

Second Floor
772 sq. ft.

Bedroom #4
15'-8" X 11'-8"

Balcony

Bedroom #2
12'-0" X 11'-3"

Bedroom #3
11'-6" X 12'-9"

Bath

First Floor
1,588 sq. ft.

Width: 73'-10"
Depth: 46'-5"

Wood Deck

Master Bedroom
15'-10" X 15'-0"

Living
18'-2" X 16'-6"

Breakfast
12'-6" X 10'-0"

Garage
21'-8" X 21'-4"

Bath

Kitchen
13'-6" X 12'-6"

Foyer

Dining
15'-4 1/4" X 12'-6"

Utility
12'-6" X 5'-6"

Porch

TO ORDER BLUEPRINTS USE THE FORM ON PAGE 15 OR CALL TOLL-FREE 1-877-671-6036
View thousands more home plans online at www.familyhandyman.com/homeplans

Eye-Appealing Design

Plan #711-015D-0032

2,917 total square feet of living area

Price Code E

Special features

- Private master bath on the second floor has a huge walk-in closet, corner soaking tub and a cheerful skylight
- Open floor plan with vaulted living and dining rooms
- Inviting covered porch
- Den/guest room is well-designed to suit needs
- The bonus room on the second floor has 313 square feet of living area and is included in the total square footage
- 3 bedrooms, 3 baths, 3-car garage
- Crawl space foundation

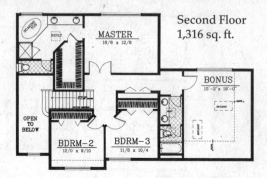

Second Floor
1,316 sq. ft.

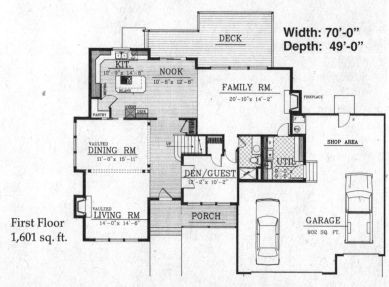

Width: 70'-0"
Depth: 49'-0"

First Floor
1,601 sq. ft.

TO ORDER BLUEPRINTS USE THE FORM ON PAGE 15 OR CALL TOLL-FREE 1-877-671-6036
View thousands more home plans online at www.familyhandyman.com/HOMEPLANS

45

Home Offers Stylish Exterior

Plan #711-007D-0041

1,700 total square feet of living area

Price Code B

Special features

- Two-story entry with T-stair is illuminated with a decorative oval window
- Skillfully designed U-shaped kitchen has a built-in pantry
- All bedrooms have generous closet storage and are common to spacious hall with walk-in cedar closet
- 4 bedrooms, 2 1/2 baths, 2-car side entry garage
- Basement foundation

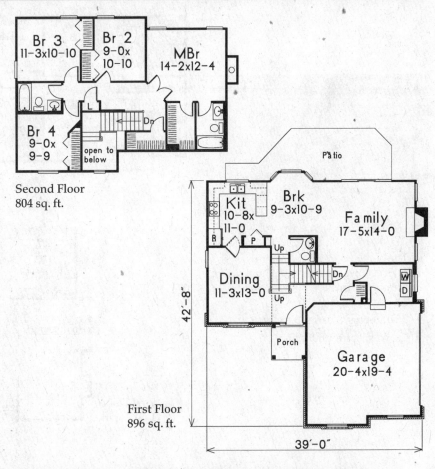

Br 3
11-3x10-10

Br 2
9-0x
10-10

MBr
14-2x12-4

Br 4
9-0x
9-9

open to below

Second Floor
804 sq. ft.

Patio

Kit
10-8x
11-0

Brk
9-3x10-9

Family
17-5x14-0

Dining
11-3x13-0

Up

Dn

Up

W
D

42'-8"

Porch

Garage
20-4x19-4

First Floor
896 sq. ft.

39'-0"

46

TO ORDER BLUEPRINTS USE THE FORM ON PAGE 15 OR CALL TOLL-FREE 1-877-671-6036
View thousands more home plans online at www.familyhandyman.com/homeplans

Step Up Into Master Bath Tub   Plan #711-019D-0016

2,678 total square feet of living area   **Price Code E**

Special features

- Elegant arched opening graces entrance
- Kitchen has double ovens, walk-in pantry and an eating bar
- Master bedroom has a beautiful bath spotlighting a step-up tub
- 4 bedrooms, 2 1/2 baths, 2-car side entry garage
- Crawl space foundation, drawings also include slab foundation

TO ORDER BLUEPRINTS USE THE FORM ON PAGE 15 OR CALL TOLL-FREE 1-877-671-6036
View thousands more home plans online at www.familyhandyman.com/homeplans

47

Covered Verandah

Plan #711-062D-0039

2,493 total square feet of living area

Price Code D

Special features

- Energy efficient home with 2" x 6" exterior walls
- Breakfast room is nestled in a bay window
- Master bedroom boasts a vaulted ceiling alcove, window seat and walk-in closet
- Sunken family room features a state-of-the-art built-in media center
- 3 bedrooms, 2 1/2 baths, 2-car garage
- Basement foundation

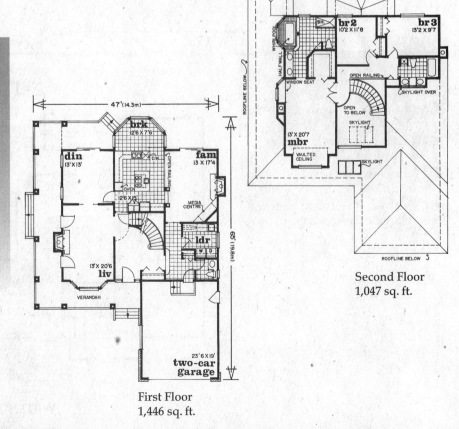

Second Floor
1,047 sq. ft.

First Floor
1,446 sq. ft.

A Great Country Farmhouse

Plan #711-049D-0010

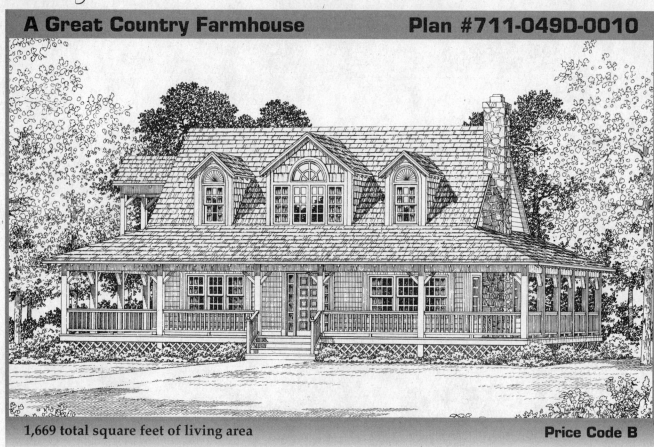

1,669 total square feet of living area

Price Code B

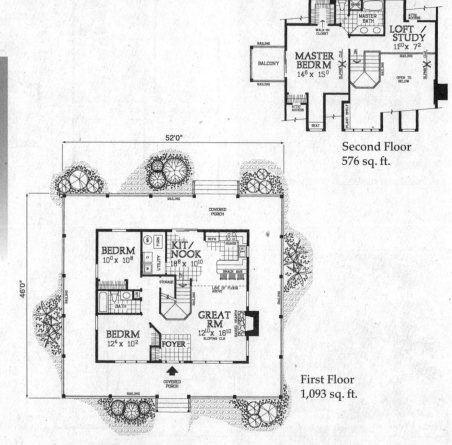

Second Floor
576 sq. ft.

Special features

- Generous use of windows add exciting visual elements to the exterior as well as plenty of natural light to the interior
- Two-story great room has a raised hearth
- Second floor loft/study would easily make a terrific home office
- 3 bedrooms, 2 baths
- Crawl space foundation

First Floor
1,093 sq. ft.

TO ORDER BLUEPRINTS USE THE FORM ON PAGE 15 OR CALL TOLL-FREE 1-877-671-6036
View thousands more home plans online at www.familyhandyman.com/homeplans

49

Balcony Enjoys Spectacular Views   Plan #711-007D-0003

2,806 total square feet of living area

Price Code E

Special features

- Harmonious charm throughout
- Sweeping balcony and vaulted ceiling soar above spacious great room and walk-in bar
- Atrium with lower level family room is a unique touch, creating an open and airy feeling
- 4 bedrooms, 2 1/2 baths, 2-car garage
- Walk-out basement foundation

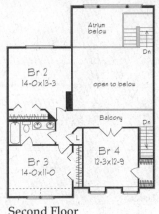

Second Floor
785 sq. ft.

First Floor
1,473 sq. ft.

Rear View

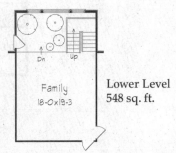

Lower Level
548 sq. ft.

TO ORDER BLUEPRINTS USE THE FORM ON PAGE 15 OR CALL TOLL-FREE 1-877-671-6036
View thousands more home plans online at www.familyhandyman.com/homeplans

Porch Adds To Farmhouse Style

Plan #711-016D-0049

1,793 total square feet of living area

Price Code B

Special features

- Beautiful foyer leads into the great room that has a fireplace flanked by two sets of beautifully transomed doors both leading to a large covered porch

- Dramatic eat-in kitchen includes an abundance of cabinets and workspace in an exciting angled shape

- Delightful master bedroom has many amenities

- Optional bonus room above the garage has an additional 779 square feet of living area

- 3 bedrooms, 2 baths, 2-car side entry garage

- Basement, crawl space or slab foundation, please specify when ordering

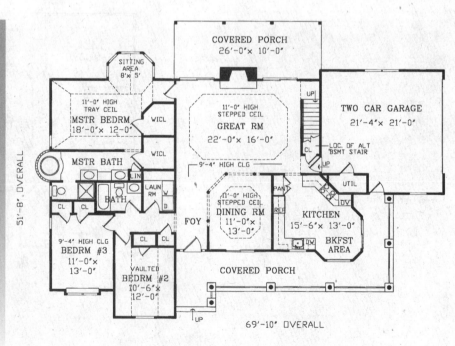

J.N. HANSEN

2,397 total square feet of living area   **Price Code E**

Special features

- Covered entrance with fountain leads to double-door entry and foyer
- Kitchen features two pantries and opens into breakfast and family rooms
- Master bath features huge walk-in closet, electric clothes carousel, double-bowl vanity and corner tub
- 3 bedrooms, 2 1/2 baths, 2-car garage
- Slab foundation

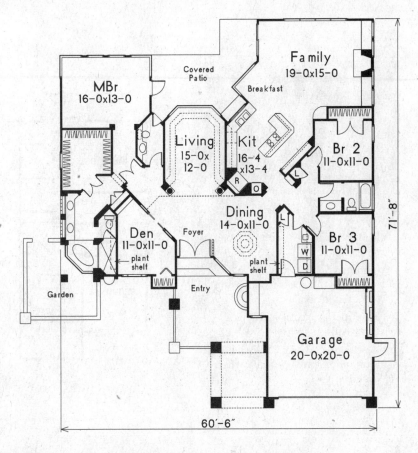

The Family Handyman

Striking Great Room
Plan #711-019D-0014

COPYRIGHT LARRY E. BELK

2,586 total square feet of living area

Price Code D

Special features

- Great room has an impressive tray ceiling and see-through fireplace into bayed breakfast room
- Master bedroom has walk-in closet and private bath
- 4 bedrooms, 3 baths, 2-car side entry garage
- Basement foundation, drawings also include crawl space and slab foundations

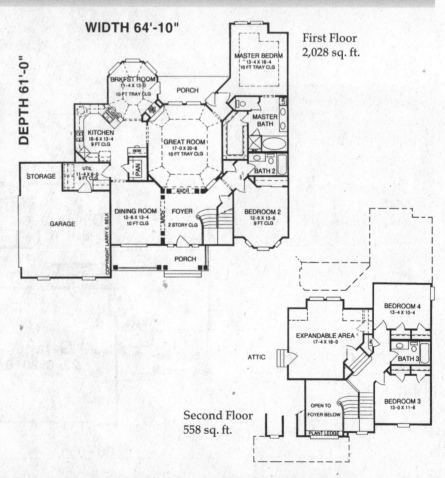

WIDTH 64'-10"

DEPTH 61'-0"

First Floor
2,028 sq. ft.

MASTER BEDRM
13-4 X 16-4
10 FT TRAY CLG

PORCH

BRKFST ROOM
17-4 X 13-0
10 FT TRAY CLG

MASTER BATH

KITCHEN
16-6 X 13-4
9 FT CLG

GREAT ROOM
17-0 X 20-6
10 FT TRAY CLG

BATH 2

DESK
PAN

UTIL
11-4 X 8-0
9 FT CLG

STORAGE

ARCH

GARAGE

DINING ROOM
12-6 X 13-4
10 FT CLG

FOYER
2 STORY CLG

BEDROOM 2
12-6 X 13-6
9 FT CLG

ARCH

PORCH

COPYRIGHT LARRY E. BELK

BEDROOM 4
13-4 X 10-4

EXPANDABLE AREA
17-4 X 18-0

ATTIC

BATH 3

OPEN TO FOYER BELOW

BEDROOM 3
13-0 X 11-6

PLANT LEDGE

Second Floor
558 sq. ft.

TO ORDER BLUEPRINTS USE THE FORM ON PAGE 15 OR CALL TOLL-FREE 1-877-671-6036
View thousands more home plans online at www.familyhandyman.com/homeplans

53

Spacious Vaulted Great Room

Plan #711-041D-0006

1,189 total square feet of living area

Price Code AA

Special features

- All bedrooms are located on the second floor
- Dining room and kitchen both have views of the patio
- Convenient half bath located near the kitchen
- Master bedroom has a private bath
- 3 bedrooms, 2 1/2 baths, 2-car garage
- Basement foundation

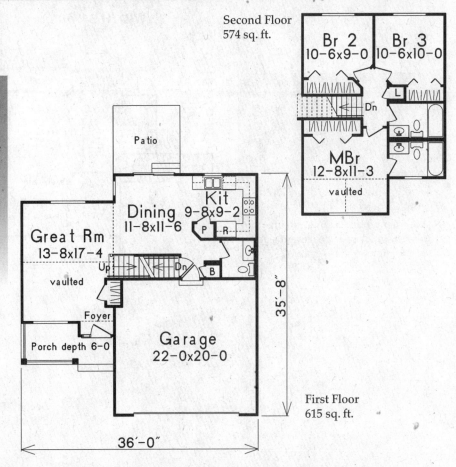

Second Floor
574 sq. ft.

Br 2
10-6x9-0

Br 3
10-6x10-0

Dn

L

MBr
12-8x11-3

vaulted

Patio

Kit
9-8x9-2

Dining
11-8x11-6

P R

Great Rm
13-8x17-4

vaulted

Up Dn B

Foyer

Porch depth 6-0

Garage
22-0x20-0

35'-8"

36'-0"

First Floor
615 sq. ft.

Bay Windows Brighten Home

Plan #711-071D-0003

2,890 total square feet of living area

Price Code E

Special features

- Formal dining and living rooms in the front of the home create a private place for entertaining
- Kitchen is designed for efficiency including a large island with cooktop and extra counterspace in route to dining room
- A stunning oversized whirlpool tub is showcased in the private master bath
- Bonus room on the second floor has an additional 240 square feet of living area
- 3 bedrooms, 3 baths, 3-car side entry garage
- Crawl space foundation

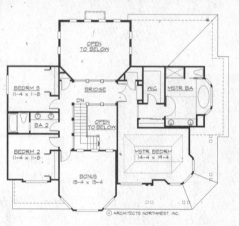

Second Floor
1,260 sq. ft.

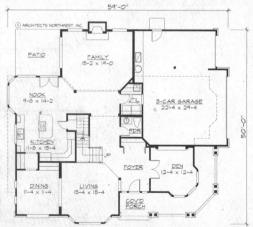

First Floor
1,630 sq. ft.

TO ORDER BLUEPRINTS USE THE FORM ON PAGE 15 OR CALL TOLL-FREE 1-877-671-6036
View thousands more home plans online at www.familyhandyman.com/homeplans

55

Handsome Facade, Compact Design   Plan #711-014D-0013

2,041 total square feet of living area

Price Code C

Special features

- Wonderful sunken family room features fireplace and accesses patio
- The kitchen with island cooktop and nook combines with family room creating an open area
- Dining room is accessible from kitchen and vaulted living room
- Bedroom #4 could easily convert to a study or den
- 4 bedrooms, 3 baths, 2-car side entry garage
- Partial basement/slab foundation

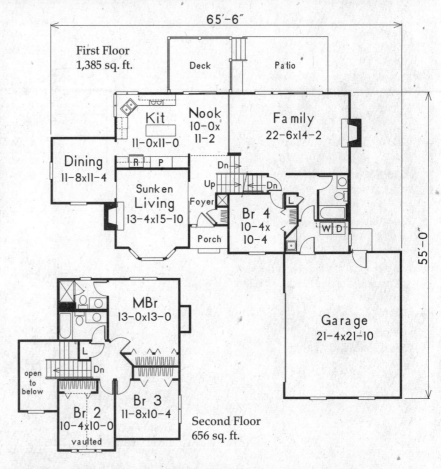

First Floor
1,385 sq. ft.

65'-6"

55'-0"

Deck   Patio

Kit
11-0x11-0

Nook
10-0x
11-2

Family
22-6x14-2

Dining
11-8x11-4

Sunken
Living
13-4x15-10

R   P

Dn

Up   Dn

Foyer

Br 4
10-4x
10-4

L

W D

Porch

Garage
21-4x21-10

MBr
13-0x13-0

L   Dn

open
to
below

Br 3
11-8x10-4

Br 2
10-4x10-0
vaulted

Second Floor
656 sq. ft.

Great Family Home

Plan #711-026D-0009

2,219 total square feet of living area

Price Code D

Special features

- The formal dining room includes a hutch and provides an elegant atmosphere for entertaining
- The great room boasts a 10' ceiling and grand fireplace
- The kitchen has an abundance of counterspace with an island and connects to the bayed breakfast room for an open area
- 4 bedrooms, 2 1/2 baths, 2-car garage with storage
- Basement foundation

First Floor
1,132 sq. ft.

© design basics inc.

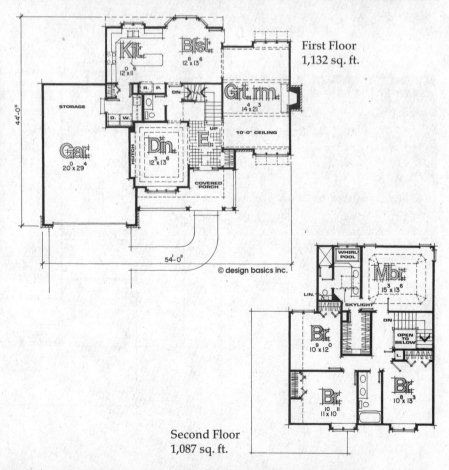

Second Floor
1,087 sq. ft.

Traditional Southern Style Home   Plan #711-028D-0004

1,785 total square feet of living area   **Price Code B**

Special features

- 9' ceilings throughout home
- Luxurious master bath includes whirlpool tub and separate shower
- Cozy breakfast area is convenient to kitchen
- 3 bedrooms, 3 baths, 2-car detached garage
- Basement, crawl space or slab foundation, please specify when ordering

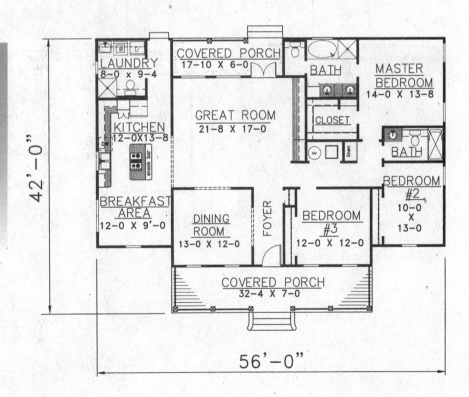

Elaborate Stonework Adds Charm   Plan #711-031D-0016

2,560 total square feet of living area

Price Code D

Special features

- See-through fireplace surrounded with shelving warms both family and living rooms
- Tall ceilings in living areas
- Bedrooms maintain privacy
- 4 bedrooms, 3 baths, 3-car side entry garage
- Slab foundation

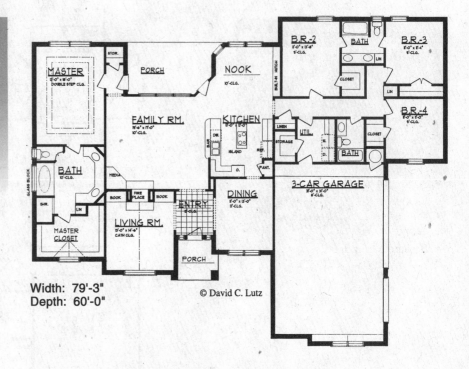

Width: 79'-3"
Depth: 60'-0"

© David C. Lutz

TO ORDER BLUEPRINTS USE THE FORM ON PAGE 15 OR CALL TOLL-FREE 1-877-671-6036
View thousands more home plans online at www.familyhandyman.com/HOMEPLANS

59

High Fashion Modern Design
Plan #711-022D-0029

2,463 total square feet of living area

Price Code D

Special features

- Exciting angular design with diagonal stairway
- Living room features vaulted ceiling, fireplace and convenient wet bar
- Generously sized family room features vaulted ceiling and easy access to kitchen
- Sunny bay window defines breakfast area which accesses deck
- 4 bedrooms, 2 1/2 baths, 2-car garage
- Basement foundation

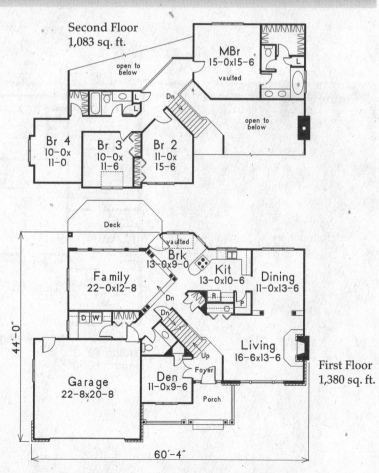

Second Floor
1,083 sq. ft.

open to below

MBr
15-0x15-6
vaulted

open to below

Br 4
10-0x
11-0

Br 3
10-0x
11-6

Br 2
11-0x
15-6

Dn

Deck

Family
22-0x12-8

Brk
13-0x9-0
vaulted

Kit
13-0x10-6

Dining
11-0x13-6

Living
16-6x13-6

Den
11-0x9-6

Garage
22-8x20-8

Foyer

Porch

Up

Dn

Dn

D W

44'-0"

60'-4"

First Floor
1,380 sq. ft.

1,945 total square feet of living area

Price Code C

Special features

- Large gathering room with corner fireplace and 12' high ceiling
- Master suite has a coffered ceiling and French door leading to the patio/deck
- Master bath has a cultured marble seat, separate shower and tub
- All bedrooms have walk-in closets
- 3 bedrooms, 2 baths, 2-car side entry garage
- Slab or crawl space foundation, please specify when ordering

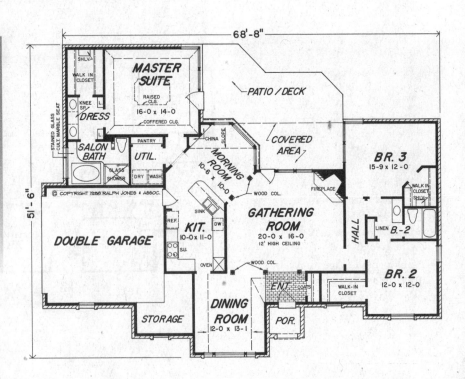

TO ORDER BLUEPRINTS USE THE FORM ON PAGE 15 OR CALL TOLL-FREE 1-877-671-6036
View thousands more home plans online at www.familyhandyman.com/homeplans

61

Optimal Family Living Layout

Plan #711-069D-0017

1,926 total square feet of living area

Price Code C

Special features

- Large covered rear porch is spacious enough for entertaining
- L-shaped kitchen is compact yet efficient and includes a snack bar for extra dining space
- Oversized utility room has counterspace, extra shelves and space for a second refrigerator
- Secluded master suite has a private bath and a large walk-in closet
- 3 bedrooms, 2 baths, 2-car side entry garage
- Slab or crawl space foundation, please specify when ordering

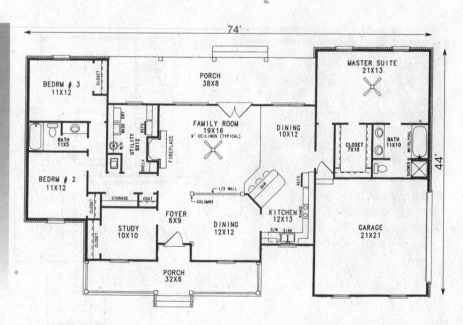

Striking Curb Appeal

Plan #711-041D-0002

2,204 total square feet of living area

Price Code D

Special features

- First floor den offers the flexibility of an office, study or fourth bedroom
- Large island kitchen with breakfast bar next to family room provides open living space
- Second floor balcony overlooks entry below
- Master bedroom features double walk-in closets, private bath with step-up tub and double-bowl vanity
- 3 bedrooms, 2 1/2 baths, 2-car garage
- Basement foundation

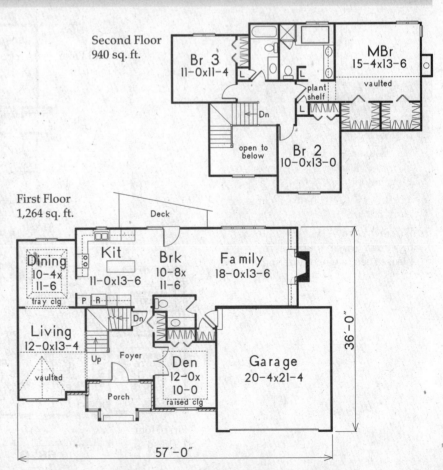

Second Floor
940 sq. ft.

Br 3
11-0x11-4

MBr
15-4x13-6
vaulted

plant shelf

Dn

open to below

Br 2
10-0x13-0

First Floor
1,264 sq. ft.

Deck

Dining
10-4x
11-6
tray clg

Kit
11-0x13-6

Brk
10-8x
11-6

Family
18-0x13-6

Living
12-0x13-4
vaulted

Up

Dn

Foyer

Den
12-0x
10-0
raised clg

Garage
20-4x21-4

Porch

36'-0"

57'-0"

TO ORDER BLUEPRINTS USE THE FORM ON PAGE 15 OR CALL TOLL-FREE 1-877-671-6036
View thousands more home plans online at www.familyhandyman.com/homeplans

63

Two-Story Has Terrific Curb Appeal   Plan #711-025D-0052

3,033 total square feet of living area

Price Code E

Special features

- Sunroom warmed by fireplace and brightened by lots of windows
- Bedroom #4 and bath #2 on second floor both lead to balcony through French doors
- 4 bedrooms, 3 1/2 baths, 2-car side entry garage
- Basement, crawl space, walk-out basement or slab foundation, please specify when ordering

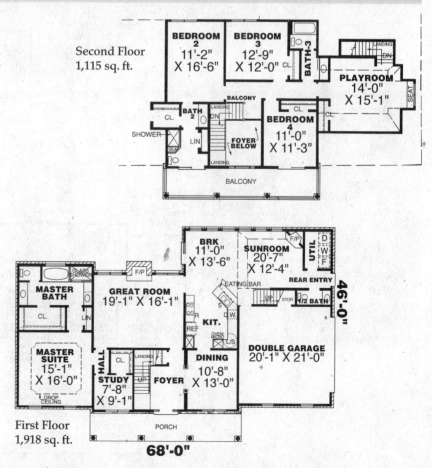

Second Floor
1,115 sq. ft.

BEDROOM 2
11'-2" X 16'-6"

BEDROOM 3
12'-9" X 12'-0"

BATH-3

PLAYROOM
14'-0" X 15'-1"

SEAT

CL.

LANDING DN

SHOWER

CL.

BATH 2

SEAT

LIN

DN

LANDING

FOYER BELOW

LANDING

BEDROOM 4
11'-0" X 11'-3"

CL.

CL.

BALCONY

BALCONY

First Floor
1,918 sq. ft.

MASTER BATH

GLASS SHOWER

CL.

LIN

F/P

BRK
11'-0" X 13'-6"

F/P

SUNROOM
20'-7" X 12'-4"

UTIL
D W F

REAR ENTRY

46'-0"

GREAT ROOM
19'-1" X 16'-1"

EATING BAR

MASTER SUITE
15'-1" X 16'-0"

DROP CEILING

HALL

CL.

LANDING

UP

STUDY
7'-8" X 9'-1"

FOYER

DINING
10'-8" X 13'-0"

KIT.

REF

OVEN MICRO

D.W.

UP

STOR

1/2 BATH

DOUBLE GARAGE
20'-1" X 21'-0"

PORCH

68'-0"

TO ORDER BLUEPRINTS USE THE FORM ON PAGE 15 OR CALL TOLL-FREE 1-877-671-6036
View thousands more home plans online at www.familyhandyman.com/homeplans

2,006 total square feet of living area

Price Code C

Special features

- Built-in bookshelves in family room add a warm feeling
- Two-story entry creates elegant appeal
- Enter French doors to a den ideal for an office
- Kitchen has eating counter and a nook
- T-stair adds easy access to entry and kitchen
- 4 bedrooms, 2 1/2 baths, 2-car rear entry garage
- Crawl space foundation

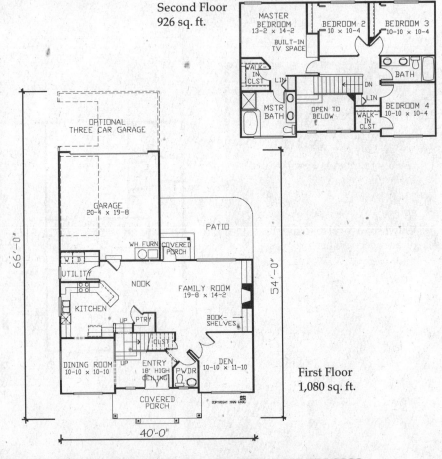

Second Floor
926 sq. ft.

MASTER BEDROOM
13-2 × 14-2

BEDROOM 2
10 × 10-4

BEDROOM 3
10-10 × 10-4

BUILT-IN TV SPACE

WALK-IN CLST

LIN

BATH

MSTR BATH

OPEN TO BELOW

DN

LIN

BEDROOM 4
10-10 × 10-4

WALK-IN CLST

OPTIONAL THREE CAR GARAGE

GARAGE
20-4 × 19-8

PATIO

WH FURN

COVERED PORCH

W/D

UTILITY

NOOK

FAMILY ROOM
19-8 × 14-2

KITCHEN

UP

PTRY

BOOK-SHELVES

DINING ROOM
10-10 × 10-10

UP

ENTRY
18' HIGH CEILING

CLST

PWDR

DEN
10-10 × 11-10

COVERED PORCH

COPYRIGHT 1999 430G

66'-0"

54'-0"

40'-0"

First Floor
1,080 sq. ft.

Fireplace Warms Home

Plan #711-055D-0014

2,216 total square feet of living area

Price Code D

Special features

- Grilling porch is a lovely addition to the breakfast room and adds convenience
- Extra storage in garage
- Gallery foyer adds a dramatic feel to the great room
- 3 bedrooms, 2 1/2 baths, 2-car garage
- Crawl space or slab foundation, please specify when ordering

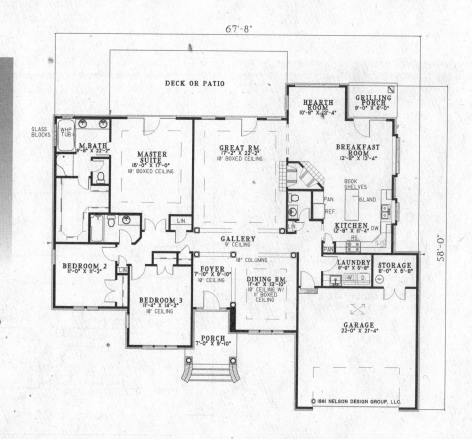

TO ORDER BLUEPRINTS USE THE FORM ON PAGE 15 OR CALL TOLL-FREE 1-877-671-6036
View thousands more home plans online at www.familyhandyman.com/homeplans

Splendid Master Bedroom

Plan #711-065D-0013

2,041 total square feet of living area

Price Code C

Special features

- Great room accesses directly onto covered rear deck with ceiling fan above
- Private master bedroom has a beautiful octagon-shaped sitting area that opens and brightens the space
- Two secondary bedrooms share a full bath
- 3 bedrooms, 2 baths, 2-car side entry garage
- Basement or walk-out basement foundation, please specify when ordering

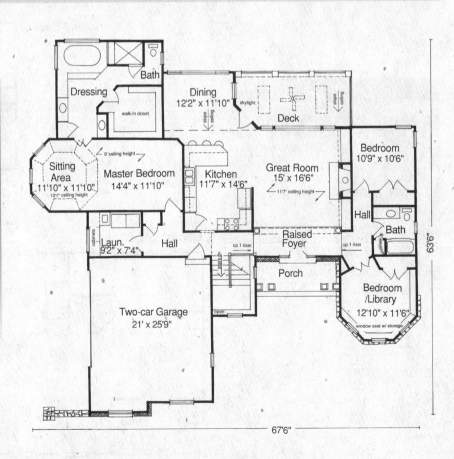

TO ORDER BLUEPRINTS USE THE FORM ON PAGE 15 OR CALL TOLL-FREE 1-877-671-6036
View thousands more home plans online at www.familyhandyman.com/homeplans

67

Ideal Design For Stunning Views

Plan #711-024D-0039

1,779 total square feet of living area

Price Code B

Special features

- Sunny living room has walls covered with windows and is attached to a sunroom with double-door entry
- Master bedroom has access to balcony through double-doors and a private bath
- Kitchen has an open feel with a center island and overlooks dining area
- 3 bedrooms, 2 1/2 baths
- Pier foundation

Second Floor
872 sq. ft.

Bedroom
11'x 9'4"

Bath

Master Bath

WIC

Bedroom
11'x 9'2"

Master Bedroom
19'x 13'4"

Balcony
14'x 8'

Width: 34'-0"
Depth: 30'-0"

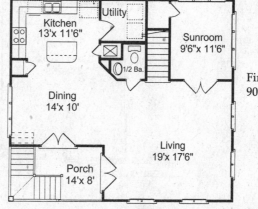

Utility

Kitchen
13'x 11'6"

Sunroom
9'6"x 11'6"

1/2 Ba.

Dining
14'x 10'

First Floor
907 sq. ft.

Living
19'x 17'6"

Porch
14'x 8'

Efficient Multi-Level Home

Plan #711-010D-0004

1,617 total square feet of living area

Price Code B

Special features

- Kitchen and breakfast area overlook great room with fireplace
- Formal dining room features vaulted ceiling and elegant circle-top window
- All bedrooms are located on the second floor for privacy
- 3 bedrooms, 2 1/2 baths, 2-car garage
- Partial crawl space/slab foundation

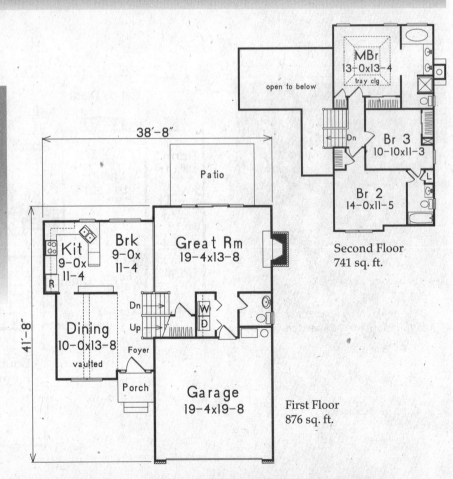

Second Floor
741 sq. ft.

First Floor
876 sq. ft.

TO ORDER BLUEPRINTS USE THE FORM ON PAGE 15 OR CALL TOLL-FREE 1-877-671-6036
View thousands more home plans online at www.familyhandyman.com/homeplans

69

Stone Accents Inviting Entry   Plan #711-052D-0047

1,869 total square feet of living area   **Price Code C**

Special features

- Bayed breakfast area walks out to a sunny patio/deck
- Master bath has intricate ceiling design, double vanity, spa tub and a large walk-in closet
- Elegant columns frame the formal dining area
- Bonus room on the second floor has an additional 336 square feet of living area
- 3 bedrooms, 2 baths, 2-car side entry garage
- Basement, crawl space or slab foundation, please specify when ordering

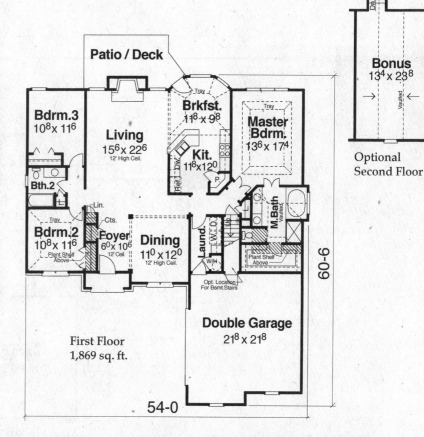

Patio / Deck

Bdrm.3
10⁸ x 11⁶

Living
15⁶ x 22⁶
12' High Ceil.

Brkfst.
11⁸ x 9⁸

Tray

Master Bdrm.
13⁶ x 17⁴

Tray

Kit.
11⁸ x 12⁰

Bth.2

Lin.

Tray

Cts.

Bdrm.2
10⁸ x 11⁶
Plant Shelf Above

Foyer
6⁰ x 10⁶
12' Ceil.

Dining
11⁰ x 12⁰
12' High Ceil.

Laund.
W/D

M.Bath
Vaulted

Plant Shelf Above

Opt. Location For Bsmt.Stairs

60-6

First Floor
1,869 sq. ft.

Double Garage
21⁸ x 21⁸

54-0

Bonus
13⁴ x 23⁸
Vaulted

Optional Second Floor

Magnificent Facade

Plan #711-048D-0010

2,887 total square feet of living area

Price Code F

Special features

- Columned foyer opens into living room which has sunken wet bar that extends into pool area
- Stunning master bedroom accesses patio and offers view of pool through curved window wall
- Dining room boasts window walls
- Second floor includes two bedrooms, bath and shared balcony deck overlooking pool area
- 3 bedrooms, 2 1/2 baths, 2-car garage
- Slab foundation

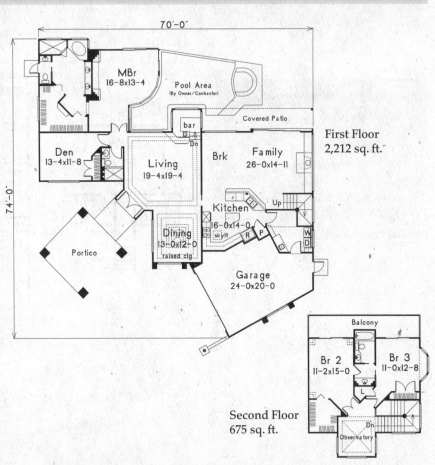

First Floor
2,212 sq. ft.

Second Floor
675 sq. ft.

TO ORDER BLUEPRINTS USE THE FORM ON PAGE 15 OR CALL TOLL-FREE 1-877-671-6036
View thousands more home plans online at www.familyhandyman.com/homeplans

71

CHARMING French Country Home

Plan #711-025D-0039

2,503 total square feet of living area

Price Code D

Special features

- The foyer opens into the expansive great room and cozy sunroom
- The kitchen, including an eating bar, connects to the dining room
- Bedroom #4 on the second floor has a private bath and walk-in closet
- 4 bedrooms, 3 baths, 2-car garage
- Slab foundation

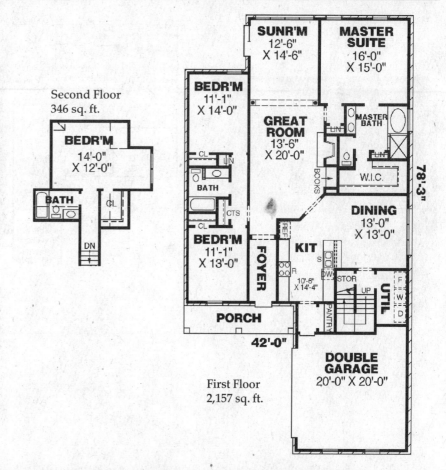

Second Floor
346 sq. ft.

BEDR'M
14'-0"
X 12'-0"

BATH

CL

DN

SUNR'M
12'-6"
X 14'-6"

MASTER
SUITE
16'-0"
X 15'-0"

BEDR'M
11'-1"
X 14'-0"

GREAT
ROOM
13'-6"
X 20'-0"

MASTER
BATH

CL

LIN

BATH

CTS

BEDR'M
11'-1"
X 13'-0"

W.I.C.

BOOKS

DINING
13'-0"
X 13'-0"

FOYER

REF

KIT
10'-6"
X 14'-4"

R

S

DW

STOR

UP

PANTRY

UTIL

F
W
D

PORCH

42'-0"

78'-3"

DOUBLE
GARAGE
20'-0" X 20'-0"

First Floor
2,157 sq. ft.

72

TO ORDER BLUEPRINTS USE THE FORM ON PAGE 15 OR CALL TOLL-FREE 1-877-671-6036
View thousands more home plans online at www.familyhandyman.com/homeplans

Warm And Inviting Ranch

Plan #711-065D-0040

1,874 total square feet of living area

Price Code C

Special features

- The bayed dining area, kitchen and great room with a fireplace combine for an open living area
- The master bedroom pampers with a corner whirlpool tub, double vanity and walk-in closet
- 9' ceilings throughout home add to the spaciousness
- Optional lower level has an additional 1,175 square feet of living area
- 3 bedrooms, 2 baths, 3-car side entry garage
- Basement or walk-out basement foundation, please specify when ordering

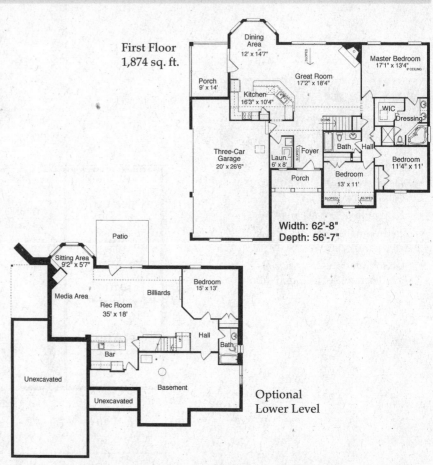

First Floor
1,874 sq. ft.

Width: 62'-8"
Depth: 56'-7"

Optional
Lower Level

TO ORDER BLUEPRINTS USE THE FORM ON PAGE 15 OR CALL TOLL-FREE 1-877-671-6036
View thousands more home plans online at www.familyhandyman.com/homeplans

73

Corner Fireplace Adds Warmth Plan #711-020D-0016

1,984 total square feet of living area

Price Code C

Special features

- Living room has sloped ceiling and corner fireplace
- Kitchen has breakfast bar overlooking dining room
- Master suite is separate from other bedrooms for privacy
- Large utility/storage area
- 3 bedrooms, 2 baths, 2-car side entry garage
- Slab foundation, drawings also include crawl space foundation

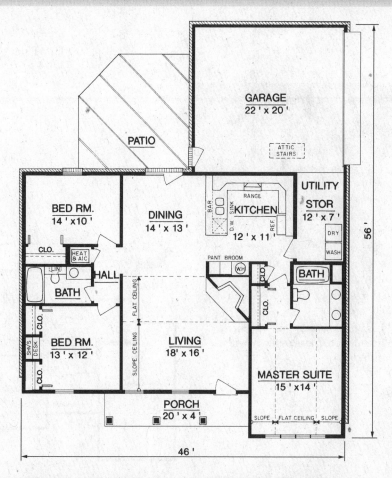

The Family Handyman

Great Traffic Flow On Both Floors
Plan #711-001D-0028

2,461 total square feet of living area

Price Code D

Special features

- Unique corner tub, double vanities and walk-in closet enhance the large master bedroom
- Fireplace provides focus in the spacious family room
- Centrally located half bath for guests
- 4 bedrooms, 2 1/2 baths, 2-car garage
- Basement foundation, drawings also include slab and crawl space foundations

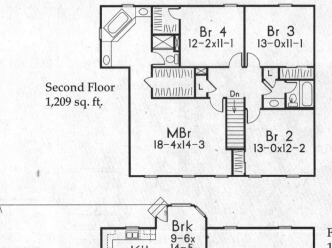

Second Floor
1,209 sq. ft.

Br 4
12-2x11-1

Br 3
13-0x11-1

Dn

MBr
18-4x14-3

Br 2
13-0x12-2

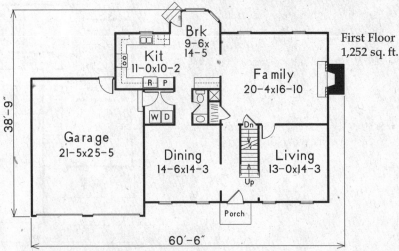

First Floor
1,252 sq. ft.

Brk
9-6x14-5

Kit
11-0x10-2

R P

W D

Family
20-4x16-10

Garage
21-5x25-5

Dn

Dining
14-6x14-3

Living
13-0x14-3

Up

Porch

38'-9"

60'-6"

TO ORDER BLUEPRINTS USE THE FORM ON PAGE 15 OR CALL TOLL-FREE 1-877-671-6036
View thousands more home plans online at www.familyhandyman.com/homeplans

75

Terrific Screened Porch   Plan #711-069D-0015

1,815 total square feet of living area   Price Code C

Special features

- Center island in kitchen creates extra dining space as well as a cooking area
- Large vaulted great room has a fireplace centered on one wall for coziness
- The second floor features a centralized sitting area ideal for casual living space
- Bonus room on the second floor has an additional 426 square feet of living area
- 3 bedrooms, 2 1/2 baths, 2-car garage
- Slab or crawl space foundation, please specify when ordering

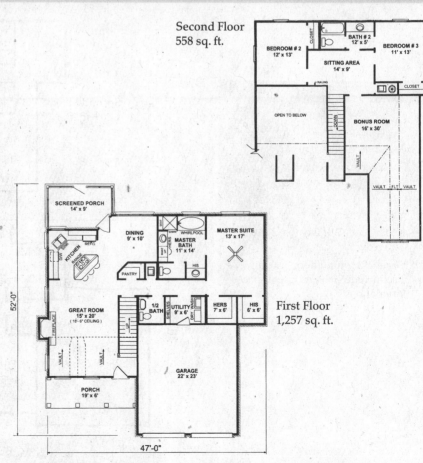

Second Floor
558 sq. ft.

First Floor
1,257 sq. ft.

1,815 total square feet of living area

Price Code C

Special features

- Well-designed kitchen opens to dining room and features raised breakfast bar
- First floor master suite has walk-in closet
- Front and back porches unite this home with the outdoors
- 3 bedrooms, 2 baths, 2-car side entry garage
- Basement, crawl space or slab foundation, please specify when ordering

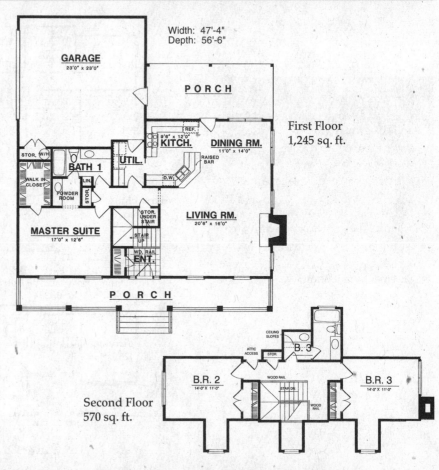

Width: 47'-4"
Depth: 56'-6"

First Floor
1,245 sq. ft.

GARAGE
23'0" x 23'0"

PORCH

STOR. W/H

BATH 1

UTIL.

KITCH.
9'6" x 12'0"

REF.

DINING RM.
11'0" x 14'0"

RAISED BAR

D.W.

WALK IN CLOSET

POWDER ROOM

LIN.

STOR

STOR. UNDER STAIR

LIVING RM.
20'6" x 16'0"

MASTER SUITE
17'0" x 12'6"

STAIR UP

WD. RAIL

ENT.

PORCH

Second Floor
570 sq. ft.

CEILING SLOPES

B. 3

ATTIC ACCESS

STOR

B.R. 2
14'0" X 11'0"

WOOD RAIL

STAIR DN.

WOOD RAIL

B.R. 3
14'0" X 11'0"

TO ORDER BLUEPRINTS USE THE FORM ON PAGE 15 OR CALL TOLL-FREE 1-877-671-6036
View thousands more home plans online at www.familyhandyman.com/homeplans

77

Terrific Three-Season Room

Plan #711-045D-0006

2,351 total square feet of living area

Price Code D

Special features

- Coffered ceiling in dining room adds elegant appeal
- Wrap-around porch creates a pleasant escape
- Cozy study with double-doors and extra storage
- Double walk-in closets balance and organize the master bedroom
- 3 bedrooms, 2 1/2 baths, 2-car garage
- Basement foundation

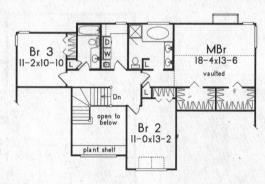

Second Floor
1,015 sq. ft.

Br 3
11-2x10-10

MBr
18-4x13-6
vaulted

Dn

open to below

Br 2
11-0x13-2

plant shelf

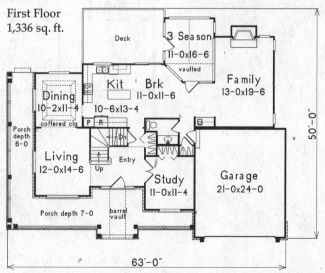

First Floor
1,336 sq. ft.

Deck

3 Season
11-0x16-6
vaulted

Family
13-0x19-6

Kit
10-6x13-4

Brk
11-0x11-6

Dining
10-2x11-4
coffered clg

Porch depth 6-0

Living
12-0x14-6

Entry

Up

Study
11-0x11-4

Garage
21-0x24-0

Porch depth 7-0

barrel vault

50'-0"

63'-0"

Multiple Porches And Decks

Plan #711-052D-0085

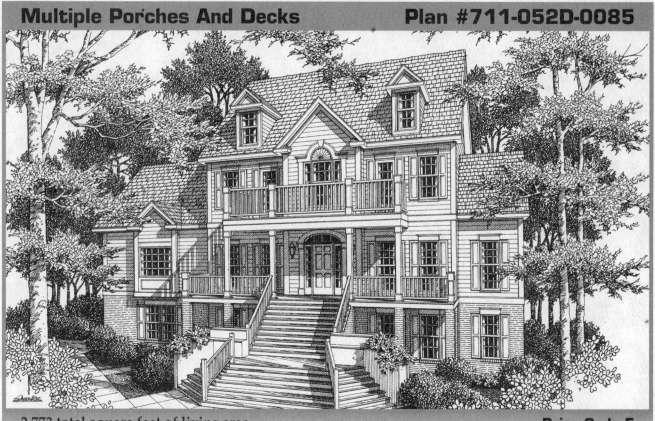

2,773 total square feet of living area

Price Code E

Special features

- First floor screened back porch with spiral staircase to second floor covered porch
- Family room and kitchen area combine for added space
- Master bedroom includes bath with large tub, separate shower, two walk-in closets and access to sundeck in back
- 4 bedrooms, 3 1/2 baths, 2-car drive under garage
- Basement foundation

Second Floor
1,152 sq. ft.

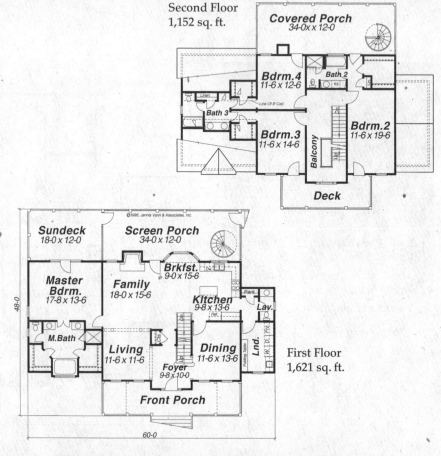

Covered Porch
34-0 x 12-0

Bath 2

Bdrm.4
11-6 x 12-6

Linen

Bath 3

Line Of 8' Ceil.

Bdrm.3
11-6 x 14-6

Balcony

Bdrm.2
11-6 x 19-6

Deck

©1998, Jannis Vann & Associates, Inc.

Sundeck
18-0 x 12-0

Screen Porch
34-0 x 12-0

Brkfst.
9-0 x 15-6

Master
Bdrm.
17-8 x 13-6

Family
18-0 x 15-6

Kitchen
9-8 x 13-6

Pant.

Lav.

48-0

M.Bath

Living
11-6 x 11-6

Dining
11-6 x 13-6

Lnd.

Foyer
9-8 x 10-0

Front Porch

First Floor
1,621 sq. ft.

60-0

TO ORDER BLUEPRINTS USE THE FORM ON PAGE 15 OR CALL TOLL-FREE 1-877-671-6036
View thousands more home plans online at www.familyhandyman.com/homeplans

79

Classic Elegance

Plan #711-007D-0062

2,483 total square feet of living area

Price Code D

Special features

- A large entry porch with open brick arches and palladian door welcomes guests
- The vaulted great room features an entertainment center alcove and the ideal layout for furniture placement
- The dining room is extra large with a stylish tray ceiling
- Study can easily be converted to a fourth bedroom
- 3 bedrooms, 2 baths, 2-car side entry garage
- Basement foundation

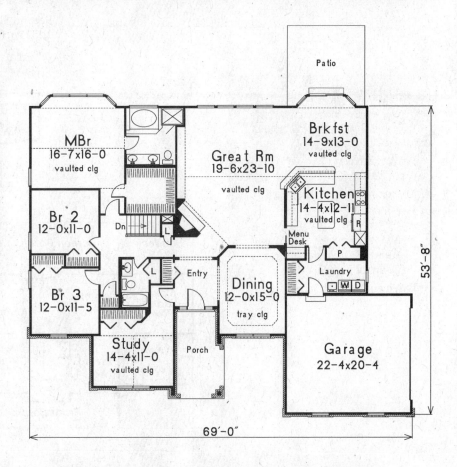

TO ORDER BLUEPRINTS USE THE FORM ON PAGE 15 OR CALL TOLL-FREE 1-877-671-6036
View thousands more home plans online at www.familyhandyman.com/homeplans

Spacious Private Master Bedroom   Plan #711-051D-0067

2,649 total square feet of living area

Price Code F

Special features

- A see-through fireplace warms the kitchen, nook and family rooms
- The kitchen features a cooktop island with rounded seating and opens into the cheerful bayed nook
- Secondary bedrooms both feature walk-in closets and share a bath
- 3 bedrooms, 2 1/2 baths, 3-car side entry garage
- Basement foundation

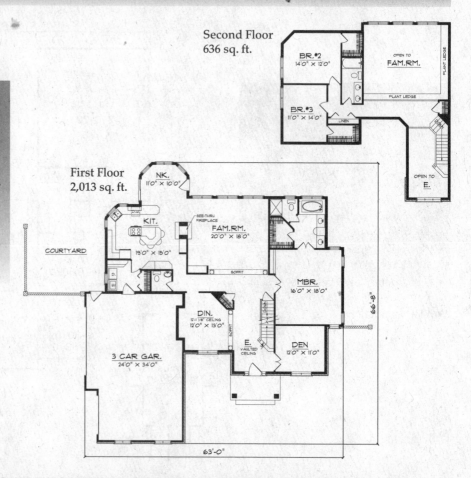

Second Floor
636 sq. ft.

First Floor
2,013 sq. ft.

TO ORDER BLUEPRINTS USE THE FORM ON PAGE 15 OR CALL TOLL-FREE 1-877-671-6036
View thousands more home plans online at www.familyhandyman.com/homeplans

81

2,468 total square feet of living area

Price Code D

Special features

- Open floor plan has family room with columns, fireplace, triple French doors and 12' ceiling
- Master bath features double walk-in closets and vanities
- Bonus room above garage has a private stairway and is included in the total square footage
- Bedrooms separate from main living space for privacy
- 3 bedrooms, 2 1/2 baths, 2-car side entry garage
- Slab foundation

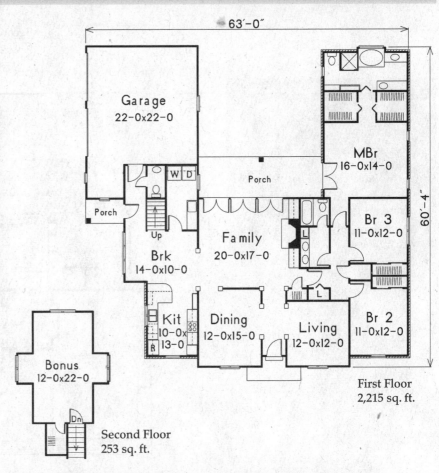

63'-0"

Garage
22-0x22-0

Porch

W D

Porch

MBr
16-0x14-0

60'-4"

Up

Family
20-0x17-0

Br 3
11-0x12-0

Brk
14-0x10-0

Kit
10-0x
13-0

Dining
12-0x15-0

Living
12-0x12-0

Br 2
11-0x12-0

First Floor
2,215 sq. ft.

Bonus
12-0x22-0

Dn

Second Floor
253 sq. ft.

Welcoming Front Porch

Plan #711-017D-0001

2,043 total square feet of living area

Price Code D

Special features

- Energy efficient home with 2" x 6" exterior walls
- Two-story central foyer includes two coat closets
- Large combined space provided by the kitchen, family and breakfast rooms
- Breakfast nook for informal dining looks out to the deck and screened porch
- 3 bedrooms, 2 1/2 baths, 2-car side entry garage
- Basement foundation, drawings also include slab foundation

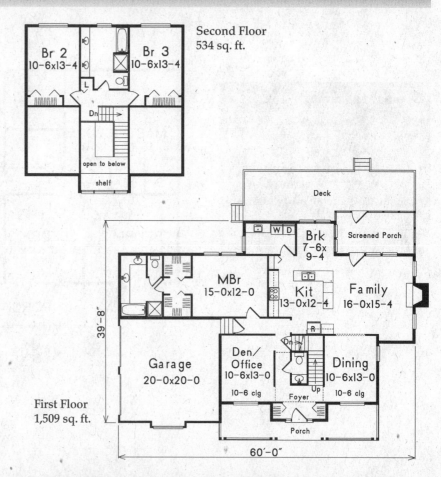

Second Floor
534 sq. ft.

Br 2
10-6x13-4

Br 3
10-6x13-4

Dn

open to below

shelf

First Floor
1,509 sq. ft.

Deck

W D

Brk
7-6x
9-4

Screened Porch

MBr
15-0x12-0

Kit
13-0x12-4

Family
16-0x15-4

39'-8"

Garage
20-0x20-0

Den/
Office
10-6x13-0

10-6 clg

Dn

Foyer

Up

Dining
10-6x13-0

10-6 clg

R

Porch

60'-0"

TO ORDER BLUEPRINTS USE THE FORM ON PAGE 15 OR CALL TOLL-FREE 1-877-671-6036
View thousands more home plans online at www.familyhandyman.com/homeplans

83

Charming Stone Accents

Plan #711-013D-0004

1,381 total square feet of living area

Price Code B

Special features

- Two walk-in closets in the master bedroom allow plenty of storage possibilities
- Cozy kitchen has space for dining and plenty of cabinet storage
- Sunny dining room has windows on two walls
- 3 bedrooms, 2 baths, 2-car garage
- Slab foundation

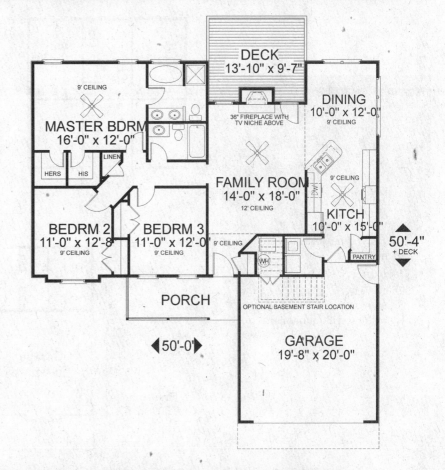

DECK
13'-10" x 9'-7"

9' CEILING

MASTER BDRM
16'-0" x 12'-0"

LINEN

HERS HIS

BEDRM 2
11'-0" x 12'-8"
9' CEILING

BEDRM 3
11'-0" x 12'-0"
9' CEILING

36" FIREPLACE WITH
TV NICHE ABOVE

DINING
10'-0" x 12'-0"
9' CEILING

FAMILY ROOM
14'-0" x 18'-0"
12' CEILING

KITCH
10'-0" x 15'-0"

9' CEILING

9' CEILING

WH

PANTRY

50'-4"
+ DECK

PORCH

OPTIONAL BASEMENT STAIR LOCATION

◄ 50'-0" ►

GARAGE
19'-8" x 20'-0"

TO ORDER BLUEPRINTS USE THE FORM ON PAGE 15 OR CALL TOLL-FREE 1-877-671-6036
View thousands more home plans online at www.familyhandyman.com/HOMEPLANS

Trio Of Dormers Add Appeal

Plan #711-031D-0011

2,164 total square feet of living area

Price Code C

Special features

- Country-styled front porch adds charm
- Plenty of counterspace in kitchen
- Large utility area meets big families' laundry needs
- Double-doors lead to covered rear porch
- 4 bedrooms, 2 1/2 baths, 2-car side entry garage
- Slab foundation

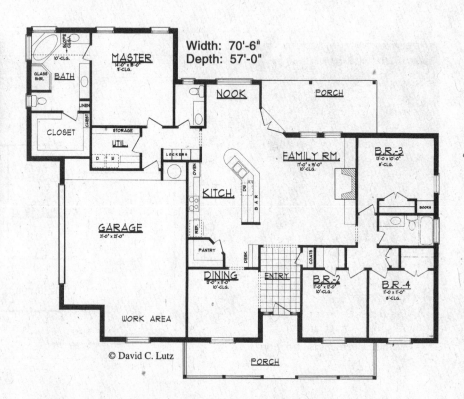

Width: 70'-6"
Depth: 57'-0"

© David C. Lutz

TO ORDER BLUEPRINTS USE THE FORM ON PAGE 15 OR CALL TOLL-FREE 1-877-671-6036
View thousands more home plans online at www.familyhandyman.com/homeplans

85

2,514 total square feet of living area

Price Code D

Special features

- Expansive porch welcomes you to the foyer, spacious dining area with bay and a gallery-sized hall with plant shelf above
- A highly functional U-shaped kitchen is open to a bayed breakfast room, study and family room with a 46' vista
- Vaulted rear sunroom has fireplace
- 1,509 square feet of optional living area on the lower level with recreation room, bedroom #4 with bath and an office with storage closet
- 3 bedrooms, 2 baths, 3-car oversized side entry garage with workshop/storage area
- Walk-out basement foundation

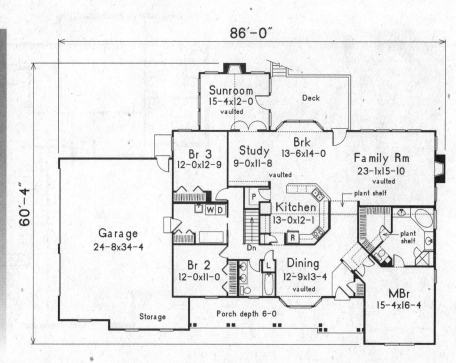

86

TO ORDER BLUEPRINTS USE THE FORM ON PAGE 15 OR CALL TOLL-FREE 1-877-671-6036
View thousands more home plans online at www.familyhandyman.com/homeplans

Traditional Home Appeal

Plan #711-058D-0042

2,356 total square feet of living area

Price Code D

Special features

- Master bedroom is located on the first floor and features lots of closet space and a luxury bath
- Plenty of extras throughout including a planning desk, large pantry, wet bar and a two-story great room
- Second floor boasts three bedrooms and a lovely view to the great room below
- 4 bedrooms, 2 1/2 baths, 2-car garage
- Basement foundation

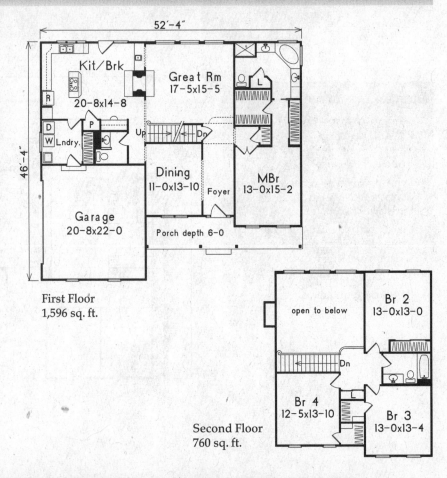

52'-4"

46'-4"

Kit/Brk
20-8x14-8

Great Rm
17-5x15-5

Up

Dn

Dining
11-0x13-10

Foyer

MBr
13-0x15-2

Lndry.

Garage
20-8x22-0

Porch depth 6-0

First Floor
1,596 sq. ft.

open to below

Br 2
13-0x13-0

Dn

Br 4
12-5x13-10

Br 3
13-0x13-4

Second Floor
760 sq. ft.

1,830 total square feet of living area

Price Code C

Special features

- A uniquely shaped galley-style kitchen shares a snack bar with the spacious gathering room that features a fireplace
- Dining room has sliding glass doors to the rear terrace as well as the master bedroom
- Master bedroom includes a luxury bath with a whirlpool tub and separate dressing room
- 3 bedrooms, 2 baths, 2-car garage
- Basement foundation

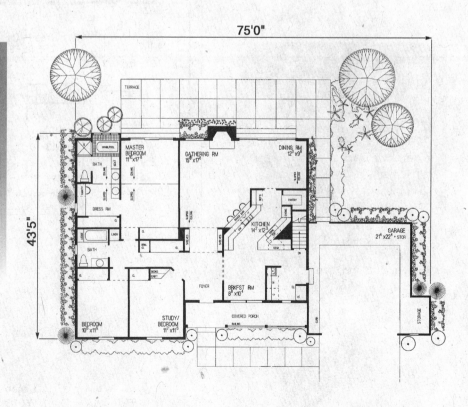

Handyman

2,018 total square feet of living area

Price Code C

Special features

- Family room is situated near dining area and kitchen creating a convenient layout
- First floor master bedroom features private bath with step-up tub and bay window
- Laundry area located on the first floor
- 4 bedrooms, 2 1/2 baths, 2-car garage
- Basement foundation

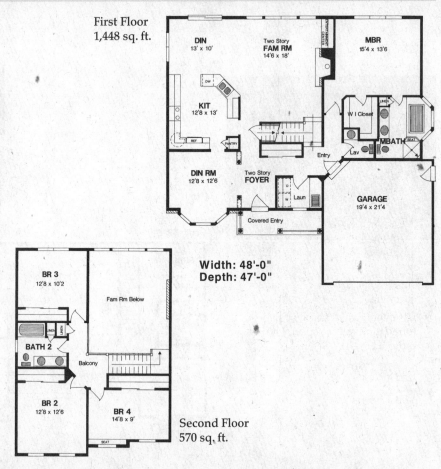

First Floor
1,448 sq. ft.

DIN
13' x 10'

Two Story
FAM RM
14'6 x 18'

MBR
15'4 x 13'6

KIT
12'8 x 13'

W I Closet

MBATH

DIN RM
12'8 x 12'6

Two Story
FOYER

Entry

Lav

Laun

GARAGE
19'4 x 21'4

Covered Entry

Width: 48'-0"
Depth: 47'-0"

BR 3
12'8 x 10'2

Fam Rm Below

BATH 2

Balcony

BR 2
12'8 x 12'6

BR 4
14'8 x 9'

Second Floor
570 sq. ft.

TO ORDER BLUEPRINTS USE THE FORM ON PAGE 15 OR CALL TOLL-FREE 1-877-671-6036
View thousands more home plans online at www.familyhandyman.com/homeplans

89

A Beautifully Balanced Facade   Plan #711-016D-0011

1,815 total square feet of living area

Price Code D

Special features

- A true great room features 10' ceiling, built-in fireplace and a bright airy feeling from several windows
- The kitchen and breakfast area are visually connected and the formal dining room is nearby for convenience
- Optional bonus room has an additional 323 square feet of living area
- 3 bedrooms, 2 baths, 2-car side entry garage
- Basement, crawl space or slab foundation, please specify when ordering

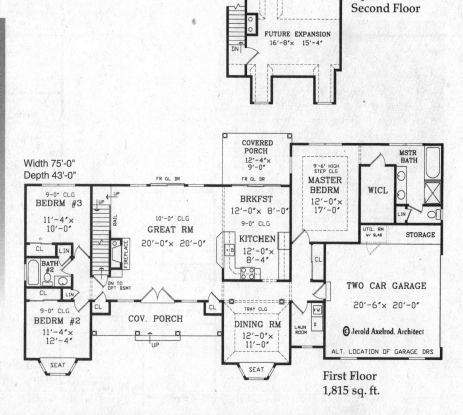

Optional Second Floor

FUTURE EXPANSION
16'-8" x 15'-4"

Width 75'-0"
Depth 43'-0"

COVERED PORCH
12'-4" x 9'-0"

BEDRM #3
11'-4" x 10'-0"
9'-0" CLG

GREAT RM
20'-0" x 20'-0"
10'-0" CLG

BRKFST
12'-0" x 8'-0"
9'-0" CLG

KITCHEN
12'-0" x 8'-4"

MASTER BEDRM
12'-0" x 17'-0"
9'-6" HIGH STEP CLG

MSTR BATH

WICL

UTIL. RM W/ SLAB

STORAGE

BATH #2

BEDRM #2
11'-4" x 12'-4"
9'-0" CLG

COV. PORCH

DINING RM
12'-0" x 11'-0"
TRAY CLG

LAUN ROOM

TWO CAR GARAGE
20'-6" x 20'-0"

© Jerold Axelrod, Architect

ALT. LOCATION OF GARAGE DRS

First Floor
1,815 sq. ft.

TO ORDER BLUEPRINTS USE THE FORM ON PAGE 15 OR CALL TOLL-FREE 1-877-671-6036
View thousands more home plans online at www.familyhandyman.com/homeplans

Secluded Master Suite

Plan #711-049D-0008

1,937 total square feet of living area

Price Code C

Special features

- Upscale great room offers a sloped ceiling, fireplace with extended hearth and built-in shelves for an entertainment center
- Gourmet kitchen includes a cooktop island counter and a quaint morning room
- Master suite features a sloped ceiling, cozy sitting room, walk-in closet and a private bath with whirlpool tub
- 3 bedrooms, 2 baths, 2-car side entry garage
- Crawl space foundation

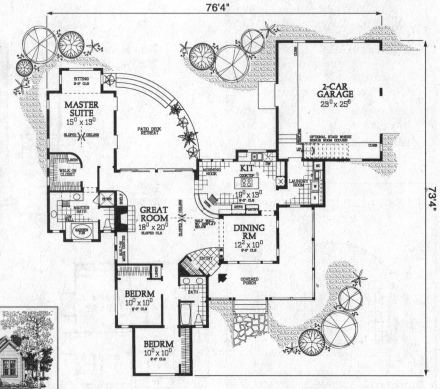

Rear View

Luxury Home

Plan #711-036D-0002

3,138 total square feet of living area

Price Code E

Special features

- Foyer opens into grand living room with vaulted ceiling and fireplace
- Study features built-in bookshelves
- Master bedroom and family room/ dining area have direct access to the outdoors onto two rear patios
- 4 bedrooms, 3 1/2 baths, 2-car side entry garage
- Slab foundation

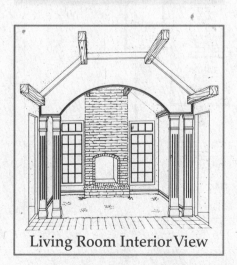

Living Room Interior View

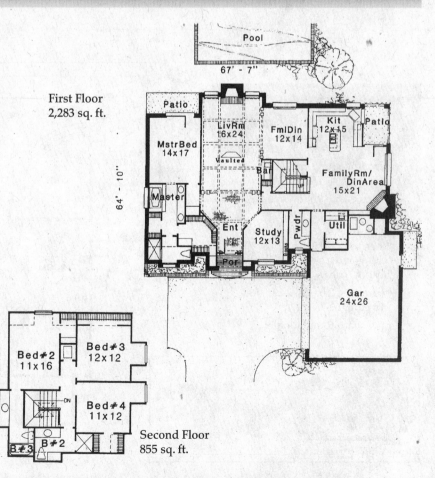

First Floor
2,283 sq. ft.

Second Floor
855 sq. ft.

TO ORDER BLUEPRINTS USE THE FORM ON PAGE 15 OR CALL TOLL-FREE 1-877-671-6036
View thousands more home plans online at www.familyhandyman.com/homeplans

High-Styled Compact Plan

Plan #711-053D-0012

2,356 total square feet of living area

Price Code D

Special features

- Impressive arched and mullioned window treatment embellishes entrance and foyer
- Fourth bedroom located over the side entry garage
- Full-size laundry facility
- Adjoining family room, breakfast area and kitchen form an extensive living area
- 4 bedrooms, 2 1/2 baths, 2-car side entry garage
- Basement foundation

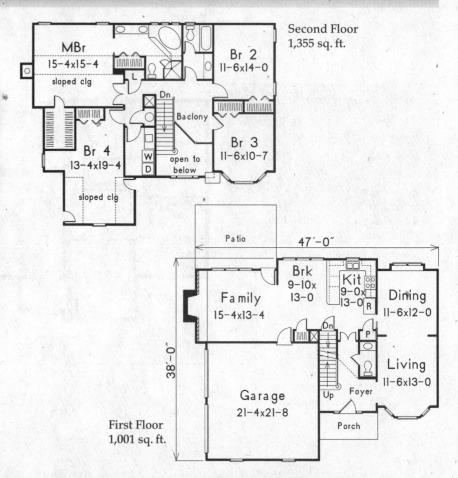

Second Floor
1,355 sq. ft.

MBr
15-4x15-4
sloped clg

Br 2
11-6x14-0

Dn

Baclony

Br 4
13-4x19-4

W D

open to below

Br 3
11-6x10-7

sloped clg

Patio

47'-0"

Brk
9-10x13-0

Kit
9-0x13-0

R

Dining
11-6x12-0

Family
15-4x13-4

Dn

P

38'-0"

Living
11-6x13-0

Garage
21-4x21-8

Up   Foyer

Porch

First Floor
1,001 sq. ft.

TO ORDER BLUEPRINTS USE THE FORM ON PAGE 15 OR CALL TOLL-FREE 1-877-671-6036
View thousands more home plans online at www.familyhandyman.com/homeplans

93

Unique Entry Has Cathedral Ceiling   Plan #711-051D-0035

1,868 total square feet of living area   **Price Code C**

Special features

- Bayed dining area has sliding glass door leading to the outdoors
- Oversized shower and tub in master bath
- Large laundry room has a half bath and a storage closet
- 3 bedrooms, 2 1/2 baths, 2-car side entry garage
- Basement foundation

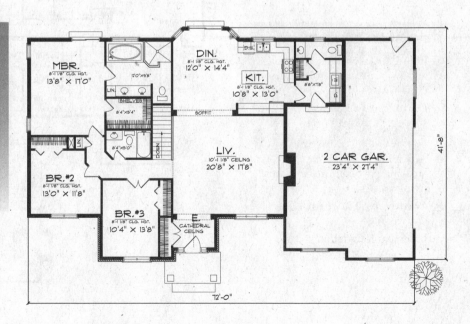

The Family Handyman

2,967 total square feet of living area

Price Code E

Special features

- An exterior with charm graced with country porch and multiple arched projected box windows
- Dining area is oversized and adjoins a fully equipped kitchen with walk-in pantry
- Two bay windows light up the enormous informal living area to the rear
- 4 bedrooms, 3 1/2 baths, 3-car side entry garage
- Basement foundation

Second Floor
1,517 sq. ft.

Br 3
13-0x14-0

Br 2
13-0x10-2

Br 4
14-9x13-1

Study
9-0x10-0

Dn

plant shelf

MBr
15-4x17-0

vaulted clg

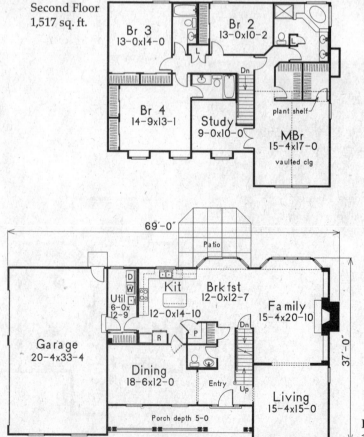

69'-0"

Patio

Util
6-0x
12-9

Kit
12-0x14-10

Brk fst
12-0x12-7

Family
15-4x20-10

D
W

Garage
20-4x33-4

P

R

Dn

37'-0"

Dining
18-6x12-0

Entry

Up

Living
15-4x15-0

Porch depth 5-0

First Floor
1,450 sq. ft.

TO ORDER BLUEPRINTS USE THE FORM ON PAGE 15 OR CALL TOLL-FREE 1-877-671-6036
View thousands more home plans online at www.familyhandyman.com/homeplans

95

COVERED PORCH ADDS APPEAL

Plan #711-032D-0040

1,480 total square feet of living area

Price Code A

Special features

- Energy efficient home with 2" x 6" exterior walls
- Cathedral ceilings in family and dining rooms
- Master bedroom has a walk-in closet and access to bath
- 2 bedrooms, 2 baths
- Basement foundation

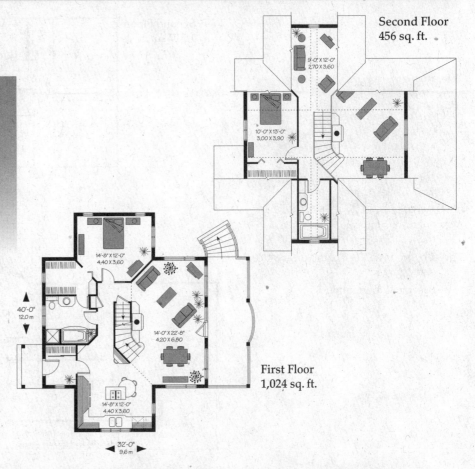

Second Floor
456 sq. ft.

First Floor
1,024 sq. ft.

2,840 total square feet of living area

Price Code F

Special features

- Secluded den has a half bath perfect for a home office
- Corner columns separate the formal dining room while maintaining openness
- Built-in bookshelves flank each side of the fireplace in the great room
- 3 bedrooms, 2 1/2 baths, 2-car garage
- Crawl space foundation

First Floor
1,744 sq. ft.

DECK

NOOK
10/0 x 11/4
(9' CLG.)

10/6 x 13/4

DESK

GREAT RM.
18/6 X 15/4
(13' CLG.)

MASTER
15/8 X 13/2
(9' CLG.)

DN.

DINING
11/0 x 13/2
(13' CLG.)

FOYER
(13' CLG.)

BUILT-INS

GARAGE
21/0 X 21/6

46'

DEN
10/6 x 13/4+
(9' CLG.)

©Alan Mascord Design Associates, Inc.

◄ 57'-6" ►

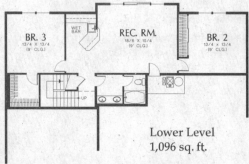

BR. 3
13/4 x 13/4
(9' CLG.)

WET BAR

REC. RM.
18/6 X 13/4
(9' CLG.)

BR. 2
13/4 x 13/4
(9' CLG.)

UP

Lower Level
1,096 sq. ft.

TO ORDER BLUEPRINTS USE THE FORM ON PAGE 15 OR CALL TOLL-FREE 1-877-671-6036
View thousands more home plans online at www.familyhandyman.com/homeplans

97

Grand Appeal With Expansive Porch   Plan #711-005D-0001

1,400 total square feet of living area

Price Code B

Special features

- Master bedroom is secluded for privacy
- Large utility room has additional cabinet space
- Covered porch provides an outdoor seating area
- Roof dormers add great curb appeal
- Living room and master bedroom feature vaulted ceilings
- Oversized two-car garage has storage space
- 3 bedrooms, 2 baths, 2-car garage
- Basement foundation, drawings also include crawl space foundation

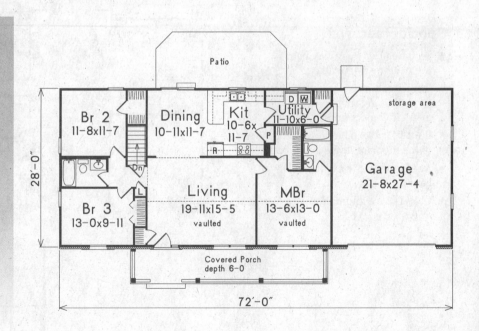

Bay Window In Master Bedroom   Plan #711-053D-0002

1,668 total square feet of living area

Price Code C

Special features

- Large bay windows in breakfast area, master bedroom and dining room
- Extensive walk-in closets and storage spaces throughout the home
- Handy covered entry porch
- Large living room has fireplace, built-in bookshelves and sloped ceiling
- 3 bedrooms, 2 baths, 2-car drive under garage
- Basement foundation

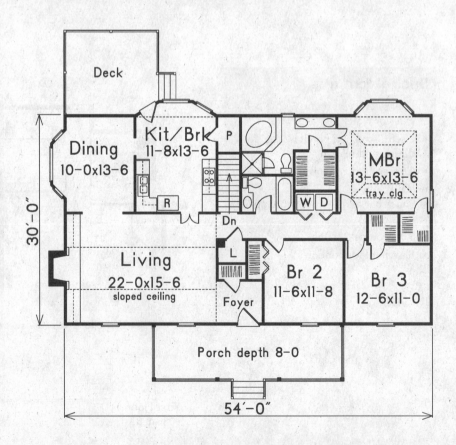

Deck

Dining
10-0x13-6

Kit/Brk
11-8x13-6

P

MBr
13-6x13-6
tray clg

30'-0"

R

W D

Dn

Living
22-0x15-6
sloped ceiling

L

Br 2
11-6x11-8

Br 3
12-6x11-0

Foyer

Porch depth 8-0

54'-0"

TO ORDER BLUEPRINTS USE THE FORM ON PAGE 15 OR CALL TOLL-FREE 1-877-671-6036
View thousands more home plans online at www.familyhandyman.com/homeplans

99

Four Seasons Cottage

Plan #711-032D-0033

1,484 total square feet of living area

Price Code A

Special features

- Energy efficient home with 2" x 6" exterior walls
- Useful screened porch is ideal for dining and relaxing
- Corner fireplace warms living room
- Snack bar adds extra counterspace in kitchen
- 3 bedrooms, 2 baths
- Basement foundation

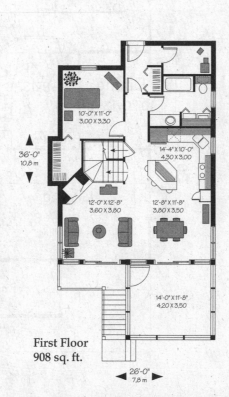

36'-0"
10,8 m

10'-0" X 11'-0"
3,00 X 3,30

14'-4" X 10'-0"
4,30 X 3,00

12'-0" X 12'-8"
3,60 X 3,80

12'-8" X 11'-8"
3,80 X 3,50

14'-0" X 11'-8"
4,20 X 3,50

First Floor
908 sq. ft.

26'-0"
7,8 m

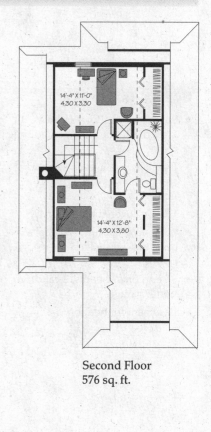

14'-4" X 11'-0"
4,30 X 3,30

14'-4" X 12'-8"
4,30 X 3,80

Second Floor
576 sq. ft.

Dormers Enhance This Home

Plan #711-052D-0089

2,911 total square feet of living area

Price Code E

Special features

- Wrap-around porch with double columns
- Optional living area and bedroom above two-car garage has 512 square feet of living area
- Beautiful master bath with corner tub, separate shower and large walk-in closet
- Large sundeck offers a great area to relax
- 3 bedrooms, 2 1/2 baths, 2-car side entry garage
- Basement foundation

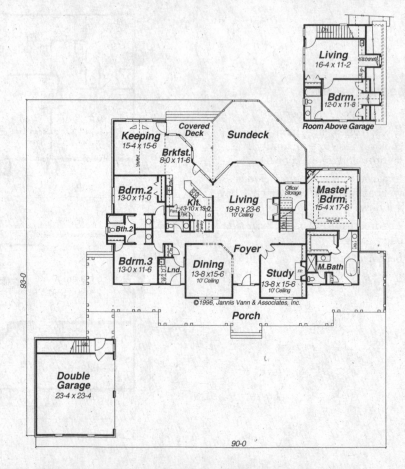

Living 16-4 x 11-2

Bdrm. 12-0 x 11-8

Room Above Garage

Keeping 15-4 x 15-6

Covered Deck

Sundeck

Brkfst. 8-0 x 11-6

Bdrm.2 13-0 x 11-0

Kit. 13-10 x 13-0

Living 19-8 x 23-6 10' Ceiling

Office/ Storage

Master Bdrm. 15-4 x 17-6

Bth.2

Foyer

Bdrm.3 13-0 x 11-6

Dining 13-8 x15-6 10' Ceiling

Study 13-8 x 15-6 10' Ceiling

M.Bath

©1996, Jannis Vann & Associates, Inc.

Porch

93-0

Double Garage 23-4 x 23-4

90-0

TO ORDER BLUEPRINTS USE THE FORM ON PAGE 15 OR CALL TOLL-FREE 1-877-671-6036
View thousands more home plans online at www.familyhandyman.com/homeplans

101

Foyer With Grand Curved Stairway   Plan #711-001D-0038

3,144 total square feet of living area   **Price Code E**

Special features

- 9' ceilings on first floor
- Kitchen offers large pantry, island cooktop and close proximity to laundry and dining rooms
- Expansive family room includes wet bar, fireplace and attractive bay window
- 4 bedrooms, 4 1/2 baths, 3-car side entry garage
- Basement foundation

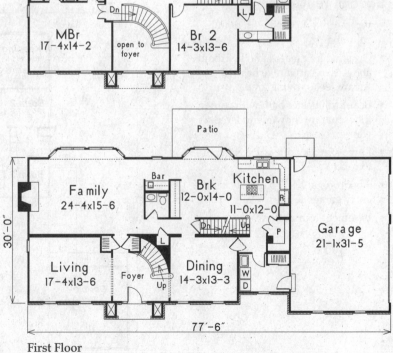

Second Floor
1,420 sq. ft.

Br 4
12-0x12-0

Br 3
12-0x12-0

MBr
17-4x14-2

open to
foyer

Br 2
14-3x13-6

Patio

Family
24-4x15-6

Bar

Brk
12-0x14-0

Kitchen

11-0x12-0

Garage
21-1x31-5

Living
17-4x13-6

Foyer

Dining
14-3x13-3

30'-0"

77'-6"

First Floor
1,724 sq. ft.

Unique Master Suite

Plan #711-028D-0014

2,340 total square feet of living area

Price Code D

Special features

- Great room shares a see-through fireplace with the dining room
- Bedrooms #2 and #3 share a split bath
- Enormous sitting area in master bedroom could easily be converted to a study or even a nursery
- 3 bedrooms, 2 1/2 baths, 2-car side entry garage
- Crawl space or slab foundation, please specify when ordering

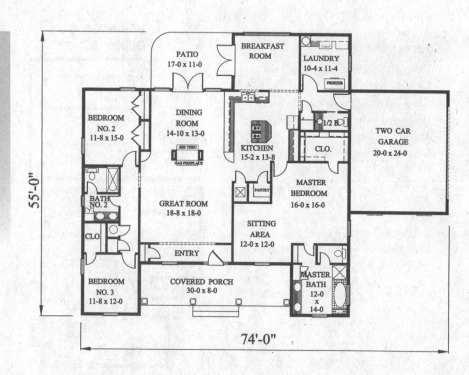

TO ORDER BLUEPRINTS USE THE FORM ON PAGE 15 OR CALL TOLL-FREE 1-877-671-6036
View thousands more home plans online at www.familyhandyman.com/homeplans

103

CRAFTSMAN COTTAGE

Plan #711-015D-0023

1,649 total square feet of living area

Price Code B

Special features

- Energy efficient home with 2" x 6" exterior walls
- Ideal design for a narrow lot
- Country kitchen includes an island and eating bar
- Master bedroom has 12' vaulted ceiling and a charming arched window
- 4 bedrooms, 2 1/2 baths, 2-car side entry garage
- Basement or crawl space foundation, please specify when ordering

Width: 30'-0"
Depth: 52'-0"

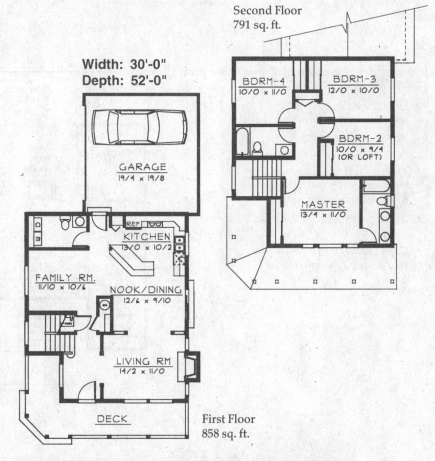

Second Floor
791 sq. ft.

BDRM-4
10/0 x 11/0

BDRM-3
12/0 x 10/0

BDRM-2
10/0 x 9/4
(OR LOFT)

MASTER
13/4 x 11/0

GARAGE
19/4 x 19/8

KITCHEN
13/0 x 10/2

FAMILY RM.
11/10 x 10/6

NOOK/DINING
12/6 x 9/10

LIVING RM.
14/2 x 11/0

DECK

First Floor
858 sq. ft.

Excellent Ranch For Country Setting   Plan #711-007D-0048

2,758 total square feet of living area

Price Code E

Special features

- Vaulted great room excels with fireplace, wet bar, plant shelves and skylights
- Fabulous master bedroom enjoys a fireplace, large bath, walk-in closet and vaulted ceiling
- Trendsetting kitchen and breakfast rooms adjoin spacious screened porch
- Convenient office near kitchen is perfect for computer room, hobby enthusiast or fifth bedroom
- 4 bedrooms, 2 1/2 baths, 3-car side entry garage
- Basement foundation

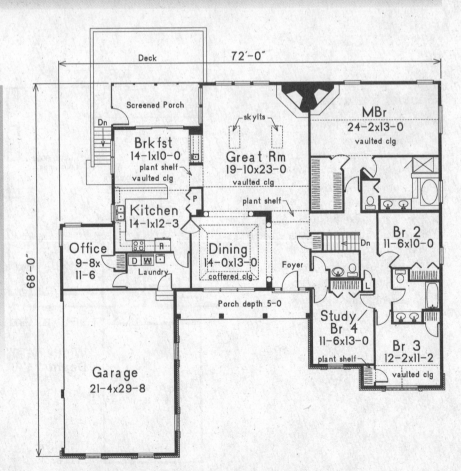

TO ORDER BLUEPRINTS USE THE FORM ON PAGE 15 OR CALL TOLL-FREE 1-877-671-6036
View thousands more home plans online at www.familyhandyman.com/homeplans

105

© 2003, Garrell Associates, Inc.

Christine Canova 2/02

2,111 total square feet of living area

Price Code H

Special features

- 9' ceilings throughout first floor
- Formal dining room has columns separating it from other areas while allowing it to maintain an open feel
- Master bedroom has privacy from other bedrooms
- Bonus room on the second floor has an additional 345 square feet of living area
- 3 bedrooms, 2 baths, 2-car side entry garage
- Basement foundation

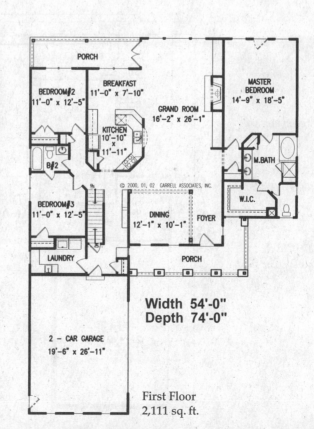

PORCH

BEDROOM#2
11'-0" x 12'-5"

BREAKFAST
11'-0" x 7'-10"

MASTER BEDROOM
14'-9" x 18'-5"

GRAND ROOM
16'-2" x 26'-1"

KITCHEN
10'-10" x 11'-11"

B.#2

M.BATH

© 2000, 01, 02 GARRELL ASSOCIATES, INC.

BEDROOM#3
11'-0" x 12'-5"

DINING
12'-1" x 10'-1"

FOYER

W.I.C.

LAUNDRY

PORCH

Width 54'-0"
Depth 74'-0"

2 - CAR GARAGE
19'-6" x 26'-11"

First Floor
2,111 sq. ft.

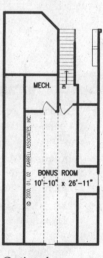

MECH.

© 2000, 01, 02 GARRELL ASSOCIATES, INC.

BONUS ROOM
10'-10" x 26'-11"

Optional
Second Floor

TO ORDER BLUEPRINTS USE THE FORM ON PAGE 15 OR CALL TOLL-FREE 1-877-671-6036
View thousands more home plans online at www.familyhandyman.com/homeplans

Exquisite Entry

Plan #711-025D-0015

1,778 total square feet of living area

Price Code B

Special features

- Angled walls in foyer add interest to this floor plan
- Secluded master suite maintains privacy
- Centralized kitchen is spacious in size with extras such as a nearby desk
- 3 bedrooms, 2 baths, 2-car side entry garage
- Slab foundation

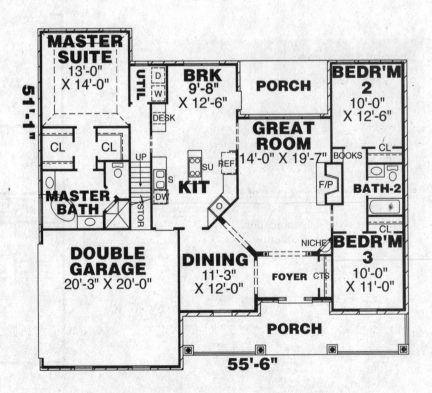

51'-1"

MASTER SUITE 13'-0" X 14'-0"

UTIL

D W DESK

BRK 9'-8" X 12'-6"

PORCH

BEDR'M 2 10'-0" X 12'-6"

CL CL

UP

GREAT ROOM 14'-0" X 19'-7"

BOOKS

CL

STOR

SU REF

F/P

BATH-2

MASTER BATH

S

DW

KIT

DOUBLE GARAGE 20'-3" X 20'-0"

DINING 11'-3" X 12'-0"

NICHE

BEDR'M 3 10'-0" X 11'-0"

FOYER CTS

CL

PORCH

55'-6"

TO ORDER BLUEPRINTS USE THE FORM ON PAGE 15 OR CALL TOLL-FREE 1-877-671-6036
View thousands more home plans online at www.familyhandyman.com/homeplans

107

Comfortable Living In This Home

Plan #711-055D-0116

1,462 total square feet of living area

Price Code A

Special features

- U-shaped kitchen has everything within reach
- All bedrooms have access to their own bath
- Master bath has double vanity, shower and a whirlpool tub with glass block window
- 3 bedrooms, 3 baths, 2-car rear entry garage
- Crawl space or slab foundation, please specify when ordering

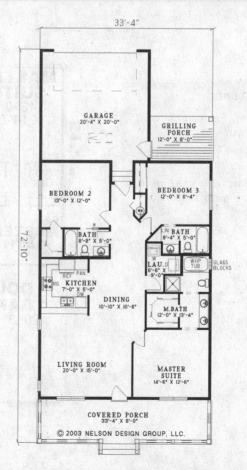

33'-4"

72'-10"

GARAGE
20'-4" X 20'-0"

GRILLING PORCH
12'-0" X 8'-0"

BEDROOM 2
13'-0" X 12'-0"

BEDROOM 3
12'-0" X 11'-4"

BATH
8'-8" X 5'-0"

BATH
9'-4" X 5'-0"

REF PAN

LAU.
6'-6" X 9'-0"

WHP TUB

GLASS BLOCKS

KITCHEN
7'-0" X 5'-0"

DINING
10'-10" X 10'-6"

M.BATH
12'-0" X 13'-4"

LIVING ROOM
20'-0" X 15'-0"

MASTER SUITE
14'-6" X 12'-6"

COVERED PORCH
33'-4" X 8'-0"

© 2003 NELSON DESIGN GROUP, LLC.

Breakfast/Family Room Combination   Plan #711-027D-0005

2,135 total square feet of living area

Price Code D

Special features

- Family room features extra space, impressive fireplace and full wall of windows that joins breakfast room creating a spacious entertainment area
- Washer and dryer are conveniently located on the second floor
- Kitchen features island counter and pantry
- 4 bedrooms, 2 1/2 baths, 2-car garage
- Basement foundation

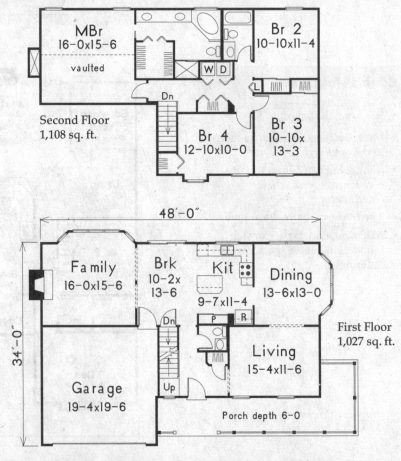

MBr
16-0x15-6
vaulted

Br 2
10-10x11-4

Second Floor
1,108 sq. ft.

Br 4
12-10x10-0

Br 3
10-10x 13-3

W D

48'-0"

Family
16-0x15-6

Brk
10-2x 13-6

Kit
9-7x11-4

Dining
13-6x13-0

34'-0"

Dn

P   R

Living
15-4x11-6

First Floor
1,027 sq. ft.

Garage
19-4x19-6

Up

Porch depth 6-0

TO ORDER BLUEPRINTS USE THE FORM ON PAGE 15 OR CALL TOLL-FREE 1-877-671-6036
View thousands more home plans online at www.familyhandyman.com/homeplans

109

Traditional Ranch With Extras   Plan #711-038D-0039

1,771 total square feet of living area   **Price Code B**

Special features

- Den has a sloped ceiling and charming window seat
- Private master bedroom has access to the outdoors
- Central kitchen allows for convenient access when entertaining
- 2 bedrooms, 2 baths, 2-car garage
- Basement, crawl space or slab foundation, please specify when ordering

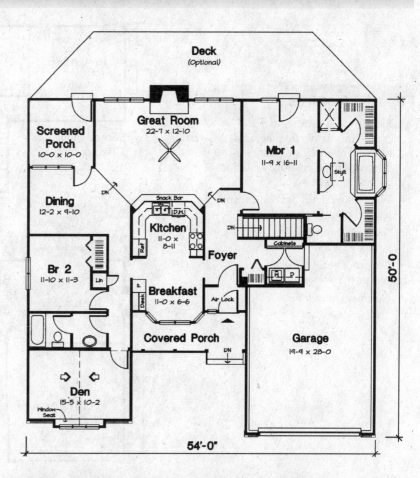

TO ORDER BLUEPRINTS USE THE FORM ON PAGE 15 OR CALL TOLL-FREE 1-877-671-6036
View thousands more home plans online at www.familyhandyman.com/homeplans

Exquisite Brick And Stone Exterior   Plan #711-065D-0037

2,241 total square feet of living area   Price Code D

Special features

- The dining and great rooms combine for a beautiful gathering place
- An island with extended counter seating defines the kitchen and breakfast area
- Bonus room on the second floor has an additional 283 square feet of living area
- 4 bedrooms, 2 1/2 baths, 2-car side entry garage
- Basement foundation

Second Floor
519 sq. ft.

Bedroom
13'2" x 11'

Bedroom
11' x 12'2"

Bath

Great Room
Below

Balcony

WALK-IN CLOSE

Bonus
Room
11'2" x 16'

First Floor
1,722 sq. ft.

Breakfast
15'2" x 8'10"

Dining Room
12'10" x 14'6"

Great Room
16' x 23'2"

Kitchen

Bath

Dressing

Laun.

Hall

Foyer

Master
Bedroom
13'3" x 16'6"

Two-Car
Garage
22' x 23'10"

Porch

First Floor Plan

55'-6"

56'-8"

TO ORDER BLUEPRINTS USE THE FORM ON PAGE 15 OR CALL TOLL-FREE 1-877-671-6036
View thousands more home plans online at www.familyhandyman.com/homeplans

111

Grand Victorian Home

Plan #711-032D-0048

2,590 total square feet of living area

Price Code D

Special features

- Energy efficient home with 2" x 6" exterior walls
- Utility room is located on the second floor for convenience
- Master bedroom has private bath with double vanity, oversized shower and freestanding tub in bay window
- Bonus room above the garage has an additional 459 square feet of living area
- 3 bedrooms, 2 1/2 baths, 2-car garage
- Basement foundation

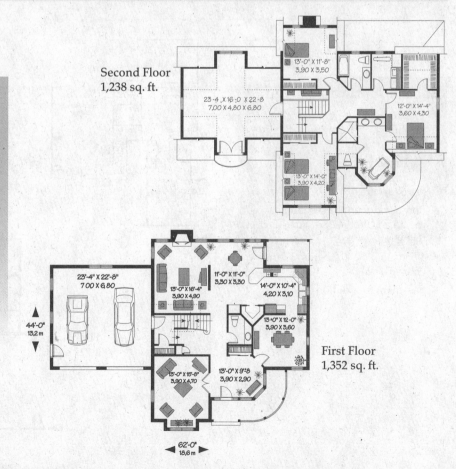

Second Floor
1,238 sq. ft.

23-4 X 16-0 X 22-8
7,00 X 4,80 X 6,80

13'-0" X 11'-8"
3,90 X 3,50

12'-0" X 14'-4"
3,60 X 4,30

13'-0" X 14'-0"
3,90 X 4,20

23'-4" X 22'-8"
7,00 X 6,80

11'-0" X 11'-0"
3,30 X 3,30

13'-0" X 16'-4"
3,90 X 4,90

14'-0" X 10'-4"
4,20 X 3,10

13'-0" X 12'-0"
3,90 X 3,60

44'-0"
13,2 m

13'-0" X 15'-8"
3,90 X 4,70

13'-0" X 9'-8"
3,90 X 2,90

First Floor
1,352 sq. ft.

62'-0"
18,6 m

Inviting Master Bedroom

Plan #711-052D-0092

3,118 total square feet of living area

Price Code E

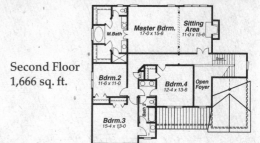

Second Floor
1,666 sq. ft.

First Floor
1,452 sq. ft.

Special features

- A warm cottage feel is created with the use of stone and an arched entry
- Second floor master bedroom has lovely sitting area with fireplace
- Spacious feel is created by cathedral ceiling in living area
- 4 bedrooms, 2 1/2 baths, 2-car side entry garage
- Walk-out basement foundation

Impressive Victorian

Plan #711-001D-0003

2,286 total square feet of living area

Price Code E

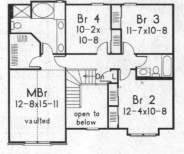

Second Floor
1,003 sq. ft.

First Floor
1,283 sq. ft.

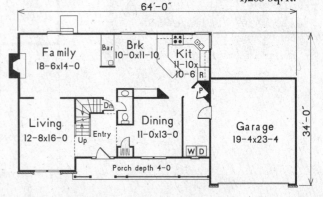

Special features

- Fine architectural detail makes this home a showplace
- Stunning two-story entry with attractive wood railing and balustrades in foyer
- Convenient wrap-around kitchen with window view, planning center and pantry
- Oversized master bedroom with walk-in closet and master bath
- 4 bedrooms, 2 1/2 baths, 2-car garage
- Basement foundation, drawings also include crawl space and slab foundations

TO ORDER BLUEPRINTS USE THE FORM ON PAGE 15 OR CALL TOLL-FREE 1-877-671-6036
View thousands more home plans online at www.familyhandyman.com/homeplans

113

Small Ranch For A Perfect Haven   Plan #711-007D-0067

1,761 total square feet of living area

Price Code B

Special features

- Exterior window dressing, roof dormers and planter boxes provide visual warmth and charm
- Great room boasts a vaulted ceiling, fireplace and opens to a pass-through kitchen
- Master bedroom is vaulted with luxury bath and walk-in closet
- Home features eight separate closets with an abundance of storage
- 4 bedrooms, 2 baths, 2-car side entry garage
- Basement foundation

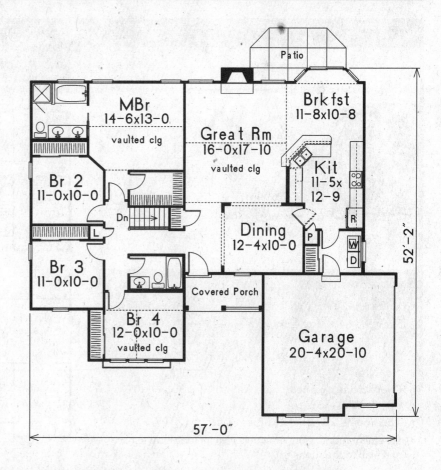

Patio

MBr
14-6x13-0
vaulted clg

Brk fst
11-8x10-8

Great Rm
16-0x17-10
vaulted clg

Kit
11-5x
12-9

Br 2
11-0x10-0

Dn

Dining
12-4x10-0

P

R

W
D

Br 3
11-0x10-0

L

Covered Porch

Br 4
12-0x10-0
vaulted clg

Garage
20-4x20-10

52'-2"

57'-0"

Spacious Style For Gracious Living

Plan #711-037D-0005

3,050 total square feet of living area

Price Code E

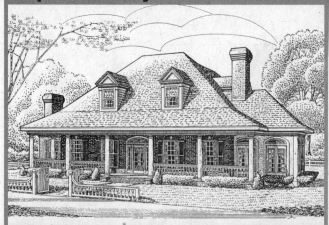

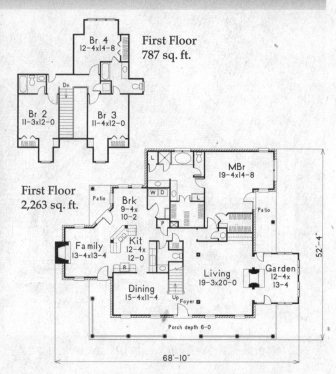

Br 4
12-4x14-8

First Floor
787 sq. ft.

Br 2
11-3x12-0

Br 3
11-4x12-0

First Floor
2,263 sq. ft.

MBr
19-4x14-8

Patio

Brk
9-4x
10-2

Family
13-4x13-4

Kit
12-4x
12-0

Living
19-3x20-0

Garden
12-4x
13-4

Dining
15-4x11-4

Foyer

Porch depth 6-0

68'-10"

52'-4"

Special features

- Sunny garden room and two-way fireplace create a bright, airy living room
- Front porch enhanced by arched transom windows and bold columns
- Sitting alcove, French door access to side patio, walk-in closets and abundant storage in master bedroom
- 4 bedrooms, 3 1/2 baths, 2-car detached garage
- Slab foundation, drawings also include crawl space foundation

Casual Living With This Design

Plan #711-062D-0053

1,405 total square feet of living area

Price Code A

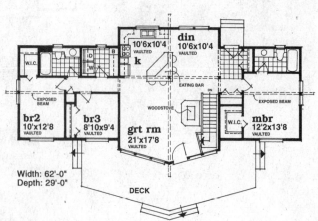

din
10'6x10'4
VAULTED

W.I.C.

10'6x10'4
VAULTED

k

EATING BAR

EXPOSED
BEAM

EXPOSED
BEAM

br2
10'x12'8
VAULTED

br3
8'10x9'4
VAULTED

WOODSTOVE

grt rm
21'x17'8
VAULTED

W.I.C.

mbr
12'2x13'8
VAULTED

Width: 62'-0"
Depth: 29'-0"

DECK

Special features

- An expansive wall of glass gives a spectacular view to the great room and accentuates the high vaulted ceilings throughout the design
- Great room is warmed by a woodstove and is open to the dining room and L-shaped kitchen
- Triangular snack bar graces kitchen
- 3 bedrooms, 2 baths
- Basement or crawl space foundation, please specify when ordering

TO ORDER BLUEPRINTS USE THE FORM ON PAGE 15 OR CALL TOLL-FREE 1-877-671-6036
View thousands more home plans online at www.familyhandyman.com/homeplans

115

3,246 total square feet of living area

Price Code F

Special features

- Cheerful sun room is surrounded with windows for added openness
- Double-door entry into the den keeps this space private
- A sink and extra counter space extends to dining room entrance for entertaining ease
- 4 bedrooms, 2 1/2 baths, 3-car side entry garage
- Basement foundation

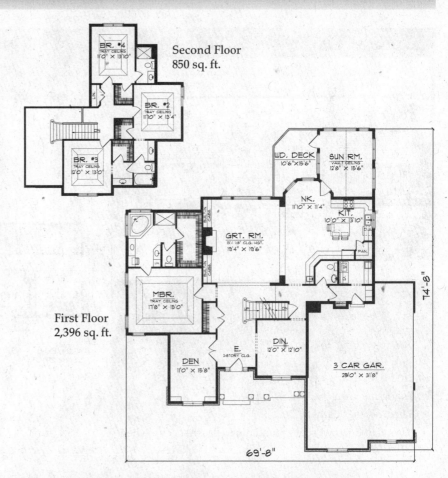

Second Floor
850 sq. ft.

BR. #4
TRAY CEILING
11'0" X 13'10"

BR. #2
TRAY CEILING
11'10" X 13'4"

BR. #3
TRAY CEILING
12'0" X 13'0"

First Floor
2,396 sq. ft.

WD. DECK
10'6" X 15'6"

SUN RM.
VAULT CEILING
12'8" X 15'6"

NK.
11'10" X 11'4"

KIT.
10'0" X 13'0"

GRT. RM.
11'-1/8" CLG. HGT.
19'4" X 19'6"

MBR.
TRAY CEILING
17'8" X 15'0"

DEN
11'0" X 15'8"

E.
2-STORY CLG.

DIN.
12'0" X 12'10"

3 CAR GAR.
29'0" X 31'8"

74'-8"

69'-8"

TO ORDER BLUEPRINTS USE THE FORM ON PAGE 15 OR CALL TOLL-FREE 1-877-671-6036
View thousands more home plans online at www.familyhandyman.com/homeplans

116

Dramatic U-Shaped Stairs

Plan #711-011D-0025

2,287 total square feet of living area

Price Code E

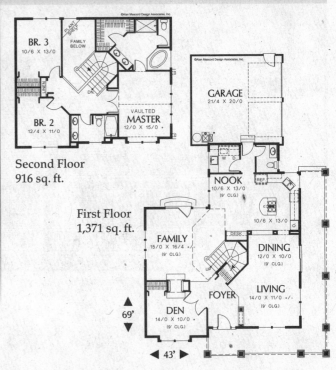

Second Floor
916 sq. ft.

First Floor
1,371 sq. ft.

Special features

- Wrap-around porch creates an inviting feeling
- First floor windows have transom windows above
- Den has see-through fireplace into the family area
- 3 bedrooms, 2 1/2 baths, 2-car side entry garage
- Crawl space foundation

Country Ranch With Open Interior

Plan #711-016D-0001

1,783 total square feet of living area

Price Code D

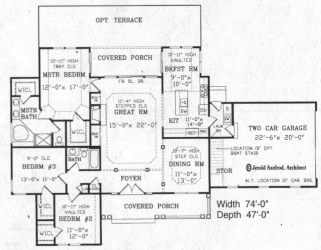

Width 74'-0"
Depth 47'-0"

Special features

- The front to rear flow of the great room, with built-ins on one side is a furnishing delight
- Bedrooms are all quietly zoned on one side
- The master bedroom is separated for privacy
- Every bedroom features walk-in closets
- 3 bedrooms, 2 baths, 2-car side entry garage
- Basement, crawl space or slab foundation, please specify when ordering

TO ORDER BLUEPRINTS USE THE FORM ON PAGE 15 OR CALL TOLL-FREE 1-877-671-6036
View thousands more home plans online at www.familyhandyman.com/homeplans

117

Porch Adds Warmth To Home

Plan #711-049D-0011

1,974 total square feet of living area

Price Code C

Special features

- Sunny bayed nook invites casual dining and shares its natural light with a snack counter and kitchen
- Spacious master bedroom occupies a bay window and offers a sumptuous bath
- Both second floor bedrooms have private balconies
- 3 bedrooms, 2 1/2 baths
- Basement or crawl space foundation, please specify when ordering

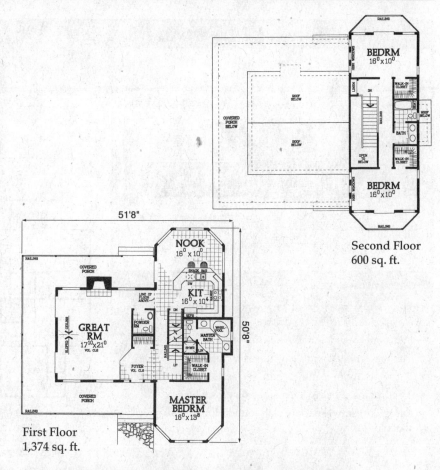

Second Floor
600 sq. ft.

First Floor
1,374 sq. ft.

TO ORDER BLUEPRINTS USE THE FORM ON PAGE 15 OR CALL TOLL-FREE 1-877-671-6036
View thousands more home plans online at www.familyhandyman.com/homeplans

Summer Home Or Year-Round

Plan #711-007D-0037

1,403 total square feet of living area

Price Code A

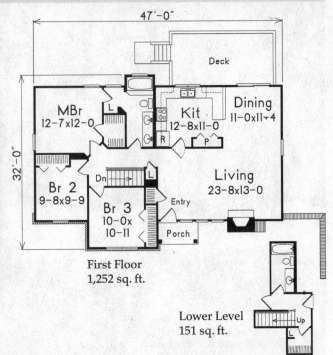

47'-0"

32'-0"

Deck

MBr
12-7x12-0

Kit
12-8x11-0

Dining
11-0x11-4

Br 2
9-8x9-9

Dn

Br 3
10-0x
10-11

Entry

Porch

Living
23-8x13-0

First Floor
1,252 sq. ft.

Lower Level
151 sq. ft.

Up

Special features

- Impressive living areas for a modest-sized home
- Special master/hall bath has linen storage, step-up tub and lots of window light
- Spacious closets everywhere you look
- 3 bedrooms, 2 baths, 2-car drive under garage
- Basement foundation

Features Generous Room Sizes

Plan #711-058D-0025

2,164 total square feet of living area

Price Code C

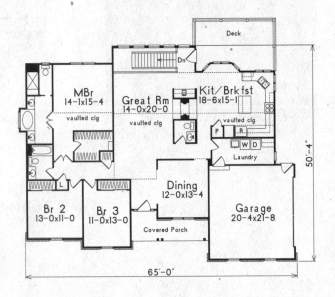

Deck

Dn

MBr
14-1x15-4
vaulted clg

Great Rm
14-0x20-0
vaulted clg

Kit/Brkfst
18-6x15-1
vaulted clg

Laundry

W D

Br 2
13-0x11-0

Br 3
11-0x13-0

Dining
12-0x13-4

Garage
20-4x21-8

Covered Porch

50'-4"

65'-0"

Special features

- Great design for entertaining with wet bar and see-through fireplace in great room
- Plenty of closet space
- Vaulted ceilings enlarge the master bedroom, great room and kitchen/breakfast area
- Great room features great view to the rear of the home
- 3 bedrooms, 2 1/2 baths, 2-car side entry garage
- Basement foundation

TO ORDER BLUEPRINTS USE THE FORM ON PAGE 15 OR CALL TOLL-FREE 1-877-671-6036
View thousands more home plans online at www.familyhandyman.com/homeplans

119

See-Through Fireplace

Plan #711-043D-0018

3,502 total square feet of living area

Price Code F

Special features

- 12' ceiling in dining room
- Interior column accents and display niches
- Living and family rooms have see-through fireplace
- Master bath has double walk-in closets
- 4 bedrooms, 2 full baths, 2 half baths, 3-car side entry garage
- Basement foundation, drawings also include crawl space foundation

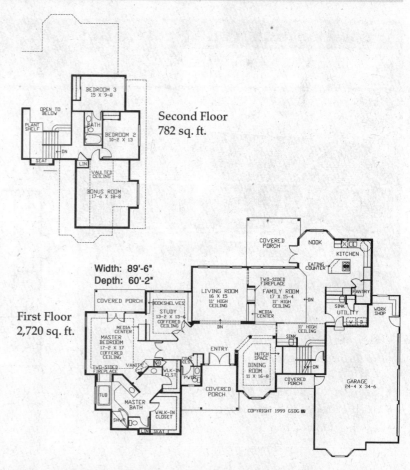

Second Floor
782 sq. ft.

Width: 89'-6"
Depth: 60'-2"

First Floor
2,720 sq. ft.

Enchanting One-Level Home

Plan #711-065D-0010

1,508 total square feet of living area

Price Code B

Special features

- Grand opening between rooms creates a spacious effect
- Additional room for quick meals or serving a larger crowd is provided at the breakfast bar
- Sunny dining area accesses the outdoors as well
- 3 bedrooms, 2 baths, 2-car garage
- Basement or crawl space foundation, please specify when ordering

Vaulted Ceilings Highlight Home

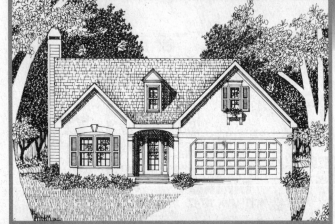

Plan #711-010D-0003

1,560 total square feet of living area

Price Code B

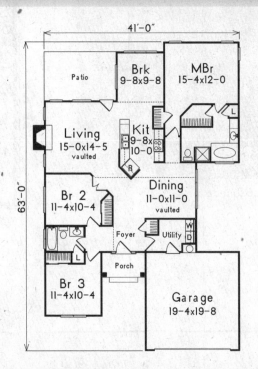

Special features

- Cozy breakfast room is tucked at the rear of this home and features plenty of windows for natural light
- Large entry has easy access to secondary bedrooms, laundry/utility, dining and living rooms
- Private master bedroom
- Kitchen overlooks living room with fireplace and patio access
- 3 bedrooms, 2 baths, 2-car garage
- Slab foundation

TO ORDER BLUEPRINTS USE THE FORM ON PAGE 15 OR CALL TOLL-FREE 1-877-671-6036
View thousands more home plans online at www.familyhandyman.com/homeplans

121

Comfortable Living In This Ranch   Plan #711-025D-0003

1,379 total square feet of living area

Price Code A

Special features

- Vaulted great room makes a lasting impression with corner fireplace and windows
- Formal dining room easily connects to kitchen making entertaining easy
- Master bath includes all the luxuries such as a spacious walk-in closet, oversized tub and separate shower
- 3 bedrooms, 2 baths, 2-car garage
- Slab foundation

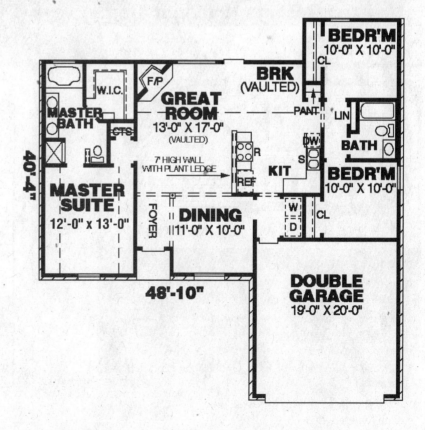

BEDR'M 10'-0" X 10'-0"

BRK (VAULTED)

GREAT ROOM 13'-0" X 17'-0" (VAULTED)

W.I.C.

MASTER BATH

40'-4"

MASTER SUITE 12'-0" X 13'-0"

7' HIGH WALL WITH PLANT LEDGE

PANT

LIN

BATH

KIT

BEDR'M 10'-0" X 10'-0"

CL

REF

FOYER

DINING 11'-0" X 10'-0"

W D

CL

48'-10"

DOUBLE GARAGE 19'-0" X 20'-0"

Economical Ranch For Easy Living

Plan #711-014D-0005

1,314 total square feet of living area

Price Code A

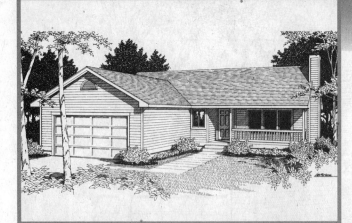

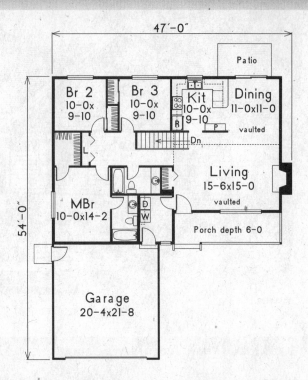

47'-0"

54'-0"

Patio

Br 2
10-0x 9-10

Br 3
10-0x 9-10

Kit
10-0x 9-10

Dining
11-0x11-0
vaulted

Dn

Living
15-6x15-0
vaulted

MBr
10-0x14-2

Porch depth 6-0

Garage
20-4x21-8

Special features

- Energy efficient home with 2" x 6" exterior walls
- Covered porch adds appeal and welcoming charm
- Open floor plan combined with a vaulted ceiling offers spacious living
- Functional kitchen complete with pantry and eating bar
- Cozy fireplace in the living room
- Master bedroom features a large walk-in closet and bath
- 3 bedrooms, 2 baths, 2-car garage
- Basement foundation

Pillars And Dormers Add Charm

Plan #711-047D-0050

2,293 total square feet of living area

Price Code D

Balc.

Bonus Rm.
21⁴ • 16⁴

Optional
Second Floor

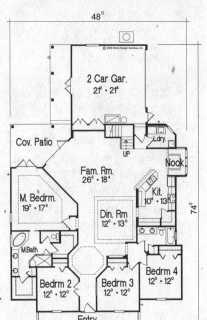

48°

2 Car Gar.
21⁸ • 21⁸

Cov. Patio

Ldry.

UP

Nook

Fam. Rm.
26³ • 18⁴

Kit.
10⁸ • 13

M. Bedrm.
19° • 17⁴

Din. Rm.
12° • 13°

M.Bath

74°

Bedrm 4
12° • 12°

Bedrm 2
12° • 12°

Bedrm 3
12° • 12°

First Floor
2,293 sq. ft.

Entry

Special features

- Formal dining area flows into large family room
- Nook off kitchen makes an ideal breakfast area
- Covered patio attaches to master bedroom and family room
- Optional second floor has an additional 509 square feet of living area
- Framing - only concrete block available
- 4 bedrooms, 2 baths, 2-car side entry garage
- Slab foundation

TO ORDER BLUEPRINTS USE THE FORM ON PAGE 15 OR CALL TOLL-FREE 1-877-671-6036
View thousands more home plans online at www.familyhandyman.com/homeplans

123

High-Style Vaulted Ranch

Plan #711-014D-0007

1,453 total square feet of living area

Price Code A

Special features

- Decorative vents, window trim, shutters and brick blend to create dramatic curb appeal
- Energy efficient home with 2" x 6" exterior walls
- Kitchen opens to living area and includes salad sink in the island, pantry and handy laundry room
- Exquisite master bedroom is highlighted by a vaulted ceiling
- Dressing area with walk-in closet, private bath and spa tub/shower
- 3 bedrooms, 2 baths, 2-car garage
- Basement foundation, drawings also include crawl space foundation

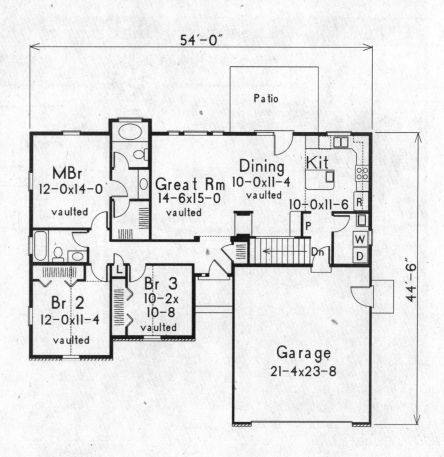

Home With Large Front Porch

Plan #711-001D-0031

1,501 total square feet of living area

Price Code B

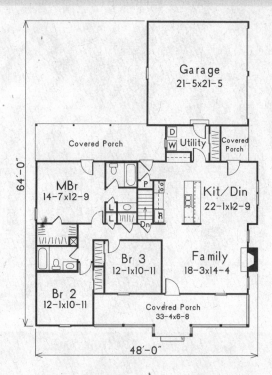

Special features

- Spacious kitchen with dining area is open to the outdoors
- Convenient utility room is adjacent to garage
- Master bedroom with private bath, dressing area and access to large covered porch
- Large family room creates openness
- 3 bedrooms, 2 baths, 2-car side entry garage
- Basement foundation, drawings also include crawl space and slab foundations

Unique Corner Fireplace

Plan #711-069D-0013

1,646 total square feet of living area

Price Code B

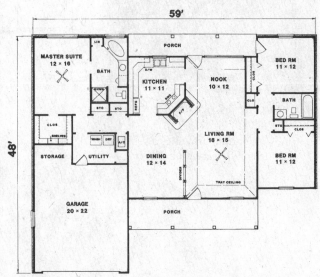

Special features

- Master suite has a luxury bath including a corner whirlpool tub
- Large living room connects to the breakfast nook adding spaciousness
- Secondary bedrooms separate from master suite for privacy
- 3 bedrooms, 2 baths, 2-car garage
- Slab or crawl space foundation, please specify when ordering

3,494 total square feet of living area   **Price Code F**

Special features

- Majestic two-story foyer opens into living and dining rooms, both framed by arched columns
- Balcony overlooks large living area featuring French doors to covered porch
- Luxurious master bedroom
- Convenient game room supports lots of activities
- 4 bedrooms, 3 1/2 baths, 3-car side entry garage
- Slab foundation, drawings also include crawl space foundation

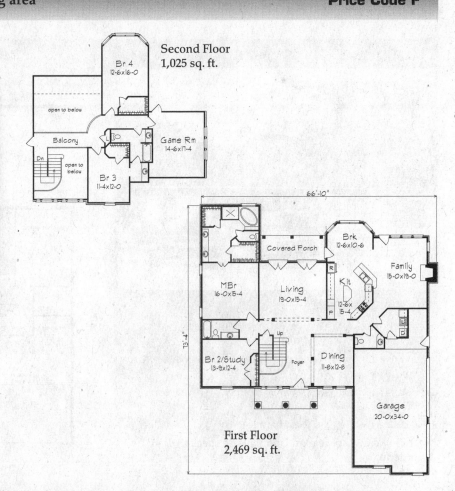

Second Floor
1,025 sq. ft.

Br 4
12-6x16-0

open to below

Balcony

Dn   open to below

Br 3
11-4x12-0

Game Rm
14-6x17-4

First Floor
2,469 sq. ft.

66'-10"

73'-4"

Covered Porch

Brk
12-6x10-6

Family
15-0x19-0

MBr
16-0x15-4

Living
19-0x15-4

Kit
12-6x
15-4

Br 2/Study
13-9x12-4

Foyer

Up

Dining
11-8x12-8

Garage
20-0x34-0

Triple Dormers And Arches

Plan #711-067D-0004

1,698 total square feet of living area

Price Code B

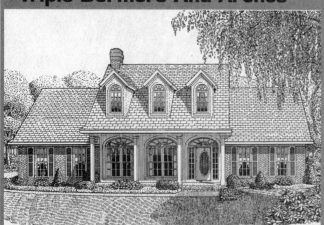

Width 59'-0"
Depth 61'-0"

Special features

- Vaulted master bedroom has a private bath and a walk-in closet
- Decorative columns flank the entrance to the dining room
- Open great room is perfect for gathering family together
- 3 bedrooms, 2 1/2 baths, 2-car side entry garage with storage
- Basement, crawl space or slab foundation, please specify when ordering

Striking Plant Shelf

Plan #711-011D-0005

1,467 total square feet of living area

Price Code C

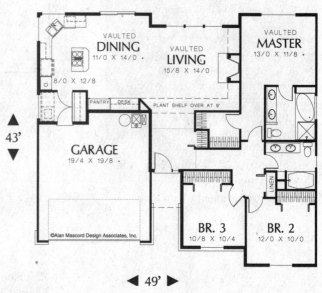

Special features

- Vaulted ceilings, an open floor plan and a wealth of windows create an inviting atmosphere
- Efficiently arranged kitchen has an island with built-in cooktop and a snack counter
- Plentiful storage and closet space throughout this home
- 3 bedrooms, 2 baths, 2-car garage
- Crawl space foundation

COUNTRY FLAVOR WITH ATRIUM

Plan #711-007D-0101

2,384 total square feet of living area

Price Code D

Special features

- Bracketed box windows create an exterior with country charm
- Massive-sized great room features a majestic atrium, fireplace, box window wall, dining balcony and vaulted ceilings
- An atrium balcony with large bay window off sundeck is enjoyed by the spacious breakfast room
- 1,038 square feet of optional living area below with family room, wet bar, bedroom #4 and bath
- 3 bedrooms, 2 1/2 baths, 2-car side entry garage
- Walk-out basement foundation

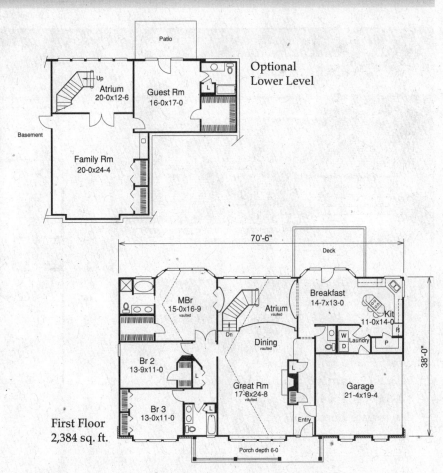

Optional Lower Level

Patio

Atrium 20-0x12-6

Guest Rm 16-0x17-0

Basement

Family Rm 20-0x24-4

First Floor 2,384 sq. ft.

70'-6"

Deck

MBr 15-0x16-9 vaulted

Atrium vaulted

Breakfast 14-7x13-0

Kit 11-0x14-0

Br 2 13-9x11-0

Dining vaulted

Laundry

Br 3 13-0x11-0

Great Rm 17-8x24-8 vaulted

Garage 21-4x19-4

38'-0"

Entry

Porch depth 6-0

TO ORDER BLUEPRINTS USE THE FORM ON PAGE 15 OR CALL TOLL-FREE 1-877-671-6036
View thousands more home plans online at www.familyhandyman.com/homeplans

128

Uncommonly Styled Ranch

Plan #711-013D-0015

1,787 total square feet of living area

Price Code B

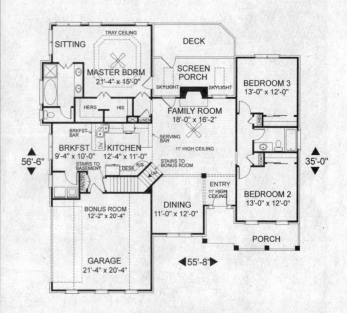

Special features

- Skylights brighten screened porch which connects to family room and deck outdoors
- Master bedroom features a comfortable sitting area, large private bath and direct access to screened porch
- Kitchen has serving bar which extends dining into family room
- 3 bedrooms, 2 baths, 2-car side entry garage
- Basement, crawl space or slab foundation, please specify when ordering

Wonderful Great Room

Plan #711-048D-0001

1,865 total square feet of living area

Price Code D

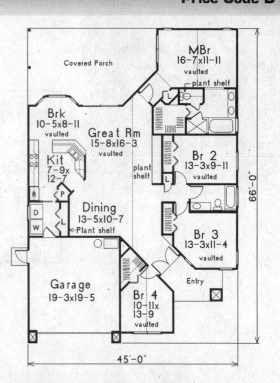

Special features

- Large foyer opens into expansive dining area and great room
- Home features vaulted ceilings throughout
- Master bedroom features an angled entry, vaulted ceiling, plant shelf and bath with double vanity, tub and shower
- 4 bedrooms, 2 baths, 2-car garage
- Slab foundation, drawings also include crawl space foundation

Handyman

2,669 total square feet of living area

Price Code E

Special features

- Nice-sized corner pantry in kitchen
- Guest bedroom, located off the great room, has a full bath and would make an excellent office
- Master bath has double walk-in closets, whirlpool tub and a large shower
- 3 bedrooms, 3 1/2 baths, 2-car side entry garage
- Basement or slab foundation, please specify when ordering

80-0 WIDE X 63-0 DEEP

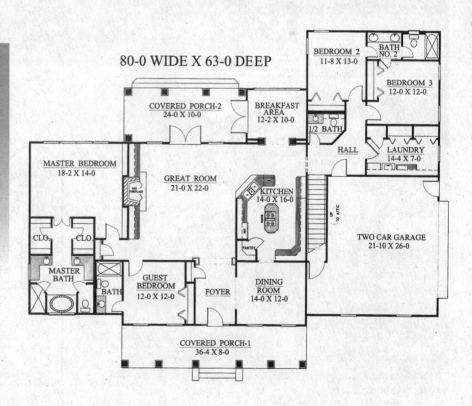

TO ORDER BLUEPRINTS USE THE FORM ON PAGE 15 OR CALL TOLL-FREE 1-877-671-6036
View thousands more home plans online at www.familyhandyman.com/homeplans

Charming Design

Special features

- Master bedroom has a private sitting area with large bay window
- Sunny breakfast room has wall of windows and easy access to kitchen
- Formal dining area has decorative columns separating it from spacious living area
- 3 bedrooms, 2 1/2 baths, 2-car garage
- Walk-out basement, slab or crawl space foundation, please specify when ordering

Plan #711-052D-0041

1,840 total square feet of living area

Price Code C

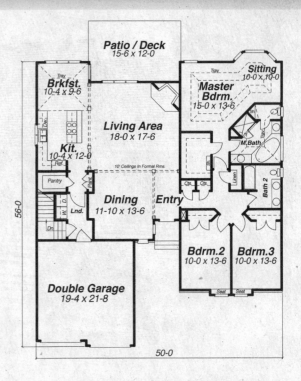

Covered Porches All Around

Special features

- Spectacular arches when entering foyer
- Dining room has double-doors leading to kitchen
- Unique desk area off kitchen ideal for computer work station
- 3 bedrooms, 2 baths, 2-car side entry garage
- Crawl space foundation, drawings also include slab foundation

Plan #711-019D-0008

1,725 total square feet of living area

Price Code B

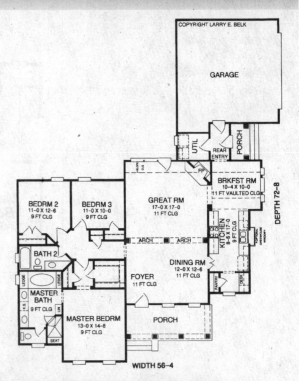

TO ORDER BLUEPRINTS USE THE FORM ON PAGE 15 OR CALL TOLL-FREE 1-877-671-6036
View thousands more home plans online at www.familyhandyman.com/homeplans

131

1,770 total square feet of living area

Price Code B

Special features

- Compartmentalized hall bath is convenient and functional
- Walk-in pantry in kitchen maintains organization
- Superb master bath is spacious and well-equipped
- 3 bedrooms, 2 baths, 2-car drive under garage
- Basement foundation

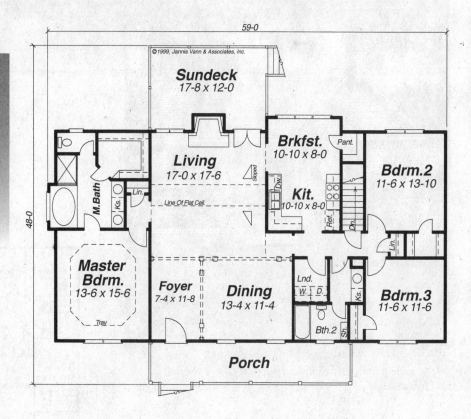

© 1999, Jannis Vann & Associates, Inc.

59-0

48-0

Sundeck
17-8 x 12-0

Living
17-0 x 17-6

Line Of Flat Ceil.

Brkfst.
10-10 x 8-0

Pant.

Kit.
10-10 x 8-0

Bdrm.2
11-6 x 13-10

M.Bath

Lin.

Ref.

Dn.

Lin.

Master Bdrm.
13-6 x 15-6

Trav

Foyer
7-4 x 11-8

Dining
13-4 x 11-4

Lnd.

W. D.

Bth.2

Sh.

Bdrm.3
11-6 x 11-6

Porch

Sloped Ceilings Enlarge Areas

Plan #711-020D-0004

1,717 total square feet of living area

Price Code B

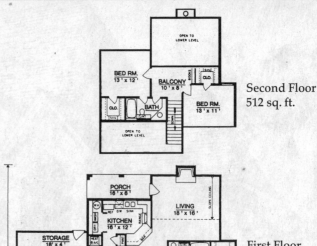

Second Floor 512 sq. ft.

First Floor 1,205 sq. ft.

Special features

- Energy efficient home with 2" x 6" exterior walls
- Kitchen has eat-in bar which overlooks gallery and living areas
- Master suite has sloped ceiling and two walk-in closets
- Covered porch connects living room to the outdoors
- 3 bedrooms, 2 baths, 2-car garage
- Crawl space foundation, drawings also include slab foundation

Wonderful Master Suite

Plan #711-055D-0085

1,989 total square feet of living area

Price Code C

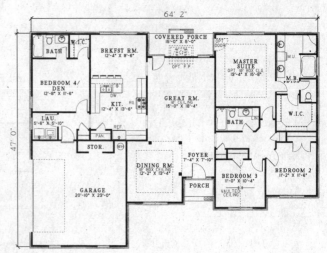

Special features

- Dining room has 8" decorative columns
- Master suite has optional door to rear covered porch
- Laundry area is convenient to kitchen and garage
- 4 bedrooms, 3 baths, 2-car side entry garage
- Crawl space or slab foundation, please specify when ordering

A Great Manor House

Plan #711-001D-0012

3,368 total square feet of living area

Price Code F

Special features

- Sunken great room with cathedral ceiling, wooden beams, skylights and a masonry fireplace
- Octagon-shaped breakfast room has domed ceiling with beams, large windows and door to patio
- Private master bedroom has a deluxe bath and dressing area
- Oversized walk-in closets and storage areas in each bedroom
- 4 bedrooms, 3 full baths, 2 half baths, 2-car side entry garage
- Basement foundation

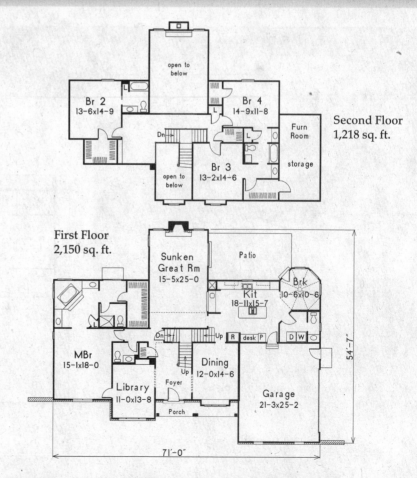

Second Floor
1,218 sq. ft.

Br 2
13-6x14-9

Br 4
14-9x11-8

Furn Room

storage

open to below

Dn

Br 3
13-2x14-6

open to below

First Floor
2,150 sq. ft.

Sunken Great Rm
15-5x25-0

Patio

Brk
10-6x10-6

Kit
18-1x15-7

MBr
15-1x18-0

Dn

Up

R desk P

D W

Dining
12-0x14-6

Library
11-0x13-8

Foyer

Garage
21-3x25-2

Porch

54'-7"

71'-0"

Lovely, Spacious Floor Plan

Plan #711-058D-0016

1,558 total square feet of living area

Price Code B

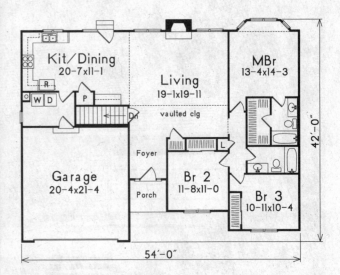

Kit/Dining
20-7x11-1

Living
19-1x19-11
vaulted clg

MBr
13-4x14-3

Foyer

Garage
20-4x21-4

Br 2
11-8x11-0

Porch

Br 3
10-11x10-4

42'-0"

54'-0"

Special features

- Spacious utility room is located conveniently between the garage and kitchen/dining area
- Bedrooms are separated from living area by hallway
- Enormous living area with fireplace and vaulted ceiling opens to kitchen and dining area
- Master bedroom is enhanced with large bay window, walk-in closet and private bath
- 3 bedrooms, 2 baths, 2-car garage
- Basement foundation

Compact, Convenient And Charming

Plan #711-021D-0008

1,266 total square feet of living area

Price Code A

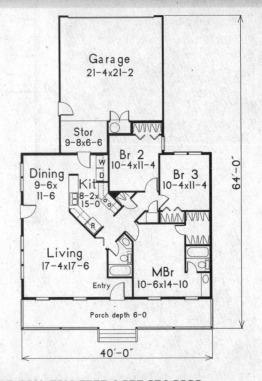

Garage
21-4x21-2

Stor
9-8x6-6

Br 2
10-4x11-4

Dining
9-6x
11-6

Kit
8-2x
15-0

Br 3
10-4x11-4

Living
17-4x17-6

MBr
10-6x14-10

Entry

Porch depth 6-0

64'-0"

40'-0"

Special features

- Narrow frontage is perfect for small lots
- Energy efficient home with 2" x 6" exterior walls
- Central hall is a convenient connection for all main rooms
- Design incorporates full-size master bedroom complete with dressing room, bath and walk-in closet
- Angled kitchen includes handy laundry facilities
- 3 bedrooms, 2 baths, 2-car rear entry garage
- Crawl space foundation, drawings also include slab foundation

TO ORDER BLUEPRINTS USE THE FORM ON PAGE 15 OR CALL TOLL-FREE 1-877-671-6036
View thousands more home plans online at www.familyhandyman.com/homeplans

135

COVERED PORCH ADDS CHARM

Plan #711-069D-0018

2,069 total square feet of living area

Price Code C

Special features

- 9' ceilings throughout this home
- Kitchen has many amenities including a snack bar
- Large front and rear porches
- 3 bedrooms, 2 1/2 baths, 2-car garage
- Slab or crawl space foundation, please specify when ordering

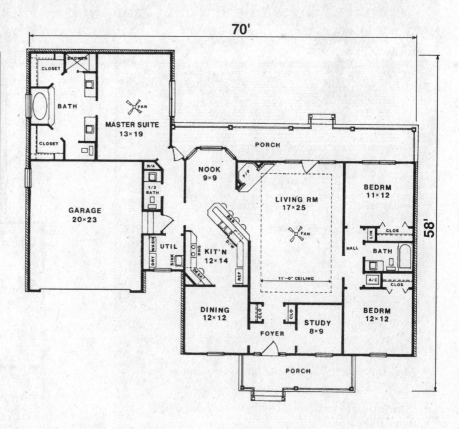

Open Design Gives Expansive Look

Plan #711-022D-0011

1,630 total square feet of living area

Price Code B

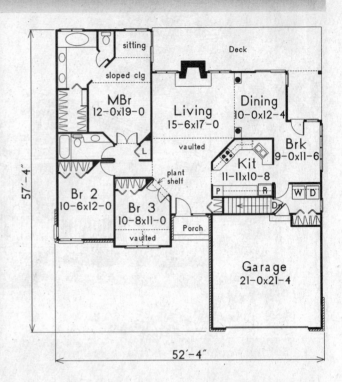

Special features

- Crisp facade and full windows front and back offer open viewing
- Wrap-around rear deck is accessible from breakfast room, dining room and master bedroom
- Vaulted ceilings in living room and master bedroom
- Sitting area and large walk-in closet complement master bedroom
- 3 bedrooms, 2 baths, 2-car garage
- Basement foundation

Country Cottage

Plan #711-056D-0001

1,624 total square feet of living area

Price Code E

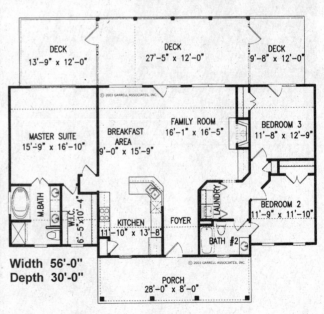

Special features

- Large covered deck leads to two uncovered decks accessible by the master bedroom and bedroom #3
- Well-organized kitchen overlooks into the breakfast area and family room
- Laundry closet located near secondary bedrooms
- 3 bedrooms, 2 baths
- Crawl space or slab foundation, please specify when ordering

Bayed Breakfast Nook

Plan #711-047D-0003

1,442 total square feet of living area

Price Code A

Special features

- Utility room includes extra counterspace and a closet for storage
- Kitchen has a useful center island creating extra workspace
- Vaulted master bedroom has unique double-door entry, private bath and a walk-in closet
- 3 bedrooms, 2 baths, 2-car side entry carport
- Slab foundation

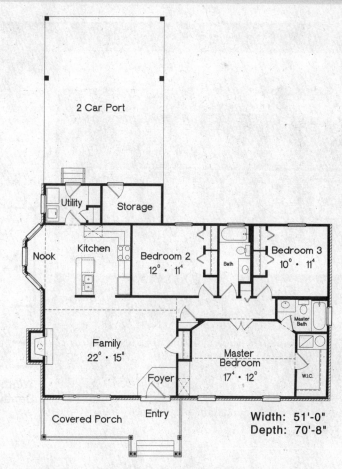

2 Car Port

Utility

Storage

Nook

Kitchen

Bedroom 2
12⁰ · 11⁴

Bath

Bedroom 3
10⁰ · 11⁴

Master
Bath

Family
22⁰ · 15⁸

Master
Bedroom
17⁴ · 12⁰

W.I.C.

Foyer

Entry

Covered Porch

Width: 51'-0"
Depth: 70'-8"

Luxurious Master Bath

Plan #711-034D-0002

1,456 total square feet of living area

Price Code A

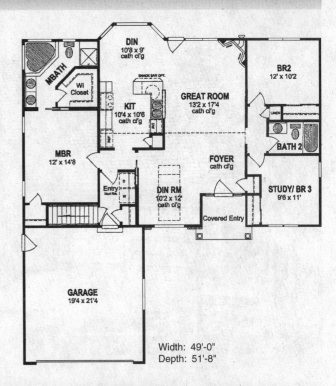

Width: 49'-0"
Depth: 51'-8"

Special features

- Open floor plan adds spaciousness to this design
- Bayed dining area creates a cheerful setting
- Corner fireplace in great room is a terrific focal point
- 3 bedrooms, 2 baths, 2-car garage
- Basement foundation

Bedroom Opens To Covered Porch

Plan #711-024D-0024

2,481 total square feet of living area

Price Code D

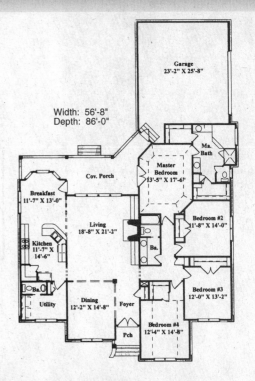

Width: 56'-8"
Depth: 86'-0"

Special features

- All bedrooms separate from main living areas for privacy
- Enormous master bath with double walk-in closets
- Unique covered porch off living area and breakfast room
- Cozy fireplace with built-in bookshelves in living area
- 4 bedrooms, 2 1/2 baths, 2-car side entry garage
- Crawl space or slab foundation, please specify when ordering

TO ORDER BLUEPRINTS USE THE FORM ON PAGE 15 OR CALL TOLL-FREE 1-877-671-6036
View thousands more home plans online at www.familyhandyman.com/homeplans

139

TrioOf Dormers Adds Light

Plan #711-039D-0011

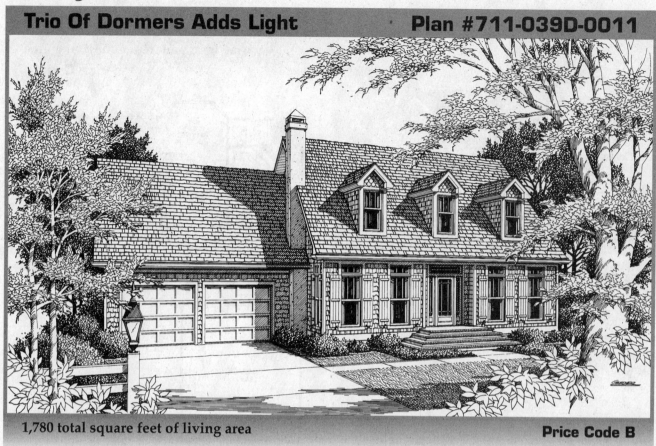

1,780 total square feet of living area

Price Code B

Special features

- Traditional styling with the comforts of home
- First floor master bedroom has walk-in closet and bath
- Large kitchen and dining area open to deck
- 3 bedrooms, 2 1/2 baths, 2-car garage
- Basement, crawl space or slab foundation, please specify when ordering

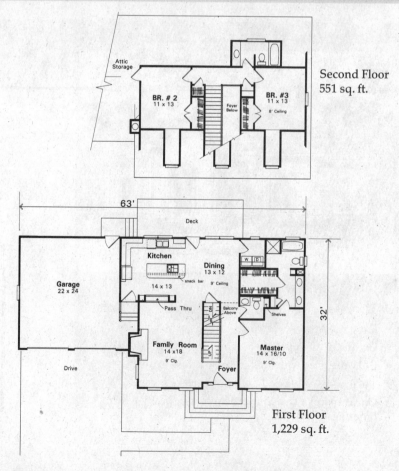

Second Floor
551 sq. ft.

Attic Storage

BR. # 2
11 x 13

Foyer Below

BR. #3
11 x 13
8' Ceiling

63'

Deck

Kitchen
14 x 13

Dining
13 x 12
9' Ceiling

W D

snack bar

Garage
22 x 24

Pass Thru

Balcony Above

Shelves

32'

Family Room
14 x18
9' Clg.

Master
14 x 16/10
9' Clg.

Drive

Foyer

First Floor
1,229 sq. ft.

Lovely Ranch Home

Plan #711-025D-0001

1,123 total square feet of living area

Price Code AA

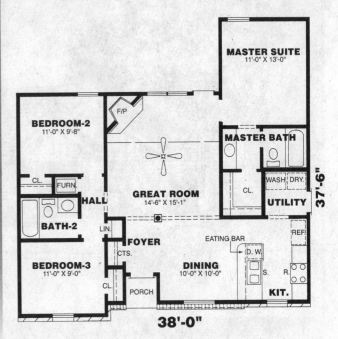

MASTER SUITE 11'-0" X 13'-0"

BEDROOM-2 11'-0" X 9'-8"

MASTER BATH

F/P

CL. FURN.

BATH-2

HALL

GREAT ROOM 14'-6" X 15'-1"

CL.

WASH. DRY.

UTILITY

LIN.

CTS.

FOYER

BEDROOM-3 11'-0" X 9'-0"

CL.

PORCH

EATING BAR

D.W.

S. R.

REF.

DINING 10'-0" X 10'-0"

KIT.

37'-6"

38'-0"

Special features

- Eating bar in kitchen extends dining area
- Dining area and great room flow together creating a sense of spaciousness
- Master suite has privacy from other bedrooms as well as a private bath
- Utility room is conveniently located near kitchen
- 3 bedrooms, 2 baths
- Crawl space or slab foundation, please specify when ordering

Quaint Box Window Seat

Plan #711-031D-0003

1,665 total square feet of living area

Price Code B

PATIO

FAMILY RM. 21'-4" X 18'-4" 10'-CLG.

MASTER 13'-2" X 11'-8"

STEP UP CLG.

LINEN

BATH

KNEE SPACE

NOOK 10'-CLG.

BAR

DW

PLANT LEDGE ABOVE

KITCH. 10'-4" X 10'-0"

ENTRY

CLOSET

UTIL.

F. REF.

B.R.-2 10'-0" X 11'-0" 10'-CLG.

BATH

POR.

GARAGE 21'-4" X 20'-0"

B.R.-3 11'-0" X 10'-0" BARN CLG.

Width: 50'-0"
Depth: 55'-0"

Special features

- Oversized family room has corner fireplace and double-doors leading to patio
- Bedroom locations give privacy from gathering areas
- 3 bedrooms, 2 baths, 2-car garage
- Slab foundation

TO ORDER BLUEPRINTS USE THE FORM ON PAGE 15 OR CALL TOLL-FREE 1-877-671-6036
View thousands more home plans online at www.familyhandyman.com/homeplans

141

Private Bedrooms

Plan #711-043D-0005

1,734 total square feet of living area

Price Code B

Special features

- Large entry with coffered ceiling and display niches
- Sunken great room has 10' ceiling
- Kitchen island includes eating counter
- 9' ceiling in master bedroom
- Master bath features corner tub and double sinks
- 3 bedrooms, 2 baths, 2-car garage
- Crawl space foundation

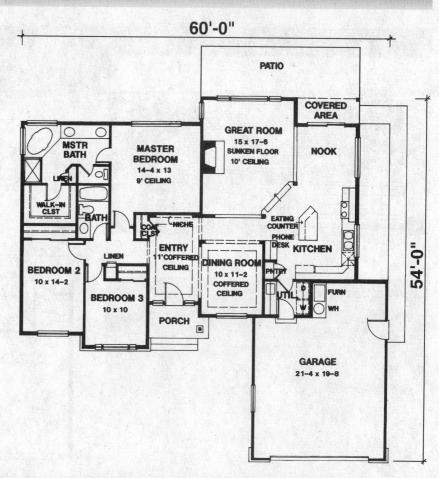

A Touch Of Home

Plan #711-028D-0007
2,052 total square feet of living area
Price Code C

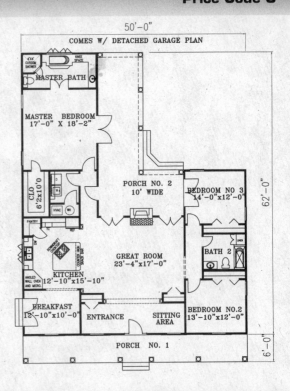

COMES W/ DETACHED GARAGE PLAN

50'-0"

62'-0"

6'-0"

MASTER BATH

KNEE SPACE

4'X4' CUSTOM SHOWER

MASTER BEDROOM
17'-0" X 18'-2"

CLO 6'2"x10'0

PORCH NO. 2
10' WIDE

BEDROOM NO 3
14'-0"x12'-0"

PANTRY

HVAC

BATH 2

GREAT ROOM
23'-4"x17'-0"

KITCHEN
12'-10"x15'-10"

BREAKFAST
12'-10"x10'-0"

ENTRANCE

SITTING AREA

BEDROOM NO.2
13'-10"x12'-0"

PORCH NO. 1

Special features

- Kitchen has large island with cooktop and snack bar
- Bedroom #3 has access to the rear porch through French doors
- Master bath has large casement windows above whirlpool tub and a 4' x 4' custom shower
- 3 bedrooms, 2 baths, 2-car detached garage
- Crawl space or slab foundation, please specify when ordering

Cozy And Convenient

Plan #711-065D-0035
1,798 total square feet of living area
Price Code B

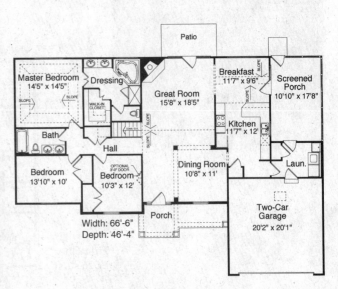

Patio

Master Bedroom
14'5" x 14'5"

Dressing

Breakfast
11'7" x 9'6"

Screened Porch
10'10" x 17'8"

SLOPE

WALK-IN CLOSET

Great Room
15'8" x 18'5"

Kitchen
11'7" x 12'

Bath

Hall

Laun.

Bedroom
13'10" x 10'

OPTIONAL 3'-0" DOOR

Bedroom
10'3" x 12'

Dining Room
10'8" x 11'

Porch

Two-Car Garage
20'2" x 20'1"

Width: 66'-6"
Depth: 46'-4"

Special features

- The expansive great room enjoys a fireplace and has access onto the rear patio
- The centrally located kitchen is easily accessible to the dining room and breakfast area
- The master bedroom boasts a sloped ceiling and deluxe bath with a corner whirlpool tub and large walk-in closet
- A screened porch offers relaxing outdoor living
- 3 bedrooms, 2 baths, 2-car garage
- Basement foundation

TO ORDER BLUEPRINTS USE THE FORM ON PAGE 15 OR CALL TOLL-FREE 1-877-671-6036
View thousands more home plans online at www.familyhandyman.com/homeplans

143

Great Curb Appeal With Gables   Plan #711-025D-0048

2,526 total square feet of living area

Price Code D

Special features

- Sunroom brightens dining areas near kitchen
- Corner whirlpool tub in master bath is a luxurious touch
- Future playroom on the second floor has an additional 341 square feet of living area
- 4 bedrooms, 3 baths, 2-car side entry garage
- Crawl space or slab foundation, please specify when ordering

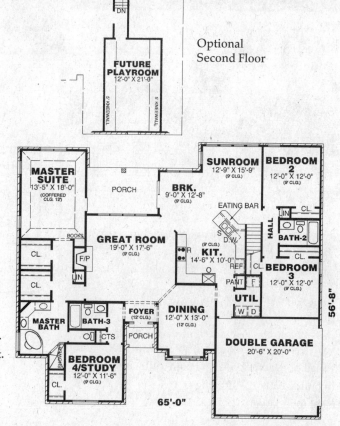

Optional Second Floor

FUTURE PLAYROOM
12'-0" X 21'-0"

5' KNEEWALL   5' KNEEWALL

DN

First Floor
2,526 sq. ft.

MASTER SUITE
13'-5" X 18'-0"
(COFFERED CLG. 12)

PORCH

BRK.
9'-0" X 12'-8"
(9' CLG.)

SUNROOM
12'-9" X 15'-9"
(9' CLG.)

BEDROOM 2
12'-0" X 12'-0"
(9' CLG.)

EATING BAR

LIN   CL.

BATH-2

GREAT ROOM
19'-0" X 17'-6"
(9' CLG.)

KIT.
14'-6" X 10'-0"

(9' CLG.)

D.W.

HALL

CL.

BEDROOM 3
12'-0" X 12'-0"
(9' CLG.)

BOOKS

CL.

F/P

LIN

REF
PANT

UTIL
W D

56'-8"

MASTER BATH

BATH-3

FOYER
(12' CLG.)

DINING
12'-0" X 13'-0"
(12' CLG.)

DOUBLE GARAGE
20'-6" X 20'-0"

CTS

PORCH

BEDROOM 4/STUDY
12'-0" X 11'-6"
(9' CLG.)

CL.

65'-0"

Spacious For A Growing Family

Plan #711-035D-0001

1,715 total square feet of living area

Price Code B

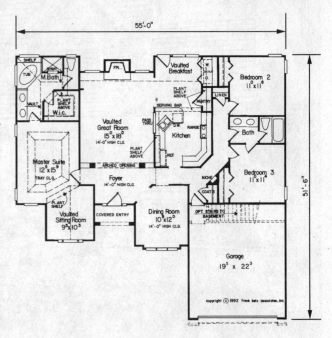

Special features

- Vaulted great room is spacious and bright
- Master suite has attached sitting room
- Kitchen has plenty of counterspace and cabinetry
- 3 bedrooms, 2 baths, 2-car garage
- Walk-out basement, crawl space or slab foundation, please specify when ordering

Colossal Great Room

Plan #711-068D-0007

1,599 total square feet of living area

Price Code B

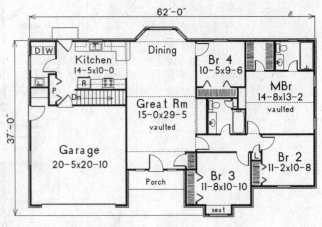

Special features

- Efficiently designed kitchen with large pantry and easy access to laundry room
- Bedroom #3 has a charming window seat
- Master bedroom has a full bath and large walk-in closet
- 4 bedrooms, 2 baths, 2-car garage
- Basement foundation, drawings also include crawl space and slab foundations

TO ORDER BLUEPRINTS USE THE FORM ON PAGE 15 OR CALL TOLL-FREE 1-877-671-6036
View thousands more home plans online at www.familyhandyman.com/homeplans

145

The Family Handyman

Window Seat In Master Bedroom   Plan #711-038D-0019

1,995 total square feet of living area

Price Code C

Second Floor
630 sq. ft.

Special features

- 9' ceilings throughout the first floor
- Pass-through from kitchen into formal dining room provides a quick and easy access
- Two-story great room has a wonderful corner fireplace
- 4 bedrooms, 2 1/2 baths, 2-car garage
- Basement, crawl space or slab foundation, please specify when ordering

First Floor
1,365 sq. ft.

146

TO ORDER BLUEPRINTS USE THE FORM ON PAGE 15 OR CALL TOLL-FREE 1-877-671-6036
View thousands more home plans online at www.familyhandyman.com/homeplans

Private Master Bedroom

Special features

- Open and airy dining room
- Secondary bedrooms share a central bath
- Optional second floor has an additional 268 square feet of living area
- 3 bedrooms, 2 baths, 2-car garage
- Basement foundation

Plan #711-070D-0002

1,700 total square feet of living area

Price Code B

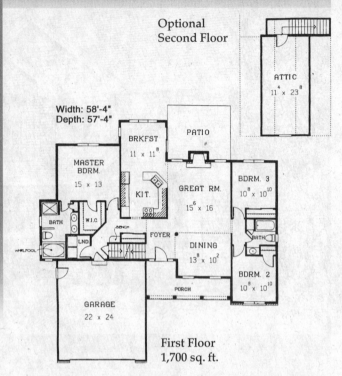

Optional Second Floor

ATTIC
11⁴ x 23⁸

Width: 58'-4"
Depth: 57'-4"

BRKFST 11 x 11⁸

PATIO

MASTER BDRM. 15 x 13

KIT.

GREAT RM. 15⁶ x 16

BDRM. 3 10⁸ x 10¹⁰

BATH

W.I.C.

BENCH

BATH

WHIRLPOOL

LND.

FOYER

DINING 13⁸ x 10²

BDRM. 2 10⁸ x 10¹⁰

PORCH

GARAGE 22 x 24

First Floor
1,700 sq. ft.

Attractive Styling

Special features

- Dining area has 10' high sloped ceiling
- Kitchen opens to large living room with fireplace and has access to a covered porch
- Master suite features private bath, double walk-in closets and whirlpool tub
- 3 bedrooms, 2 baths, 2-car garage
- Slab or crawl space foundation, please specify when ordering

Plan #711-030D-0004

1,791 total square feet of living area

Price Code B

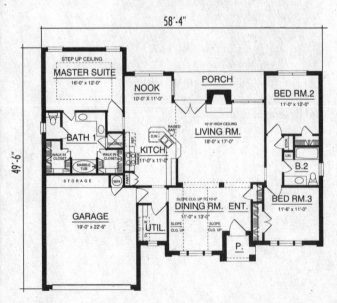

58'-4"

49'-6"

STEP UP CEILING
MASTER SUITE
16'-0" x 12'-0"

NOOK
10'-0" X 11'-0"

PORCH

BED RM.2
11'-0" x 12'-0"

BATH 1

WALK IN CLOSET

MARBLE TUB

WALK IN CLOSET

KITCH.
11'-0" x 11'-0"

LIVING RM.
18'-0" x 17'-0"

B.2

STORAGE

RAISED BAR

10'-0" HIGH CEILING

BED RM.3
11'-6" x 11'-0"

GARAGE
19'-0" x 22'-6"

UTIL.

DINING RM.
11'-0" x 13'-0"

ENT.

P.

SLOPE CLG. UP TO 10'-0"

SLOPE CLG. UP

SLOPE CLG. UP

TO ORDER BLUEPRINTS USE THE FORM ON PAGE 15 OR CALL TOLL-FREE 1-877-671-6036
View thousands more home plans online at www.familyhandyman.com/homeplans

147

Popular T-Stair

Plan #711-007D-0005

2,336 total square feet of living area

Price Code D

Special features

- Stately sunken living room with partially vaulted ceiling and classic arched transom windows
- Family room features plenty of windows and a fireplace with flanking bookshelves
- 4 bedrooms, 2 1/2 baths, 2-car garage
- Basement foundation

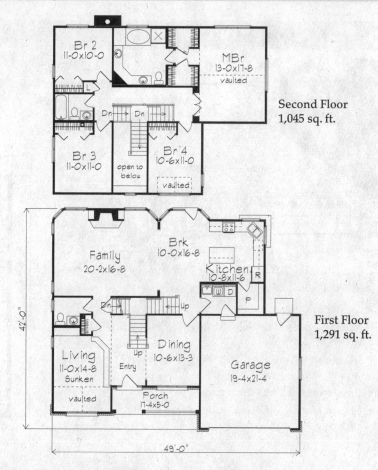

Second Floor
1,045 sq. ft.

First Floor
1,291 sq. ft.

TO ORDER BLUEPRINTS USE THE FORM ON PAGE 15 OR CALL TOLL-FREE 1-877-671-6036
View thousands more home plans online at www.familyhandyman.com/homeplans

Vaulted Rooms Throughout

Plan #711-035D-0017

1,373 total square feet of living area

Price Code A

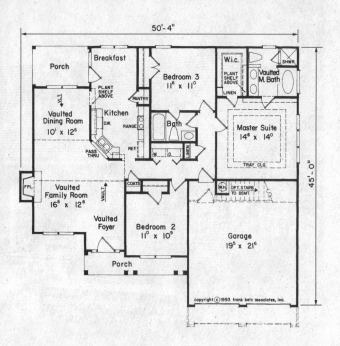

Special features

- 9' ceilings throughout this home
- Sunny breakfast room is very accessible to kitchen
- Kitchen has pass-through to vaulted family room
- 3 bedrooms, 2 baths, 2-car garage
- Crawl space or walk-out basement foundation, please specify when ordering

Cottage-Style Adds Charm

Plan #711-043D-0008

1,496 total square feet of living area

Price Code A

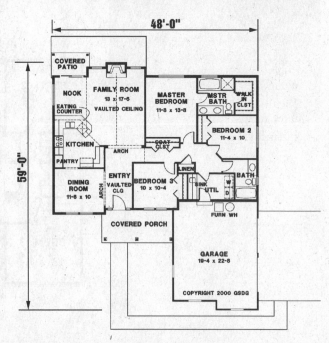

Special features

- Large utility room with sink and extra counterspace
- Covered patio off breakfast nook extends dining to the outdoors
- Eating counter in kitchen overlooks vaulted family room
- 3 bedrooms, 2 baths, 2-car side entry garage
- Crawl space foundation

TO ORDER BLUEPRINTS USE THE FORM ON PAGE 15 OR CALL TOLL-FREE 1-877-671-6036
View thousands more home plans online at www.familyhandyman.com/homeplans

149

Great Room Entertainment Center Plan #711-070D-0004

1,791 total square feet of living area

Price Code B

Special features

- A whirlpool tub adds luxury to the master bath
- Breakfast nook leads to a covered porch
- Double closets create plenty of storage in the foyer
- 3 bedrooms, 2 baths, 2-car side entry garage
- Basement foundation

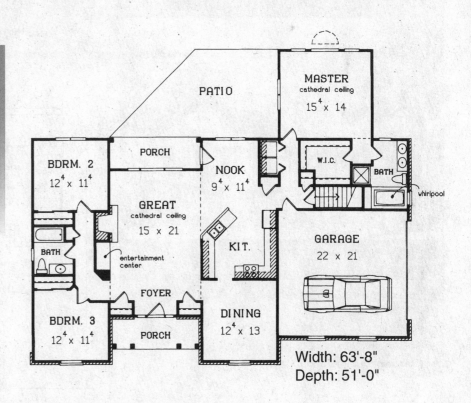

PATIO

MASTER
cathedral ceiling
15⁴ x 14

PORCH

NOOK
9⁴ x 11⁴

W.I.C.

BATH

whirlpool

BDRM. 2
12⁴ x 11⁴

GREAT
cathedral ceiling
15 x 21

KIT.

GARAGE
22 x 21

BATH

entertainment center

FOYER

DINING
12⁴ x 13

BDRM. 3
12⁴ x 11⁴

PORCH

Width: 63'-8"
Depth: 51'-0"

Whirlpool With Skylight Above

Plan #711-026D-0112

1,911 total square feet of living area

Price Code C

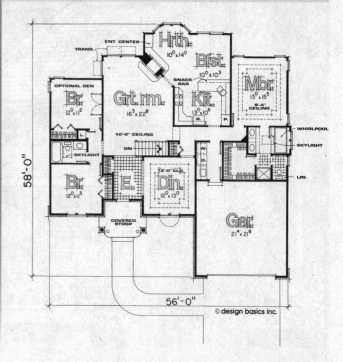

© design basics inc.

Special features

- Large entry opens into a beautiful great room with an angled see-through fireplace
- Terrific design includes kitchen and breakfast area with adjacent sunny bayed hearth room
- Private master bedroom with bath features skylight and walk-in closet
- 3 bedrooms, 2 baths, 2-car garage
- Basement foundation

Traditional Ranch With Extras

Plan #711-035D-0004

1,425 total square feet of living area

Price Code A

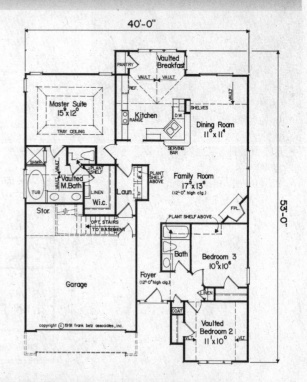

copyright © 1991 frank betz associates, inc.

Special features

- Kitchen and vaulted breakfast room are the center of activity
- Corner fireplace warms spacious family room
- Oversized serving bar extends seating in dining room
- 3 bedrooms, 2 baths, 2-car garage
- Crawl space, slab or walk-out basement foundation, please specify when ordering

TO ORDER BLUEPRINTS USE THE FORM ON PAGE 15 OR CALL TOLL-FREE 1-877-671-6036
View thousands more home plans online at www.familyhandyman.com/homeplans

151

Charming Covered Front Porch   Plan #711-058D-0046

2,547 total square feet of living area

Price Code D

Special features

- Second floor makes economical use of area above garage allowing for three bedrooms and a study/fourth bedroom
- First floor study is ideal for a home office
- Large pantry is located in efficient kitchen
- 3 bedrooms, 2 1/2 baths, 2-car garage
- Basement foundation

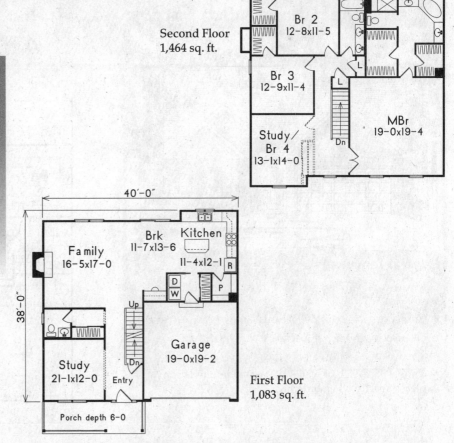

Second Floor
1,464 sq. ft.

Br 2
12-8x11-5

Br 3
12-9x11-4

Study/
Br 4
13-1x14-0

MBr
19-0x19-4

40'-0"

38'-0"

Family
16-5x17-0

Brk
11-7x13-6

Kitchen
11-4x12-1

Study
21-1x12-0

Garage
19-0x19-2

Up

Dn

Entry

Porch depth 6-0

First Floor
1,083 sq. ft.

TO ORDER BLUEPRINTS USE THE FORM ON PAGE 15 OR CALL TOLL-FREE 1-877-671-6036
View thousands more home plans online at www.familyhandyman.com/homeplans

152

Fireplace Warms This Home

Plan #711-038D-0034

1,625 total square feet of living area

Price Code B

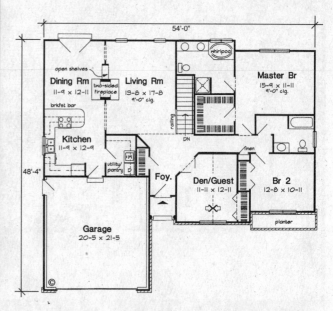

Special features

- Double-door in corner of den/guest room creates an interesting entry
- Spacious master bath has both a whirlpool tub and a shower
- Welcoming planter boxes in front add curb appeal
- 3 bedrooms, 2 baths, 2-car garage
- Basement or crawl space foundation, please specify when ordering

Windowed Dining Room

Plan #711-041D-0001

2,003 total square feet of living area

Price Code D

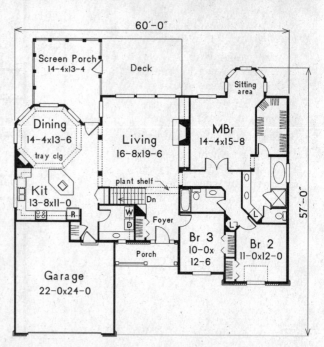

Special features

- Octagon-shaped dining room with tray ceiling and deck overlook
- L-shaped island kitchen serves living and dining rooms
- Master bedroom boasts luxury bath and walk-in closet
- Living room features columns, elegant fireplace and 10' ceiling
- 3 bedrooms, 2 baths, 2-car garage
- Basement foundation

Convenient Grilling Porch

Plan #711-055D-0034

1,787 total square feet of living area

Price Code B

Special features

- Covered grilling porch offers a convenient place for grilling or entertaining off the great room
- Columns around dining room create a sense of enclosure while maintaining spaciousness
- A sunny bay window is a nice accent to the breakfast room
- 3 bedrooms, 2 baths, 2-car garage
- Walk-out basement, basement, crawl space or slab foundation, please specify when ordering

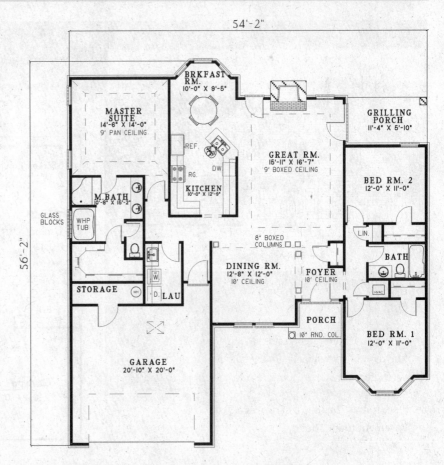

Private Bedroom Area

Plan #711-039D-0007

1,550 total square feet of living area

Price Code B

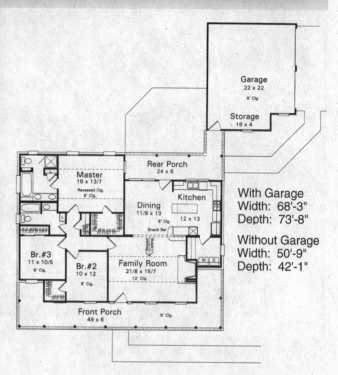

Garage
22 x 22
8' Clg.

Storage
16 x 4

Rear Porch
24 x 6

Master
16 x 13/7
Recessed Clg.
9' Clg.

Kitchen
12 x 13

Dining
11/8 x 13
8' Clg.

Snack Bar

Br.#3
11 x 10/5
8' Clg.

Br.#2
10 x 12
8' Clg.

Family Room
21/8 x 15/7
12' Clg.

Sloped Ceiling

W D

Front Porch
49 x 6
8' Clg.

With Garage
Width: 68'-3"
Depth: 73'-8"

Without Garage
Width: 50'-9"
Depth: 42'-1"

Special features

- Wrap-around front porch is an ideal gathering place
- Handy snack bar is positioned so kitchen flows into family room
- Master bedroom has many amenities
- 3 bedrooms, 2 baths, 2-car detached side entry garage
- Slab or crawl space foundation, please specify when ordering

Beautiful Brickwork Adds Elegance

Plan #711-031D-0009

1,960 total square feet of living area

Price Code C

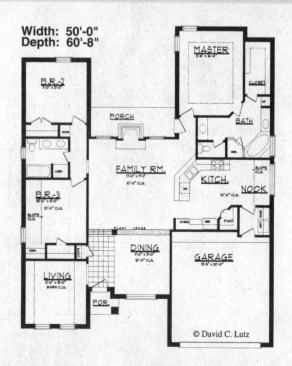

Width: 50'-0"
Depth: 60'-8"

MASTER

CLOSET

B.R.-2

PORCH

BATH

FAMILY RM.
10'-0" CLG.

KITCH.
10'-0" CLG.

NOOK

B.R.-3
10'-0" CLG.

PLANT LEDGE

OVEN REF. PANT.

DINING
10'-0" CLG.

GARAGE

LIVING
BARN CLG.

POR.

© David C. Lutz

Special features

- Open floor plan suitable for an active family
- Desk space in bedroom #3 is ideal for young student
- Effective design creates an enclosed courtyard in the rear of the home
- 3 bedrooms, 2 baths, 2-car garage
- Slab foundation

TO ORDER BLUEPRINTS USE THE FORM ON PAGE 15 OR CALL TOLL-FREE 1-877-671-6036
View thousands more home plans online at www.familyhandyman.com/homeplans

155

Brick Traditional

Plan #711-056D-0019

2,737 total square feet of living area

Price Code E

Special features

- T-stairs make any room easily accessible
- Two-story ceilings in foyer and grand room create a spacious feeling
- Master bedroom has gorgeous bay window and a sitting area
- Bedroom #4 has its own private bath
- 5 bedrooms, 4 baths, 2-car side entry garage
- Basement foundation

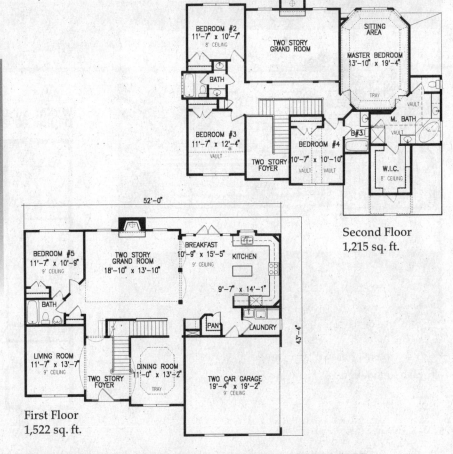

BEDROOM #2
11'-7" x 10'-7"
8' CEILING

TWO STORY
GRAND ROOM

SITTING AREA

MASTER BEDROOM
13'-10" x 19'-4"
TRAY

BATH

BEDROOM #3
11'-7" x 12'-4"
VAULT

TWO STORY
FOYER

BEDROOM #4
10'-7" x 10'-10"
VAULT   VAULT

B#3
VAULT

M. BATH

W.I.C.
8' CEILING

Second Floor
1,215 sq. ft.

52'-0"

BEDROOM #5
11'-7" x 10'-9"
9' CEILING

TWO STORY
GRAND ROOM
18'-10" x 13'-10"

BREAKFAST
10'-9" x 15'-5"
9' CEILING

KITCHEN

9'-7" x 14'-1"

BATH

43'-4"

LIVING ROOM
11'-7" x 13'-7"
9' CEILING

TWO STORY
FOYER

DINING ROOM
11'-0" x 13'-2"
TRAY

PAN

LAUNDRY

TWO CAR GARAGE
19'-4" x 19'-2"
9' CEILING

First Floor
1,522 sq. ft.

Relax In The Glorious Sunroom

Plan #711-070D-0011

2,198 total square feet of living area

Price Code C

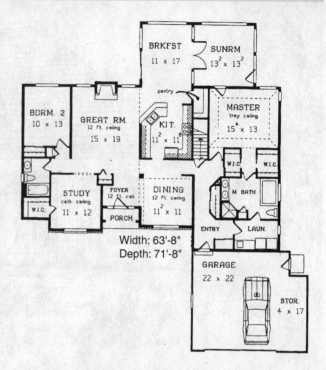

BRKFST 11 x 17

SUNRM 13² x 13²

pantry

MASTER tray ceiling 15⁴ x 13

BDRM. 2 10 x 13

GREAT RM. 12 ft. ceiling 15 x 19

KIT. 11² x 11

W.I.C. W.I.C.

STUDY cath. ceiling 11 x 12

FOYER 12 ft. ceil.

DINING 12 ft. ceiling 11² x 11

M. BATH

W.I.C.

PORCH

ENTRY LAUN.

Width: 63'-8"
Depth: 71'-8"

GARAGE 22 x 22

STOR. 4 x 17

Special features

- Double walk-in closets in the master bedroom as well as direct access to the laundry room
- Varied ceiling heights throughout this home
- Large study includes a walk-in closet and cathedral ceiling
- 2 bedrooms, 2 baths, 2-car garage
- Basement foundation

Charm Wrapped In A Veranda

Plan #711-037D-0009

2,059 total square feet of living area

Price Code C

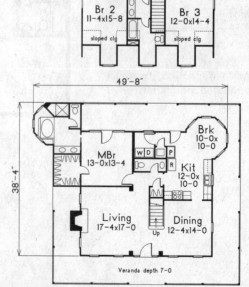

Second Floor 751 sq. ft.

Sit 10-0x 10-4

Br 2 11-4x15-8

Dn

Br 3 12-0x14-4

sloped clg sloped clg

49'-8"

38'-4"

Brk 10-0x 10-0

MBr 13-0x13-4

W D P
R

Kit 12-0x 10-0

Living 17-4x17-0

Dining 12-4x14-0

Up

Veranda depth 7-0

First Floor 1,308 sq. ft.

Special features

- Octagon-shaped breakfast room offers plenty of windows and creates a view to the veranda
- First floor master bedroom has large walk-in closet and deluxe bath
- 9' ceilings throughout the home
- Secondary bedrooms and bath feature dormers and are adjacent to cozy sitting area
- 3 bedrooms, 2 1/2 baths, 2-car detached garage
- Slab foundation, drawings also include basement and crawl space foundations

TO ORDER BLUEPRINTS USE THE FORM ON PAGE 15 OR CALL TOLL-FREE 1-877-671-6036
View thousands more home plans online at www.familyhandyman.com/homeplans

157

Open Living

Plan #711-020D-0005

1,770 total square feet of living area

Price Code B

Special features

- Open floor plan makes this home feel spacious
- 12' ceilings in kitchen, living, breakfast and dining areas
- Kitchen is the center of activity with views into all gathering places
- 3 bedrooms, 2 baths, 2-car side entry garage
- Crawl space foundation, drawings also include slab foundation

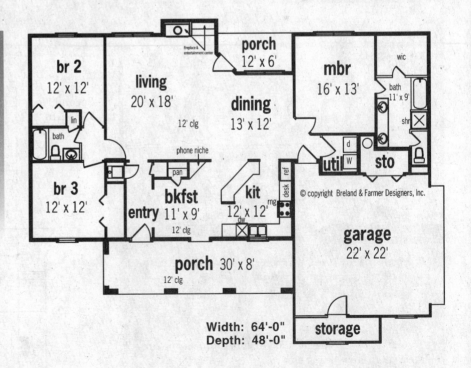

br 2
12' x 12'

living
20' x 18'
12' clg

porch
12' x 6'

mbr
16' x 13'

wic

bath
11' x 9'

dining
13' x 12'

phone niche

lin

bath

shr

br 3
12' x 12'

pan

bkfst
11' x 9'

kit
12' x 12'

desk   ref

util

sto

entry

12' clg

rng

d
w

© copyright Breland & Farmer Designers, Inc.

dw

porch
30' x 8'
12' clg

garage
22' x 22'

Width: 64'-0"
Depth: 48'-0"

storage

Dramatic Cathedral Ceilings

Plan #711-034D-0001

1,436 total square feet of living area

Price Code A

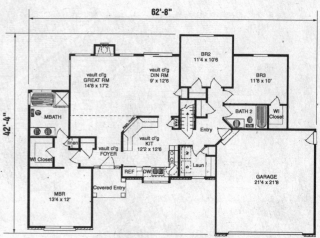

62'-8"

47'-4"

BR2 11'4 x 10'6

vault cl'g GREAT RM 14'8 x 17'2

vault cl'g DIN RM 9' x 12'6

BR3 11'8 x 10'

MBATH

BATH 2

WI Closet

Entry

linen

vault cl'g KIT 12'2 x 12'6

vault cl'g FOYER

WI Closet

REF DW

Laun

GARAGE 21'4 x 21'8

MBR 13'4 x 12'

Covered Entry

Special features

- Covered entry is inviting
- Kitchen has handy breakfast bar which overlooks great room and dining room
- Private master bedroom with bath and walk-in closet is separate from other bedrooms
- 3 bedrooms, 2 baths, 2-car garage
- Basement foundation

Master Bedroom With Sitting Area

Plan #711-026D-0142

2,188 total square feet of living area

Price Code C

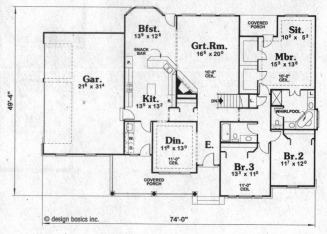

49'-4"

Bfst. 13'9 x 12'8

Grt.Rm. 16'6 x 20'0

COVERED PORCH

Sit. 10'0 x 5'3

Mbr. 15'3 x 13'6

SNACK BAR

10'-0" CEIL.

10'-0" CEIL.

Gar. 21'8 x 31'4

P.

Kit. 13'9 x 13'2

R.

DN

WHIRLPOOL

W. D.

Din. 11'8 x 13'0

E.

Br.3 13'3 x 11'0

Br.2 11'7 x 12'0

11'-0" CEIL.

11'-0" CEIL.

COVERED PORCH

© design basics inc.

74'-0"

Special features

- Master bedroom includes a private covered porch, sitting area and two large walk-in closets
- Spacious kitchen has center island, snack bar and laundry access
- Great room has a 10' ceiling and a dramatic corner fireplace
- 3 bedrooms, 2 baths, 3-car side entry garage
- Basement foundation

1,588 total square feet of living area

Price Code B

Special features

- Workshop in garage is ideal for storage and projects
- 12' vaulted master suite has double closets as well as a lovely bath with bayed soaking tub and compartmentalized shower and toilet area
- Lovely arched entry to 14' vaulted great room flows into the dining room and sky-lit kitchen
- 3 bedrooms, 2 baths, 2-car garage
- Basement foundation

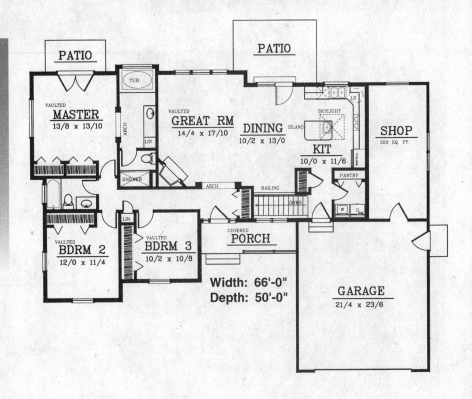

PATIO

PATIO

VAULTED
MASTER
13/8 x 13/10

TUB

VAULTED
GREAT RM
14/4 x 17/10

DINING
10/2 x 13/0

ISLAND

SKYLIGHT

SHOP
222 SQ FT

KIT
10/0 x 11/6

PANTRY

LIN

SHOWER

ARCH

RAILING

VAULTED
BDRM 2
12/0 x 11/4

LIN

VAULTED
BDRM 3
10/2 x 10/8

COVERED
PORCH

Width: 66'-0"
Depth: 50'-0"

GARAGE
21/4 x 23/6

Cozy Covered Front Porch

Plan #711-035D-0045

1,749 total square feet of living area

Price Code B

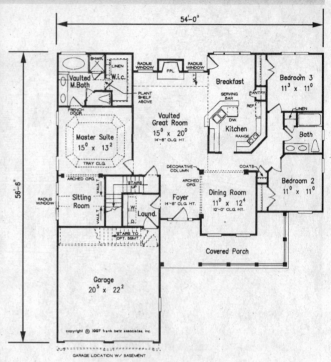

Special features

- Tray ceiling in master bedroom
- Breakfast bar overlooks vaulted great room
- Additional bedrooms are located away from master suite for privacy
- Optional bonus room above the garage has an additional 308 square feet of living area
- 3 bedrooms, 2 baths, 2-car garage
- Walk-out basement, slab or crawl space foundation, please specify when ordering

Terrific Home With Many Extras

Plan #711-047D-0004

1,550 total square feet of living area

Price Code B

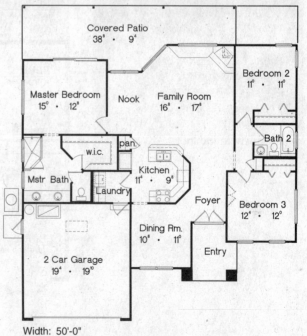

Special features

- 10' ceilings throughout this home
- U-shaped kitchen is centered between the formal dining room and the family room
- Master bedroom is secluded for privacy
- 3 bedrooms, 2 baths, 2-car garage
- Slab foundation

Width: 50'-0"
Depth: 55'-0"

TO ORDER BLUEPRINTS USE THE FORM ON PAGE 15 OR CALL TOLL-FREE 1-877-671-6036
View thousands more home plans online at www.familyhandyman.com/homeplans

161

The Family Handyman

GRAND ENTRY FOYER

Plan #711-015D-0044

2,148 total square feet of living area

Price Code C

Special features

- 9' ceilings throughout this home
- 11' ceilings in great room, kitchen, nook and foyer
- Eating bar in kitchen extends the dining space for extra guests or casual seating
- 3 bedrooms, 2 baths, 2-car side entry garage
- Basement foundation

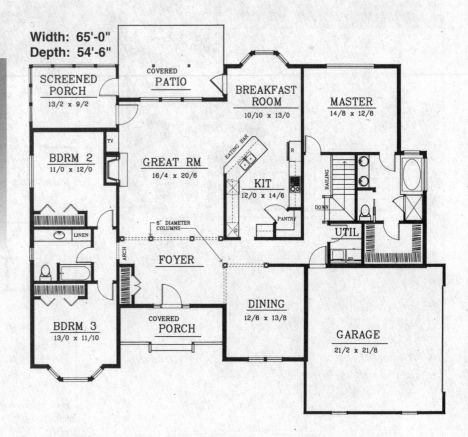

Width: 65'-0"
Depth: 54'-6"

SCREENED PORCH
13/2 x 9/2

COVERED PATIO

BREAKFAST ROOM
10/10 x 13/0

MASTER
14/8 x 12/8

BDRM 2
11/0 x 12/0

TV

GREAT RM
16/4 x 20/6

EATING BAR

KIT
12/0 x 14/6

R

RAILING

DOWN

LINEN

8" DIAMETER COLUMNS

PANTRY

UTIL

FOYER

ARCH

BDRM 3
13/0 x 11/10

COVERED PORCH

DINING
12/6 x 13/8

GARAGE
21/2 x 21/8

See-Through Fireplace

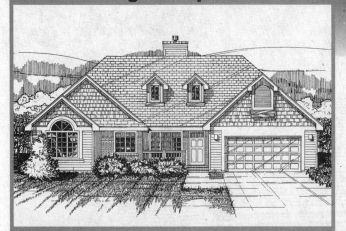

Special features

- Convenient double-doors in dining area provide access to a large deck
- Family room features several large windows for brightness
- Bedrooms separate from living areas for privacy
- Master bedroom offers a bath with walk-in closet, double-bowl vanity and both a shower and a whirlpool tub
- 3 bedrooms, 2 1/2 baths, 2-car garage
- Basement foundation

Plan #711-045D-0009

1,684 total square feet of living area

Price Code B

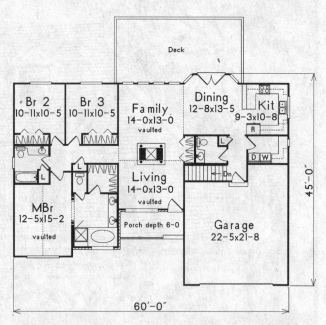

Fireplaces Are Unique Focal Points

Special features

- Varied ceiling heights throughout this home
- Master bedroom features built-in desk and pocket door entrance into large master bath
- Master bath includes corner vanity and garden tub
- Breakfast area accesses courtyard
- 3 bedrooms, 2 baths, 3-car side entry garage
- Slab foundation

Plan #711-037D-0025

2,481 total square feet of living area

Price Code D

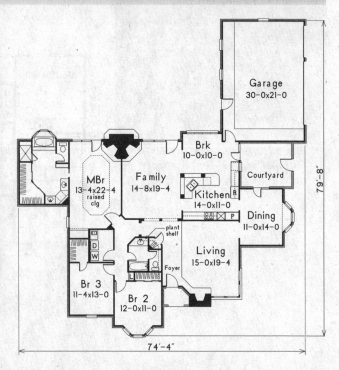

TO ORDER BLUEPRINTS USE THE FORM ON PAGE 15 OR CALL TOLL-FREE 1-877-671-6036
View thousands more home plans online at www.familyhandyman.com/homeplans

163

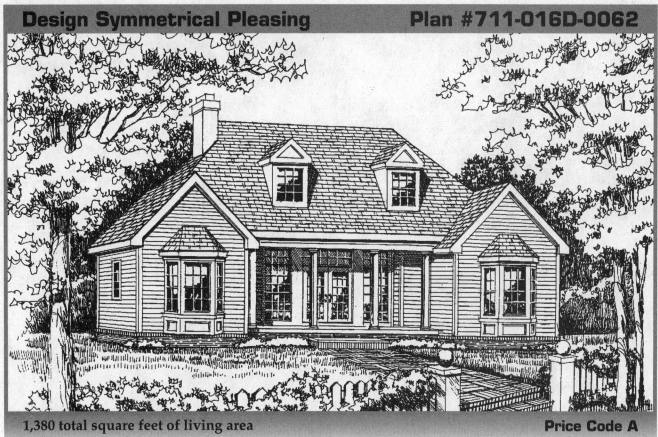

1,380 total square feet of living area

Price Code A

Special features

- Built-in bookshelves complement fireplace in great room
- Lots of storage space near laundry room and kitchen
- Covered porch has views of the backyard
- 3 bedrooms, 2 baths, optional 2-car side entry garage
- Basement, crawl space or slab foundation, please specify when ordering

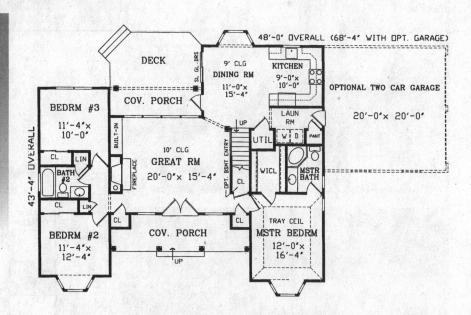

Carport With Storage

Plan #711-039D-0002

1,333 total square feet of living area

Price Code A

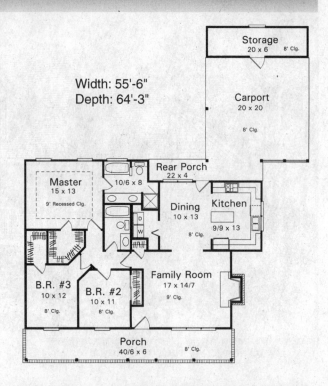

Width: 55'-6"
Depth: 64'-3"

Storage 20 x 6 · 8' Clg.

Carport 20 x 20 · 8' Clg.

Master 15 x 13 · 9' Recessed Clg.

10/6 x 8

Rear Porch 22 x 4

Dining 10 x 13 · 8' Clg.

Kitchen 9/9 x 13

B.R. #3 10 x 12 · 8' Clg.

B.R. #2 10 x 11 · 8' Clg.

Family Room 17 x 14/7 · 9' Clg.

Porch 40/6 x 6 · 8' Clg.

Special features

- Country charm with covered front porch
- Dining area looks into family room with fireplace
- Master suite has walk-in closet and private bath
- 3 bedrooms, 2 baths, 2-car attached carport
- Slab or crawl space foundation, please specify when ordering

Open Living In This Ranch

COPYRIGHT 1991 LARRY E. BELK

Plan #711-019D-0005

1,575 total square feet of living area

Price Code B

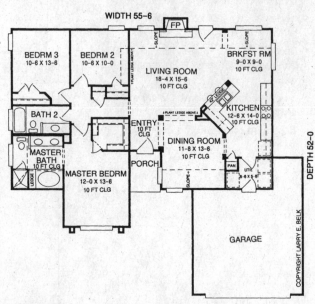

WIDTH 55-6

FP

BEDRM 3 10-6 x 13-6

BEDRM 2 10-6 x 10-0

LIVING ROOM 18-4 X 15-6 10 FT CLG

BRKFST RM 9-0 X 9-0 10 FT CLG

BATH 2

ENTRY 10 FT CLG

KITCHEN 12-6 X 14-0 10 FT CLG

MASTER BATH 10 FT CLG

MASTER BEDRM 12-0 X 13-6 10 FT CLG

DINING ROOM 11-8 X 13-6 10 FT CLG

PORCH

PAN

UTIL

DEPTH 52-0

GARAGE

COPYRIGHT LARRY E. BELK

Special features

- Decorative columns separate dining room from living room and foyer
- Kitchen has plenty of workspace
- Spacious walk-in closet in master bedroom
- 3 bedrooms, 2 baths, 2-car garage
- Crawl space foundation, drawings also include slab foundation

Classy Master Bedroom

Plan #711-052D-0058

2,012 total square feet of living area

Price Code C

Special features

- Kitchen with eat-in breakfast bar overlooks breakfast room
- Sunny living room is open and airy with vaulted ceiling
- Secondary bedrooms with convenient vanities skillfully share bath
- 3 bedrooms, 2 1/2 baths, 2-car side entry garage
- Basement foundation

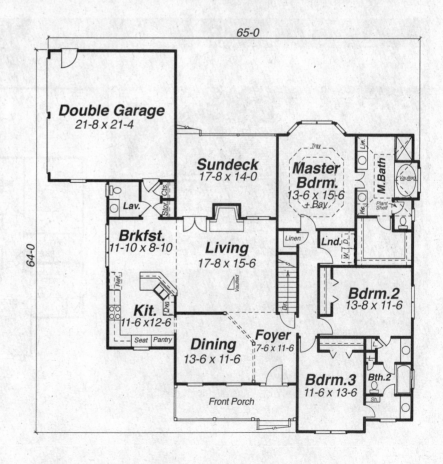

Comfortable Dinette

Plan #711-020D-0002

1,434 total square feet of living area

Price Code A

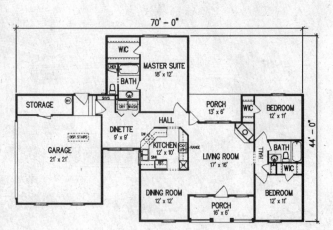

Special features

- Isolated master suite for privacy includes walk-in closet and bath
- Elegant formal dining room
- Efficient kitchen has an adjacent dining area which includes shelves and access to laundry facilities
- Extra storage in garage
- 3 bedrooms, 2 baths, 2-car side entry garage
- Crawl space foundation, drawings also include slab foundation

Symmetry Dominates Design

Plan #711-007D-0046

1,712 total square feet of living area

Price Code B

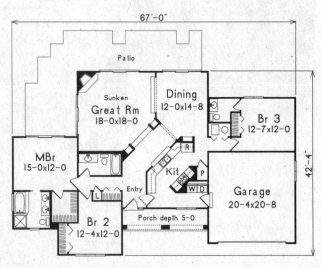

Special features

- Stylish stucco exterior enhances curb appeal
- Sunken great room offers corner fireplace flanked by 9' wide patio doors
- Well-designed kitchen features ideal view of great room and fireplace through breakfast bar opening
- 3 bedrooms, 2 1/2 baths, 2-car garage
- Crawl space foundation

TO ORDER BLUEPRINTS USE THE FORM ON PAGE 15 OR CALL TOLL-FREE 1-877-671-6036
View thousands more home plans online at www.familyhandyman.com/homeplans

167

ARCH Windows Grace Facade

Plan #711-023D-0007

2,993 total square feet of living area

Price Code E

Special features

- 10' ceilings on first floor, 9' ceilings on second floor
- Second floor bedrooms include private dressing areas, walk-in closets and share a bath
- Generous family room and kitchen combine for activity center
- 4 bedrooms, 3 baths, 2-car side entry garage
- Slab foundation, drawings also include crawl space foundation

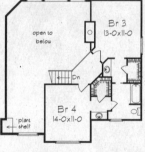

Second Floor
624 sq. ft

Br 3
13-0x11-0

open to below

Br 4
14-0x11-0

plant shelf

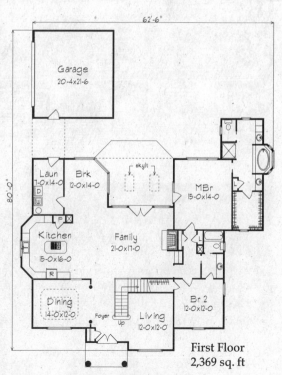

62'-6"

Garage
20-4x21-6

80'-0"

Laun
7-0x14-0

Brk
12-0x14-0

skylt

MBr
15-0x14-0

Kitchen
15-0x16-0

Family
21-0x17-0

Dining
14-0x12-0

Foyer

Living
12-0x12-0

Br 2
12-0x12-0

First Floor
2,369 sq. ft

168

TO ORDER BLUEPRINTS USE THE FORM ON PAGE 15 OR CALL TOLL-FREE 1-877-671-6036
View thousands more home plans online at www.familyhandyman.com/homeplans

The Family Handyman

Tall Windows Make An Impression

Plan #711-022D-0003

1,351 total square feet of living area

Price Code A

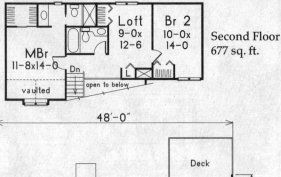

Second Floor
677 sq. ft.

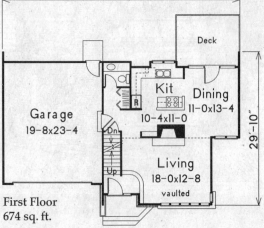

First Floor
674 sq. ft.

Special features

- Roof lines and vaulted ceilings make this home appear larger
- Central fireplace provides a focal point for dining and living areas
- Master bedroom features a roomy window seat and a walk-in closet
- Loft can easily be converted to a third bedroom
- 2 bedrooms, 2 1/2 baths, 2-car garage
- Basement foundation

Circle-Top Details

Plan #711-019D-0013

1,932 total square feet of living area

Price Code C

Special features

- Double arches form entrance to this elegantly styled home
- Two palladian windows add distinction to facade
- Kitchen has an angled eating bar opening to the breakfast and living rooms
- 3 bedrooms, 2 baths, 2-car side entry garage
- Crawl space foundation, drawings also include slab foundation

TO ORDER BLUEPRINTS USE THE FORM ON PAGE 15 OR CALL TOLL-FREE 1-877-671-6036
View thousands more home plans online at www.familyhandyman.com/homeplans

169

Bright Garden Room   Plan #711-026D-0141

1,814 total square feet of living area   **Price Code C**

Special features

- Handy bench located outside laundry area for changing
- Charming garden room located off great room brings in the outdoors
- Kitchen features lots of cabinetry and counterspace
- 4 bedrooms, 2 1/2 baths, 3-car garage
- Basement foundation

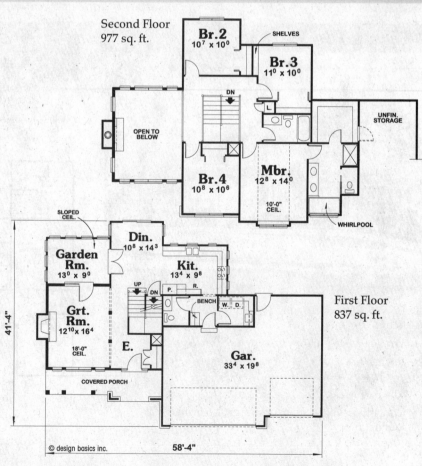

Second Floor
977 sq. ft.

Br. 2
10⁷ x 10⁰

SHELVES

Br. 3
11⁰ x 10⁰

DN

OPEN TO BELOW

UNFIN. STORAGE

Br. 4
10⁸ x 10⁶

Mbr.
12⁸ x 14⁰

10'-0" CEIL.

WHIRLPOOL

SLOPED CEIL.

Din.
10⁸ x 14³

Garden Rm.
13⁰ x 9⁰

Kit.
13⁴ x 9⁸

UP

DN

P.

R.

BENCH

W. D.

Grt. Rm.
12¹⁰ x 16⁴

18'-0" CEIL.

E.

41'-4"

First Floor
837 sq. ft.

Gar.
33⁴ x 19⁸

COVERED PORCH

© design basics inc.   58'-4"

Exterior Employs Innovative Planning Plan #711-007D-0049

1,791 total square feet of living area
Price Code C

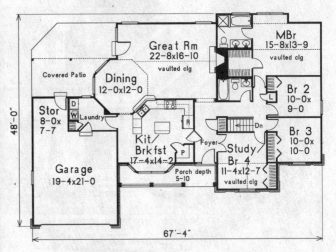

Great Rm
22-8x16-10
vaulted clg

MBr
15-8x13-9
vaulted clg

Covered Patio

Dining
12-0x12-0

Br 2
10-0x
9-0

Stor
8-0x
7-7

D W Laundry

Kit/
Brkfst
17-4x14-2

Br 3
10-0x
10-0

Dn

Foyer

Study
Br 4
11-4x12-7
vaulted clg

Garage
19-4x21-0

Porch depth
5-10

48'-0"

67'-4"

Special features

- Vaulted great room and octagon-shaped dining area enjoy views of covered patio
- Kitchen features a pass-through to dining area, center island, large walk-in pantry and breakfast room with large bay window
- Master bedroom is vaulted with sitting area
- 4 bedrooms, 2 baths, 2-car garage with storage
- Basement foundation, drawings also include crawl space and slab foundations

Spacious Family Living Area Plan #711-001D-0030

1,416 total square feet of living area
Price Code A

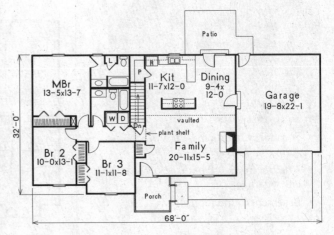

Patio

MBr
13-5x13-7

Kit
11-7x12-0

Dining
9-4x
12-0

Garage
19-8x22-1

W D

Dn

vaulted

plant shelf

Br 2
10-0x13-1

Br 3
11-1x11-8

Family
20-11x15-5

Porch

32'-0"

68'-0"

Special features

- Family room includes fireplace, elevated plant shelf and vaulted ceiling
- Patio is accessible from dining area and garage
- Centrally located laundry area
- Oversized walk-in pantry
- 3 bedrooms, 2 baths, 2-car garage
- Basement foundation, drawings also include crawl space and slab foundations

TO ORDER BLUEPRINTS USE THE FORM ON PAGE 15 OR CALL TOLL-FREE 1-877-671-6036
View thousands more home plans online at www.familyhandyman.com/homeplans

171

Kitchen Is Centrally Located

Plan #711-053D-0051

2,731 total square feet of living area

Price Code E

Special features

- Isolated master bedroom with double walk-in closets, coffered ceiling and an elegant bath
- Both dining and living rooms feature coffered ceilings and bay windows
- Breakfast room includes dramatic vaulted ceiling and plenty of windows
- Family room features fireplace flanked by shelves, vaulted ceiling and access to rear deck
- Secondary bedrooms are separate from living areas
- 4 bedrooms, 3 1/2 baths, 2-car side entry garage
- Basement foundation

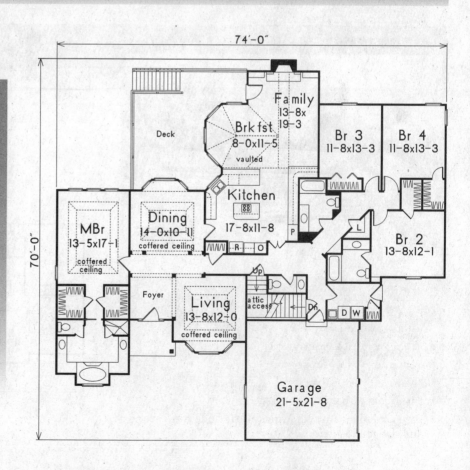

74'-0"

70'-0"

Deck

Family
13-8x
19-3

Brk fst
8-0x11-5
vaulted

Br 3
11-8x13-3

Br 4
11-8x13-3

Kitchen
17-8x11-8

MBr
13-5x17-1
coffered
ceiling

Dining
14-0x10-11
coffered ceiling

Br 2
13-8x12-1

Foyer

Living
13-8x12-0
coffered ceiling

Up

attic
access

Dn

D W

Garage
21-5x21-8

Warm And Inviting

Plan #711-019D-0011

1,955 total square feet of living area

Price Code C

WIDTH 65-0

DEPTH 58-8

MASTER BEDRM
12-8 X 14-6
10 FT CLG

MASTER BATH
10 FT CLG

BATH 2

BEDRM 2
11-0 X 13-6

BEDRM 3
12-6 X 13-4

FOYER
10 FT CLG

GREAT ROOM
18-6 X 15-6
10 FT CLG

BRKFST RM
12-0 X 10-0
10 FT CLG

KITCHEN
12-6 X 14-0
10 FT CLG

DINING ROOM
12-2 X 14-0
10 FT CLG

UTIL
6-8 X 8-6

PAN

PORCH

GARAGE

COPYRIGHT LARRY E. BELK

Special features

- Porch adds outdoor area to this design
- Dining and great rooms are visible from foyer through a series of elegant archways
- Kitchen overlooks great room and breakfast room
- 3 bedrooms, 2 baths, 2-car side entry garage
- Crawl space foundation, drawings also include slab foundation

Large Windows Grace This Home

Plan #711-010D-0007

1,427 total square feet of living area

Price Code A

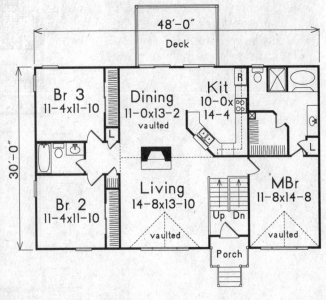

48'-0"

Deck

30'-0"

Br 3
11-4x11-10

Dining
11-0x13-2
vaulted

Kit
10-0x
14-4

Br 2
11-4x11-10

Living
14-8x13-10
vaulted

MBr
11-8x14-8
vaulted

Up Dn

Porch

Special features

- Practical storage space situated in the garage
- Convenient laundry closet located on lower level
- Kitchen and dining area both have sliding doors that access the deck
- Large expansive space created by vaulted living and dining rooms
- 3 bedrooms, 2 baths, 2-car drive under garage
- Basement foundation

TO ORDER BLUEPRINTS USE THE FORM ON PAGE 15 OR CALL TOLL-FREE 1-877-671-6036
View thousands more home plans online at www.familyhandyman.com/homeplans

173

Luxurious Bay-Shaped Master Bath   Plan #711-047D-0051

2,962 total square feet of living area

Price Code E

Special features

- Vaulted breakfast nook is adjacent to the kitchen for convenience
- Bedroom #4 is an ideal guest suite with private bath
- Master bedroom includes see-through fireplace, bayed vanity and massive walk-in closet
- 4 bedrooms, 3 baths, 3-car side entry garage
- Slab foundation

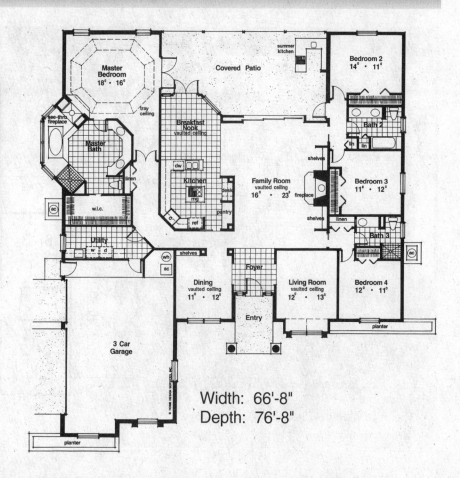

Width: 66'-8"
Depth: 76'-8"

Charming Cedar Shakes

Plan #711-039D-0013

1,842 total square feet of living area

Price Code C

Width: 56'-4"
Depth: 68'-6"

Special features

- Vaulted family room features a fireplace and an elegant bookcase
- Island countertop in kitchen makes cooking convenient
- Rear facade has an intimate porch area ideal for relaxing
- 3 bedrooms, 2 baths, 2-car garage
- Slab or crawl space foundation, please specify when ordering

Sleek Contemporary

Plan #711-047D-0034

2,010 total square feet of living area

Price Code C

Width: 62'-8"
Depth: 56'-0"

Special features

- Perfect family plan is spacious and open
- Three secondary bedrooms are separated from master bedroom
- Fireplace in family room flanked by shelves that are ideal for displaying books or other keepsakes
- 4 bedrooms, 2 baths, 2-car garage
- Slab foundation

TO ORDER BLUEPRINTS USE THE FORM ON PAGE 15 OR CALL TOLL-FREE 1-877-671-6036
View thousands more home plans online at www.familyhandyman.com/homeplans

175

Handsome Accents

Plan #711-001D-0013

1,882 total square feet of living area

Price Code D

Special features

- Wide, handsome entrance opens to the vaulted great room with fireplace
- Living and dining areas are conveniently joined but still allow privacy
- Private covered porch extends breakfast area
- Practical passageway runs through laundry and mud room from garage to kitchen
- Vaulted ceiling in master bedroom
- 3 bedrooms, 2 baths, 2-car garage
- Basement foundation

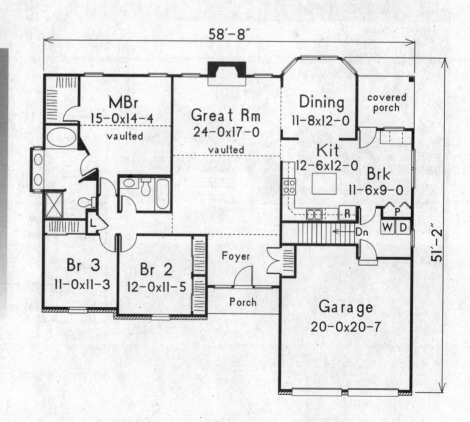

58'-8"

MBr
15-0x14-4
vaulted

Great Rm
24-0x17-0
vaulted

Dining
11-8x12-0

covered porch

Kit
12-6x12-0

Brk
11-6x9-0

Foyer

Dn

W D

Br 3
11-0x11-3

Br 2
12-0x11-5

Porch

Garage
20-0x20-7

51'-2"

Plenty Of Bright, Vaulted Spaces

Plan #711-022D-0025

2,847 total square feet of living area

Price Code E

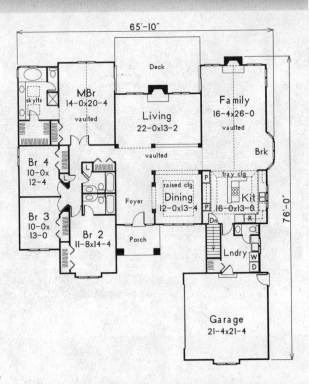

Special features

- Master bedroom includes skylighted bath, deck access and double closets
- Bedroom #2 converts to guest room with private bath
- Impressive foyer and gallery opens into large living room with fireplace
- Kitchen features desk area, center island, adjacent bayed breakfast area and access to laundry room with half bath
- 4 bedrooms, 3 1/2 baths, 2-car side entry garage
- Basement foundation

Vaulted Ceilings Add Dimension

Plan #711-048D-0011

1,550 total square feet of living area

Price Code B

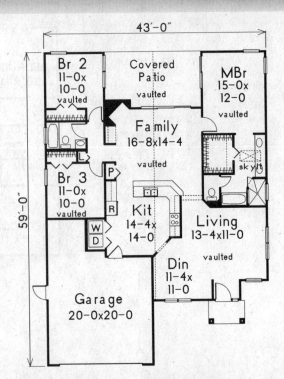

Special features

- Cozy corner fireplace provides focal point in family room
- Master bedroom features large walk-in closet, skylight and separate tub and shower
- Convenient laundry closet
- Kitchen with pantry and breakfast bar connects to family room
- Family room and master bedroom access covered patio
- 3 bedrooms, 2 baths, 2-car garage
- Slab foundation

1,992 total square feet of living area

Price Code C

Special features

- Bayed breakfast room overlooks outdoor deck and connects to screened porch
- Private formal living room in the front of the home could easily be converted to a home office or study
- Compact, yet efficient kitchen is conveniently situated between the breakfast and dining rooms
- 3 bedrooms, 2 1/2 baths, 3-car side entry garage
- Basement, crawl space or slab foundation, please specify when ordering

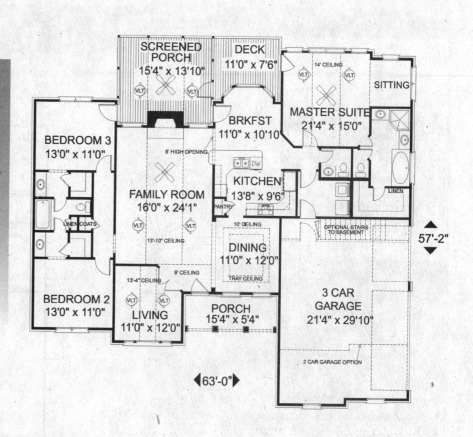

Stylish Living For A Narrow Lot

Special features

- Inviting porch leads to spacious living and dining rooms
- Kitchen with corner windows features an island snack bar, attractive breakfast room bay, convenient laundry and built-in pantry
- A luxury bath and walk-in closet adorn master bedroom suite
- 3 bedrooms, 2 1/2 baths, 2-car garage
- Basement foundation, drawings also include crawl space and slab foundations

Plan #711-007D-0054

1,575 total square feet of living area

Price Code B

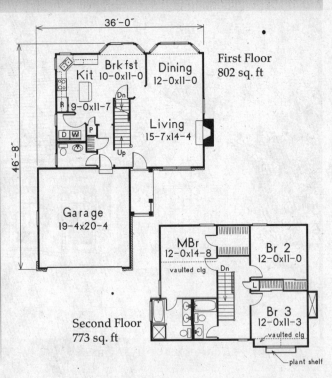

First Floor
802 sq. ft

Second Floor
773 sq. ft

Arched Windows Enhance Facade

Special features

- Open living spaces allow for dining area, great room and breakfast room to flow together
- Bedroom #4 has unique design with double closets and a built-in desk
- Plenty of closet space throughout
- 4 bedrooms, 2 baths, 2-car garage
- Crawl space or slab foundation, please specify when ordering

Plan #711-055D-0114

2,050 total square feet of living area

Price Code C

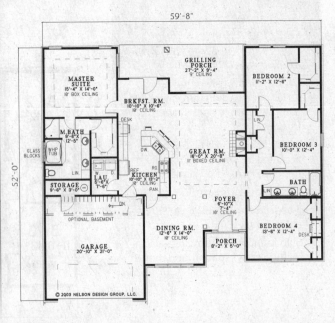

TO ORDER BLUEPRINTS USE THE FORM ON PAGE 15 OR CALL TOLL-FREE 1-877-671-6036
View thousands more home plans online at www.familyhandyman.com/homeplans

179

Open Living Areas

Plan #711-021D-0007

1,868 total square feet of living area

Price Code D

Special features

- Luxurious master bath is impressive with an angled quarter-circle tub, separate vanities and large walk-in closet
- Energy efficient home with 2" x 6" exterior walls
- Dining room is surrounded by a series of arched openings which complement the open feeling of this design
- Living room has a 12' ceiling accented by skylights and a large fireplace flanked by sliding doors
- Large storage areas
- 3 bedrooms, 2 baths, 2-car side entry garage
- Slab foundation, drawings also include crawl space foundation

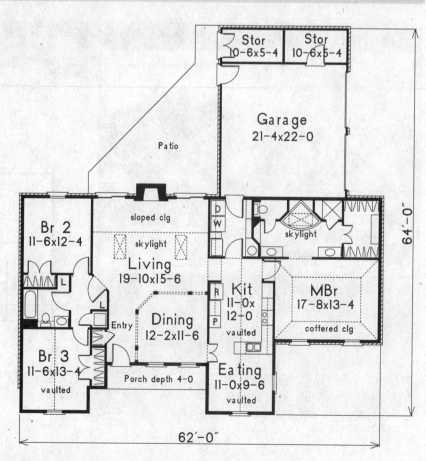

TO ORDER BLUEPRINTS USE THE FORM ON PAGE 15 OR CALL TOLL-FREE 1-877-671-6036
View thousands more home plans online at www.familyhandyman.com/homeplans

Corner Fireplace In Grand Room

Plan #711-056D-0009

1,606 total square feet of living area

Price Code B

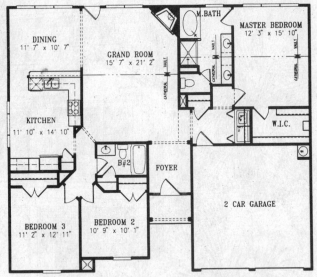

DINING 11' 7" x 10' 7"

GRAND ROOM 15' 7" x 21' 2"

M. BATH

MASTER BEDROOM 12' 3" x 15' 10"

KITCHEN 11' 10" x 14' 10"

W.I.C.

B #2

FOYER

2 CAR GARAGE

BEDROOM 3 11' 2" x 12' 11"

BEDROOM 2 10' 9" x 10' 1"

Width: 50'-0"
Depth: 42'-0"

Special features

- Kitchen has snack bar which overlooks dining area for convenience
- Master bedroom has lots of windows with a private bath and large walk-in closet
- Cathedral vault in great room adds spaciousness
- 3 bedrooms, 2 baths, 2-car garage
- Slab foundation

Sunken Family Room

Plan #711-026D-0156

2,029 total square feet of living area

Price Code C

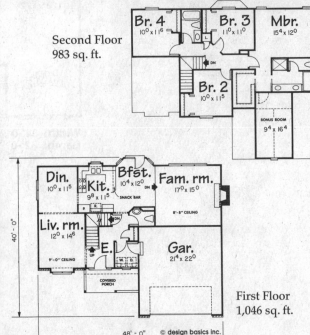

Second Floor 983 sq. ft.

Br. 4 10⁰ x 11⁶

Br. 3 11⁰ x 11⁰

Mbr. 15⁴ x 12⁰

Br. 2 10⁰ x 11⁵

BONUS ROOM 9⁴ x 16⁴

Din. 10⁰ x 11⁵

Kit. 9⁸ x 11⁵

Bfst. 10⁴ x 12⁰

SNACK BAR

Fam. rm. 17⁰ x 15⁰

8'-8" CEILING

Liv. rm. 12⁰ x 14⁶

9'-0" CEILING

E.

UP

Gar. 21⁴ x 22⁰

COVERED PORCH

First Floor 1,046 sq. ft.

40'-0"

48'-0"

© design basics inc.

Special features

- Oversized rooms throughout
- Breakfast room has access to the outdoors
- Dining and living rooms combine to create an ideal gathering place
- Master bedroom has all the amenities
- Second floor bonus room has an additional 165 square feet of living area
- 4 bedrooms, 2 1/2 baths, 2-car garage
- Basement foundation

The Family Handyman

LOTS OF WINDOWS BRING OUTDOORS IN   Plan #711-024D-0038

1,743 total square feet of living area   **Price Code B**

Special features

- 9' ceilings on first floor
- Covered porch off living area is spacious enough for entertaining
- Private study on second floor is ideal for a computer area or office
- 3 bedrooms, 3 baths, 2-car drive under carport
- Pier foundation

First Floor
912 sq. ft.

Utility
9'7"x 6'10"

1/2 Ba.

Kitchen
12'8"x 12'2"

Living
14'2"x 19'6"

Dining
11'4"x 12'

Porch
22'x8'

Width: 34'-0"
Depth: 32'-0"

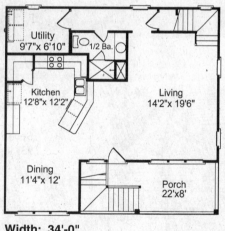

Bath

Bedroom
11'x 10'

Master
Bath

Bedroom
10'6"x 10'6"

Study
9'x 7'3"

Master
Bedroom
13'x 14'

Second Floor
831 sq. ft.

Balcony
13'6"x 5'

TO ORDER BLUEPRINTS USE THE FORM ON PAGE 15 OR CALL TOLL-FREE 1-877-671-6036
View thousands more home plans online at www.familyhandyman.com/homeplans

Secluded Living Room

Plan #711-035D-0021

1,978 total square feet of living area

Price Code C

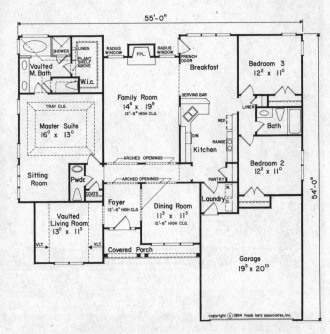

Special features

- Elegant arched openings throughout interior
- Vaulted living room off foyer
- Master suite with cheerful sitting room and a private bath
- 3 bedrooms, 2 1/2 baths, 2-car garage
- Walk-out basement, slab or crawl space foundation, please specify when ordering

Two-Story With Victorian Feel

Plan #711-038D-0044

1,982 total square feet of living area

Price Code C

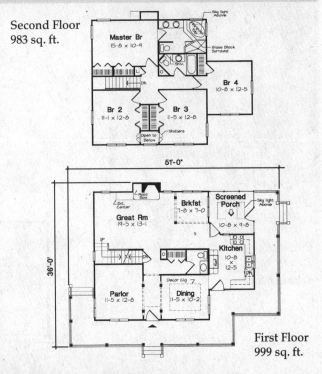

Special features

- Spacious master bedroom has bath with corner whirlpool tub and sunny skylight above
- Breakfast area overlooks into great room
- Screened porch with skylight above extends the home outdoors and allows for another entertainment area
- 4 bedrooms, 2 1/2 baths
- Crawl space or slab foundation, please specify when ordering

TO ORDER BLUEPRINTS USE THE FORM ON PAGE 15 OR CALL TOLL-FREE 1-877-671-6036
View thousands more home plans online at www.familyhandyman.com/homeplans

183

2,452 total square feet of living area

Price Code D

Special features

- Cheery and spacious home office room with private entrance and bath, two closets, vaulted ceiling and transomed window perfect shown as a home office or a fourth bedroom
- Delightful great room with vaulted ceiling, fireplace, extra storage closets and patio doors to sundeck
- Extra-large kitchen features walk-in pantry, cooktop island and bay window
- Vaulted master bedroom includes transomed windows, walk-in closet and luxurious bath
- 3 bedrooms, 2 1/2 baths, 3-car garage
- Basement foundation

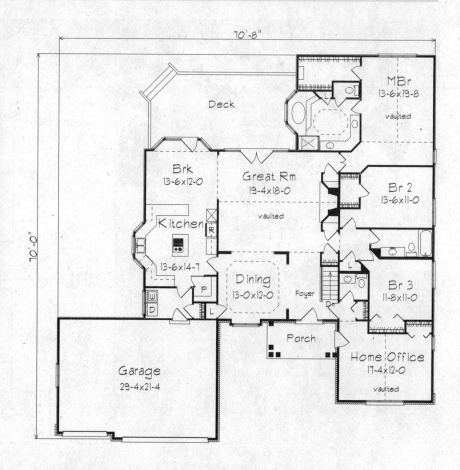

Classic Three Bedroom

Special features

- Convenient entrance from garage into home through laundry room
- Master bedroom features walk-in closet and double-door entrance into master bath with oversized tub
- Formal dining room with tray ceiling
- Kitchen features island cooktop and adjacent breakfast room
- 3 bedrooms, 2 baths, 2-car garage
- Basement foundation

Plan #711-027D-0003

2,061 total square feet of living area

Price Code D

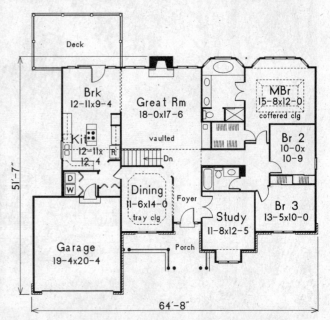

Traditional Styling

Special features

- Living room immersed in sunlight from wall of windows
- Master suite with amenities like double walk-in closets, private bath and view onto covered porch
- Cozy family room with built-in shelves and fireplace
- 3 bedrooms, 2 baths, 2-car side entry garage
- Slab or crawl space foundation, please specify when ordering

Plan #711-030D-0007

2,050 total square feet of living area

Price Code C

TO ORDER BLUEPRINTS USE THE FORM ON PAGE 15 OR CALL TOLL-FREE 1-877-671-6036
View thousands more home plans online at www.familyhandyman.com/homeplans

185

Luxurious Master Bedroom
Plan #711-007D-0007

2,523 total square feet of living area

Price Code D

Special features

- Entry with high ceiling leads to massive vaulted great room with wet bar, plant shelves, pillars and fireplace with a harmonious window trio
- Elaborate kitchen with bay and breakfast bar adjoins morning room with fireplace-in-a-bay
- Vaulted master bedroom features fireplace, book and plant shelves, large walk-in closet and double baths
- 3 bedrooms, 2 baths, 3-car garage
- Basement foundation

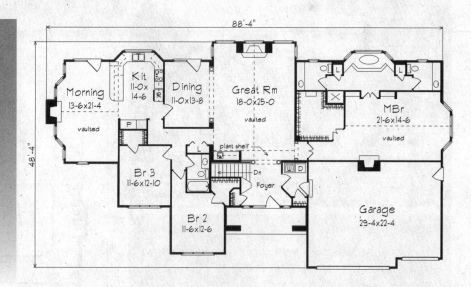

TO ORDER BLUEPRINTS USE THE FORM ON PAGE 15 OR CALL TOLL-FREE 1-877-671-6036
View thousands more home plans online at www.familyhandyman.com/homeplans

Features Designed For Entertaining

Plan #711-065D-0004

1,710 total square feet of living area

Price Code B

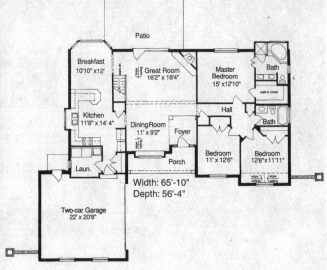

Width: 65'-10"
Depth: 56'-4"

Special features

- Expansive kitchen provides an abundance of counterspace and a pantry for extra storage
- The great room enjoys a sloped ceiling, corner fireplace and access onto the rear patio
- Windows surround the breakfast area providing warm natural light
- 3 bedrooms, 2 baths, 2-car side entry garage
- Basement foundation

Brick And Siding Enhance Home

Plan #711-010D-0006

1,170 total square feet of living area

Price Code AA

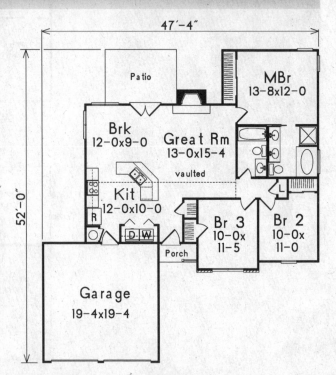

Special features

- Master bedroom enjoys privacy at the rear of this home
- Kitchen has an angled bar that overlooks great room and breakfast area
- Living areas combine to create a greater sense of spaciousness
- Great room has a cozy fireplace
- 3 bedrooms, 2 baths, 2-car garage
- Slab foundation

2,121 total square feet of living area

Price Code C

Special features

- Delightful kitchen overlooks dining and family rooms
- Optional study on the first floor has an additional 148 square feet of living area
- Garage is a useful secondary entrance
- Optional bonus room on the second floor has an additional 334 square feet of living area
- 4 bedrooms, 3 1/2 baths, 2-car garage
- Basement foundation

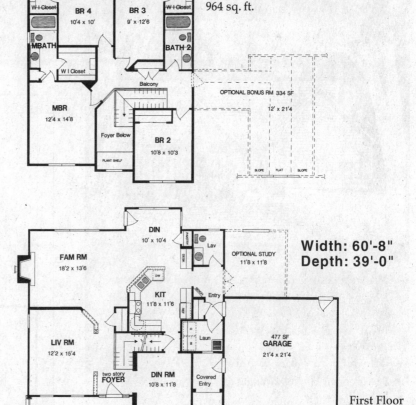

Second Floor
964 sq. ft.

W I Closet BR 4 10'4 x 10' BR 3 9' x 12'6 W I Closet

MBATH BATH 2

W I Closet Balcony OPTIONAL BONUS RM 334 SF 12' x 21'4

MBR 12'4 x 14'8

Foyer Below BR 2 10'8 x 10'3

PLANT SHELF SLOPE FLAT SLOPE

DIN 10' x 10'4 Lav PANTRY DESK OPTIONAL STUDY 11'8 x 11'8

Width: 60'-8"
Depth: 39'-0"

FAM RM 18'2 x 13'6

DW Entry

KIT 11'8 x 11'6

LIV RM 12'2 x 15'4 Laun 477 SF GARAGE 21'4 x 21'4

two story FOYER DIN RM 10'8 x 11'8 Covered Entry

First Floor
1,157 sq. ft.

188

TO ORDER BLUEPRINTS USE THE FORM ON PAGE 15 OR CALL TOLL-FREE 1-877-671-6036
View thousands more home plans online at www.familyhandyman.com/homeplans

Great Room Is Core Of Home

Plan #711-027D-0006

2,076 total square feet of living area

Price Code C

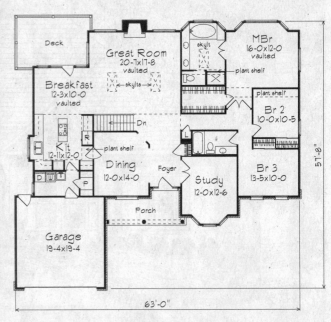

Special features

- Vaulted great room has fireplace flanked by windows and skylights that welcome the sun
- Kitchen leads to vaulted breakfast room and rear deck
- Study located off foyer provides great location for home office
- Large bay windows grace master bedroom and bath
- 3 bedrooms, 2 baths, 2-car garage
- Basement foundation

Mother-In-Law Suite

Plan #711-007D-0066

2,408 total square feet of living area

Price Code D

First Floor
2,408 sq. ft.

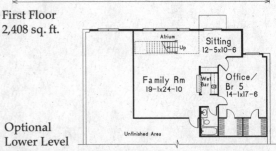

Optional
Lower Level

Special features

- Large vaulted great room overlooks atrium and window wall, adjoins dining room, spacious breakfast room with bay and pass-through kitchen
- A special private bedroom with bath, separate from other bedrooms, is perfect for mother-in-law suite or children home from college
- Atrium opens to 1,100 square feet of optional living area below
- 4 bedrooms, 3 baths, 3-car side entry garage
- Walk-out basement foundation

TO ORDER BLUEPRINTS USE THE FORM ON PAGE 15 OR CALL TOLL-FREE 1-877-671-6036
View thousands more home plans online at www.familyhandyman.com/homeplans

189

Spaciously Designed Floor Plan   Plan #711-035D-0009

1,575 total square feet of living area

Price Code B

Special features

- 9' ceilings throughout this home
- Plant shelves accent the vaulted breakfast room and dining room
- Enormous serving bar in great room is ideal for entertaining
- 3 bedrooms, 2 baths, 2-car garage
- Crawl space or walk-out basement foundation, please specify when ordering

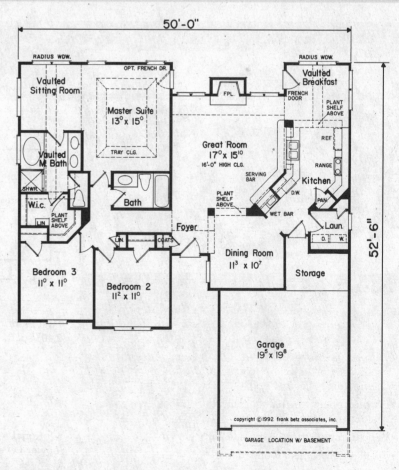

Graceful Southern Hospitality

Plan #711-049D-0006

1,771 total square feet of living area

Price Code B

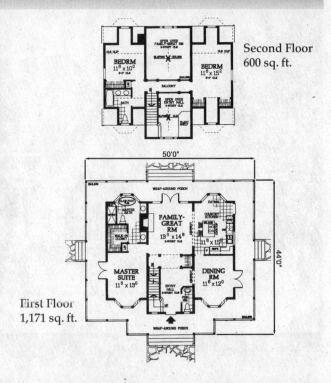

Second Floor
600 sq. ft.

First Floor
1,171 sq. ft.

Special features

- Efficient country kitchen shares space with a bayed eating area
- Two-story family/great room is warmed by a fireplace in winter and open to outdoor country comfort in the summer with double French doors
- First floor master suite offers a bay window and access to the porch through French doors
- 3 bedrooms, 2 1/2 baths, optional 2-car detached garage
- Basement foundation

Dramatic Central Staircase

Plan #711-071D-0004

3,085 total square feet of living area

Price Code F

Second Floor
1,460 sq. ft.

First Floor
1,625 sq. ft.

Special features

- Enter the foyer to find symmetrical formal living and dining rooms both with decorative columns
- Two-story family room is spectacular with fireplace and beamed ceiling
- Unique see-through area from master bedroom into bath
- Bonus room on the second floor has an additional 315 square feet of living area
- 4 bedrooms, 2 1/2 baths, 3-car tandem garage
- Crawl space foundation

Terrific Master Bedroom

Plan #711-018D-0003

2,517 total square feet of living area

Price Code D

Special features

- Energy efficient home with 2" x 6" exterior walls
- Central living room with large windows and attractive transoms
- Varied ceiling heights throughout home
- Secluded master bedroom features double-door entry, luxurious bath with separate shower, step-up whirlpool tub, double vanities and walk-in closets
- Kitchen with walk-in pantry overlooks large family room with fireplace and unique octagon-shaped breakfast room
- 4 bedrooms, 2 1/2 baths, 2-car garage
- Slab foundation, drawings also include crawl space foundation

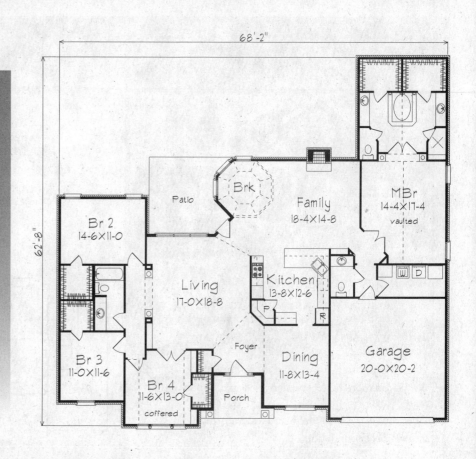

68'-2"

62'-8"

Br 2
14-6×11-0

Patio

Brk

Family
18-4×14-8

MBr
14-4×17-4
vaulted

Living
17-0×18-8

Kitchen
13-8×12-6

Br 3
11-0×11-6

Foyer

Dining
11-8×13-4

Garage
20-0×20-2

Br 4
11-6×13-0
coffered

Porch

Home Has A Custom Feel

Plan #711-026D-0164

3,072 total square feet of living area

Price Code E

Special features

- Charming window seats accent all the secondary bedrooms
- Master bedroom has a luxurious bath and an enormous walk-in closet
- Double-doors in both the study and the formal dining room lead to the covered front porch
- 4 bedrooms, 3 1/2 baths, 3-car side entry garage
- Basement, slab or crawl space foundation, please specify when ordering

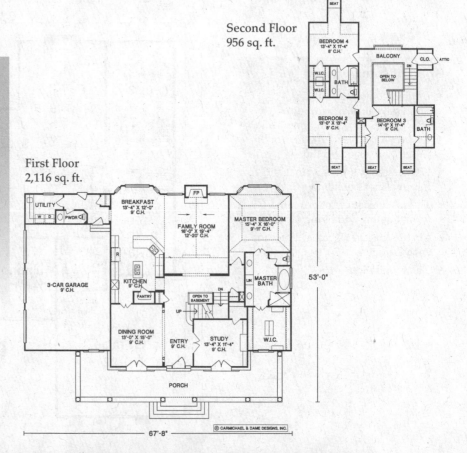

Second Floor
956 sq. ft.

First Floor
2,116 sq. ft.

TO ORDER BLUEPRINTS USE THE FORM ON PAGE 15 OR CALL TOLL-FREE 1-877-671-6036
View thousands more home plans online at www.familyhandyman.com/homeplans

193

2,287 total square feet of living area

Price Code E

Special features

- Double-doors lead into an impressive master bedroom which accesses covered porch and features a deluxe bath with double closets and a step-up tub
- Kitchen easily serves formal and informal areas of home
- The spacious foyer opens into formal dining and living rooms
- 4 bedrooms, 2 1/2 baths, 2-car side entry garage
- Slab foundation

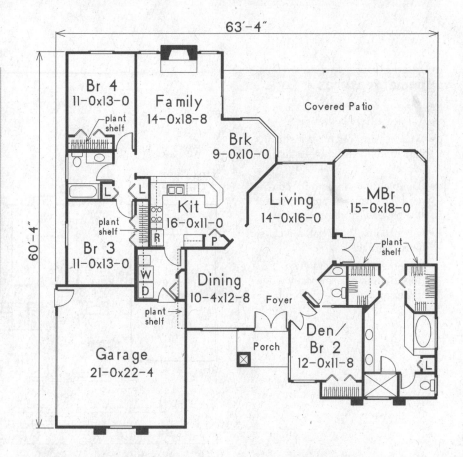

63'-4"

60'-4"

Br 4
11-0x13-0

plant shelf

Family
14-0x18-8

Covered Patio

Brk
9-0x10-0

Living
14-0x16-0

MBr
15-0x18-0

plant shelf

Kit
16-0x11-0

plant shelf

R

P

Br 3
11-0x13-0

W
D

Dining
10-4x12-8

Foyer

plant shelf

Garage
21-0x22-4

Porch

Den/ Br 2
12-0x11-8

L

Stylish And Functional

Plan #711-025D-0054

3,046 total square feet of living area

Price Code E

Special features

- Secluded hearth room is tucked away from main living areas creating a cozy feeling
- Master suite maintains lots of privacy and has a luxurious feel
- Future playroom on the second floor has an additional 298 square feet of living area
- 4 bedrooms, 3 baths, 2-car side entry garage
- Slab foundation

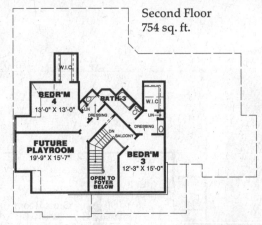

Second Floor
754 sq. ft.

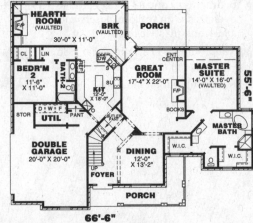

First Floor
2,292 sq. ft.

TO ORDER BLUEPRINTS USE THE FORM ON PAGE 15 OR CALL TOLL-FREE 1-877-671-6036
View thousands more home plans online at www.familyhandyman.com/homeplans

195

French Country Flavor

Plan #711-007D-0117

2,695 total square feet of living area

Price Code E

Special features

- A grandscale great room features a fireplace with flanking shelves, handsome entry foyer with staircase and opens to large kitchen and breakfast room
- Roomy master bedroom has a bay window, huge walk-in closet and bath with a shower built for two
- Bedrooms #2 and #3 are generously oversized with walk-in closets and a Jack and Jill style bath
- 3 bedrooms, 2 1/2 baths, 2-car side entry garage
- Basement foundation

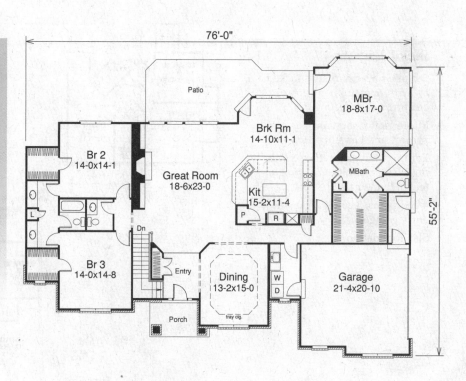

COUNTRY CHARMER

Plan #711-016D-0058

2,874 total square feet of living area

Price Code G

Special features

- Openness characterizes the casual areas
- The kitchen is separated from the bayed breakfast nook by an island workspace
- Stunning great room has dramatic vaulted ceiling and a corner fireplace
- Unfinished loft on the second floor has an additional 300 square feet of living area
- 4 bedrooms, 3 baths, 3-car side entry garage
- Basement, crawl space or slab foundation, please specify when ordering

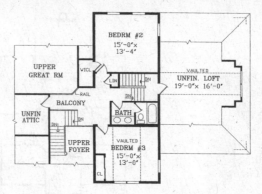

Second Floor
728 sq. ft.

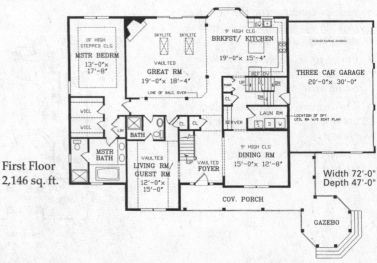

First Floor
2,146 sq. ft.

Width 72'-0"
Depth 47'-0"

TO ORDER BLUEPRINTS USE THE FORM ON PAGE 15 OR CALL TOLL-FREE 1-877-671-6036
View thousands more home plans online at www.familyhandyman.com/homeplans

197

Extravagant Classic Traditional

Plan #711-071D-0011

5,800 total square feet of living area

Price Code H

Special features

- Covered porch accesses several rooms and features a cozy fireplace for outdoor living
- A spectacular foyer leads directly to a central rotunda with a circular stair
- Luxury amenities on the first floor include a computer room, mud room and butler's pantry
- Bonus room on the second floor has an additional 500 square feet of living area
- 4 bedrooms, 5 1/2 baths, 2-car side entry garage and 2-car detached garage
- Crawl space foundation

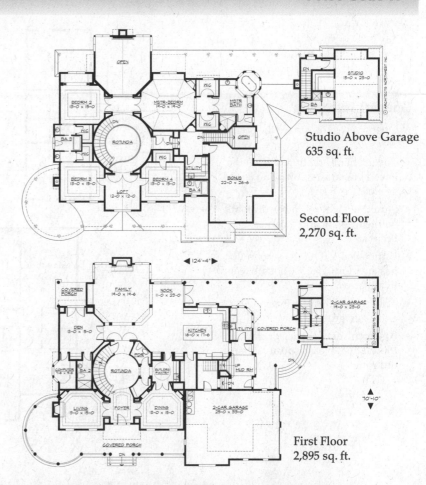

Studio Above Garage
635 sq. ft.

Second Floor
2,270 sq. ft.

First Floor
2,895 sq. ft.

2,173 total square feet of living area

Price Code D

Special features

- Enormous family room off kitchen has a fireplace surrounded by media shelves for state-of-the-art living
- The master bath has double walk-in closets as well as an oversized shower and whirlpool tub
- An arched entry graces the formal dining room
- 3 bedrooms, 2 1/2 baths, 3-car side entry garage
- Slab foundation

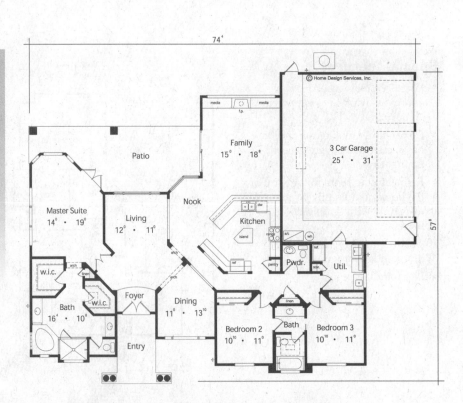

TO ORDER BLUEPRINTS USE THE FORM ON PAGE 15 OR CALL TOLL-FREE 1-877-671-6036
View thousands more home plans online at www.familyhandyman.com/homeplans

199

Stunning Southern Home

Plan #711-024D-0034

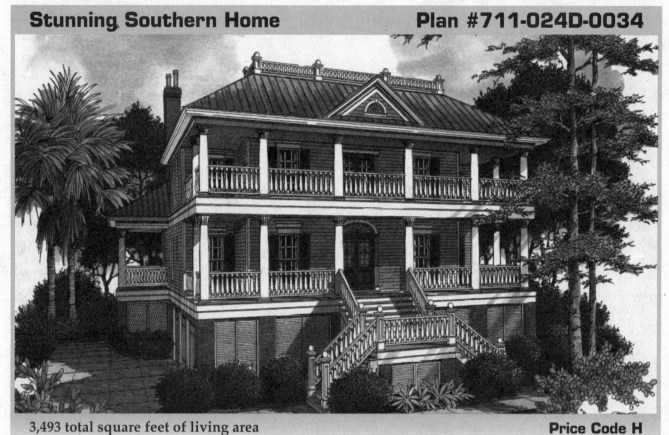

3,493 total square feet of living area

Price Code H

Special features

- First floor master bedroom has enormous walk-in closet and a lavish bath
- Cozy sitting nook on second floor has access onto covered second floor balcony
- Formal living room in the front of the home could easily be converted to a study with double-doors for privacy
- 4 bedrooms, 3 1/2 baths, 3-car drive under garage
- Pier foundation

Width: 46'-0"
Depth: 55'-0"

Porch 25'6"x 10'

Family 24'6"x 17'2"

Master Bedroom 20'2"x 16'10"

Breakfast 15'6"x 9'8"

Utility

Master Bath

1/2 Bath

Walk-In Closet

Kitchen 15'6"x 14'2"

Dining 11'x 13'8"

Foyer

Living 11'6"x 13'8"

Porch 46'x 8'

First Floor
2,327 sq. ft.

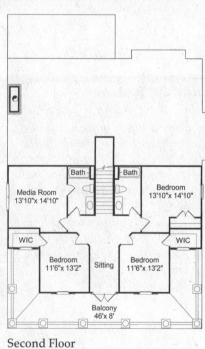

Media Room 13'10"x 14'10"

Bath

Bath

Bedroom 13'10"x 14'10"

WIC

WIC

Bedroom 11'6"x 13'2"

Sitting

Bedroom 11'6"x 13'2"

Balcony 46'x 8'

Second Floor
1,166 sq. ft.

TO ORDER BLUEPRINTS USE THE FORM ON PAGE 15 OR CALL TOLL-FREE 1-877-671-6036
View thousands more home plans online at www.familyhandyman.com/homeplans

ARCHED ELEGANCE

Plan #711-006D-0002

3,222 total square feet of living area

Price Code F

Special features

- Two-story foyer features central staircase and views to second floor, dining and living rooms
- Built-in breakfast booth surrounded by windows
- Gourmet kitchen with view to the great room
- Two-story great room features large fireplace and arched openings to the second floor
- Elegant master bedroom has separate reading room with bookshelves and fireplace
- 4 bedrooms, 3 1/2 baths, 2-car side entry garage
- Basement foundation, drawings also include crawl space and slab foundations

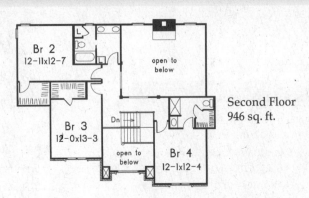

Br 2
12-11x12-7

open to below

Br 3
12-0x13-3

Dn

open to below

Br 4
12-1x12-4

Second Floor
946 sq. ft.

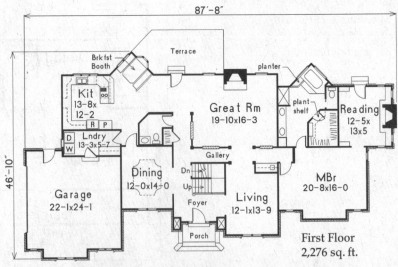

87'-8"

Brkfst Booth

Terrace

planter

Kit
13-8x
12-2

R P

Great Rm
19-10x16-3

plant-shelf

Reading
12-5x
13-5

D W

Lndry
13-3x5-7

46'-10"

Gallery

Dining
12-0x14-0

Dn
Up

Garage
22-1x24-1

Foyer

Living
12-1x13-9

MBr
20-8x16-0

Porch

First Floor
2,276 sq. ft.

TO ORDER BLUEPRINTS USE THE FORM ON PAGE 15 OR CALL TOLL-FREE 1-877-671-6036
View thousands more home plans online at www.familyhandyman.com/homeplans

201

Quaint Exterior, Full Front Porch — Plan #711-053D-0030

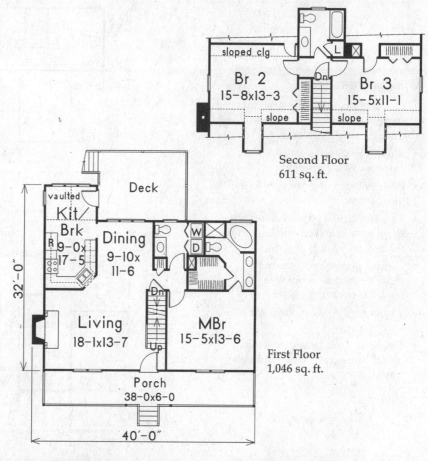

1,657 total square feet of living area

Price Code B

Special features

- Stylish pass-through between living and dining areas
- Master bedroom is secluded from living area for privacy
- Large windows in breakfast and dining areas
- 3 bedrooms, 2 1/2 baths, 2-car drive under garage
- Basement foundation

Second Floor
611 sq. ft.

Br 2
15-8x13-3

Br 3
15-5x11-1

sloped clg

slope

First Floor
1,046 sq. ft.

Deck

vaulted

Kit/ Brk
9-0x 17-5

Dining
9-10x 11-6

Living
18-1x13-7

MBr
15-5x13-6

Porch
38-0x6-0

32'-0"

40'-0"

Appealing Victorian Accents

Plan #711-062D-0045

2,516 total square feet of living area

Price Code D

Special features

- Living room has a fireplace, while the formal dining room has a buffet alcove and access to the verandah
- A cozy sitting area and tray ceiling accent the master bedroom
- Spacious bedrooms make this a wonderful family home
- 4 bedrooms, 2 1/2 baths, 2-car side entry garage
- Basement or crawl space foundation, please specify when ordering

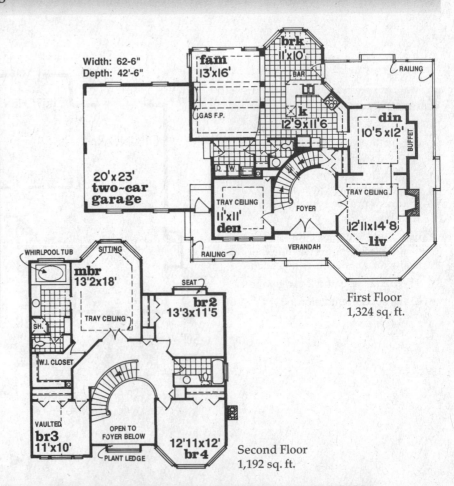

Width: 62'-6"
Depth: 42'-6"

RAILING

fam 13'x16'

brk 11'x10'

BAR

GAS F.P.

k 12'9"x11'6"

din 10'5"x12'

BUFFET

20'x23' **two-car garage**

TRAY CEILING

TRAY CEILING

FOYER

11'x11' **den**

12'11"x14'8" **liv**

RAILING

VERANDAH

First Floor 1,324 sq. ft.

WHIRLPOOL TUB

SITTING

mbr 13'2"x18'

br2 13'3"x11'5

SEAT

TRAY CEILING

SH.

W.I. CLOSET

VAULTED

br3 11'x10'

OPEN TO FOYER BELOW

PLANT LEDGE

12'11"x12' **br4**

Second Floor 1,192 sq. ft.

TO ORDER BLUEPRINTS USE THE FORM ON PAGE 15 OR CALL TOLL-FREE 1-877-671-6036
View thousands more home plans online at www.familyhandyman.com/homeplans

203

A Great Layout For Family Living   Plan #711-011D-0002

1,557 total square feet of living area

Price Code C

Special features

- Vaulted dining room extends off the great room and features an eye-catching plant shelf above

- Double closets adorn the vaulted master bedroom which also features a private bath with tub and shower

- Bedroom #3/den has the option to add double-doors creating the feeling of a home office if needed

- 3 bedrooms, 2 baths, 2-car garage

- Crawl space foundation

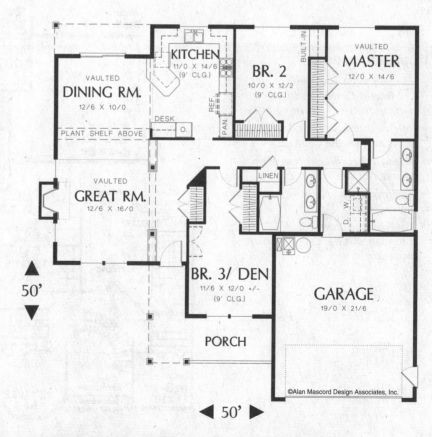

50'

50'

KITCHEN
11/0 X 14/6
(9' CLG.)

VAULTED
DINING RM.
12/6 X 10/0

DESK

PLANT SHELF ABOVE

VAULTED
GREAT RM.
12/6 X 16/0

BR. 2
10/0 X 12/2
(9' CLG.)

BUILT-IN

VAULTED
MASTER
12/0 X 14/6

REF
PAN.
O.

LINEN

D. W.

BR. 3/ DEN
11/6 X 12/0 +/-
(9' CLG.)

GARAGE
19/0 X 21/6

PORCH

©Alan Mascord Design Associates, Inc.

TO ORDER BLUEPRINTS USE THE FORM ON PAGE 15 OR CALL TOLL-FREE 1-877-671-6036
View thousands more home plans online at www.familyhandyman.com/homeplans

Two-Story Great Room

Plan #711-026D-0133

3,040 total square feet of living area

Price Code E

DESIGNERS' INK

Special features

- Cozy hearth room is the heart of the design with see-through fireplace connecting it to the two-story great room
- Den has a fireplace
- Large master bedroom has an oversized walk-in closet
- Bonus room on the second floor has an additional 186 square feet of living area
- 4 bedrooms, 3 1/2 baths, 3-car side entry garage
- Basement foundation

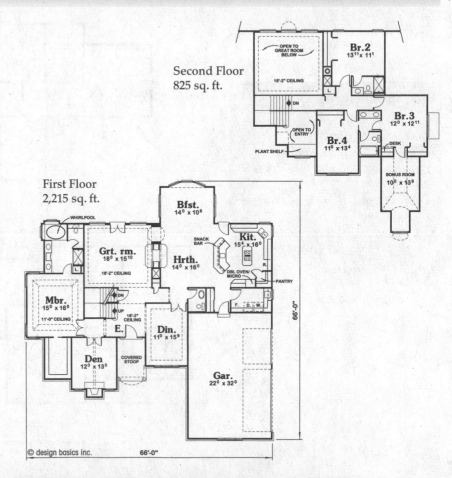

Second Floor
825 sq. ft.

First Floor
2,215 sq. ft.

© design basics inc.

205

Wrap-Around Porch   **Plan #711-040D-0027**

1,597 total square feet of living area   **Price Code C**

Special features

- Spacious family room includes fireplace and coat closet
- Open kitchen and dining room provide breakfast bar and access to the outdoors
- Convenient laundry area is located near kitchen
- Secluded master bedroom with walk-in closet and private bath
- 4 bedrooms, 2 1/2 baths, 2-car detached garage
- Basement foundation

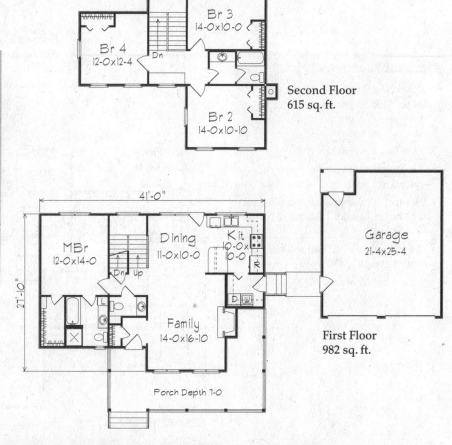

Br 4
12-0x12-4

Br 3
14-0x10-0

Dn

Second Floor
615 sq. ft.

Br 2
14-0x10-10

41'-0"

MBr
12-0x14-0

Dining
11-0x10-0

Kit
10-0x
10-0

Garage
21-4x25-4

Dn Up

21'-10"

Family
14-0x16-10

First Floor
982 sq. ft.

Porch Depth 7-0

TO ORDER BLUEPRINTS USE THE FORM ON PAGE 15 OR CALL TOLL-FREE 1-877-671-6036
View thousands more home plans online at www.familyhandyman.com/homeplans

Gables Draw Attention

Plan #711-071D-0009

4,650 total square feet of living area

Price Code G

Special features

- Two-story foyer, living and family rooms create a sense of spaciousness throughout the first floor
- Double walk-in closets create plenty of storage in the master bath
- The second floor media room is sure to be a gathering place near the bedrooms
- 5 bedrooms, 4 1/2 baths, 3-car rear entry garage
- Crawl space foundation

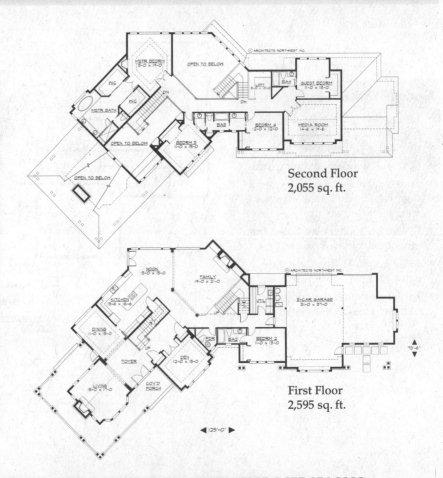

Second Floor
2,055 sq. ft.

First Floor
2,595 sq. ft.

TO ORDER BLUEPRINTS USE THE FORM ON PAGE 15 OR CALL TOLL-FREE 1-877-671-6036
View thousands more home plans online at www.familyhandyman.com/homeplans

207

Porch Has Charm And Warmth

Plan #711-017D-0007

1,567 total square feet of living area

Price Code C

Special features

- Living room flows into dining room shaped by an angled pass-through into the kitchen
- Cheerful, windowed dining area
- Future area available on the second floor has an additional 338 square feet of living area
- Master bedroom is separated from other bedrooms for privacy
- 3 bedrooms, 2 baths, 2-car side entry garage
- Basement foundation, drawings also include slab foundation

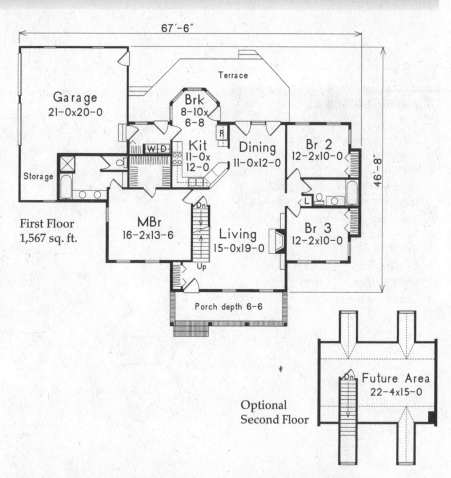

67'-6"

Garage
21-0x20-0

Terrace

Brk
8-10x
6-8

Kit
11-0x
12-0

Dining
11-0x12-0

Br 2
12-2x10-0

W/D

R

Storage

46'-8"

First Floor
1,567 sq. ft.

MBr
16-2x13-6

Dn

Living
15-0x19-0

Br 3
12-2x10-0

Up

Porch depth 6-6

Dn

Future Area
22-4x15-0

Optional
Second Floor

FUN Game Room

COPYRIGHT 1993

2,721 total square feet of living area

Price Code E

Special features

- Large foyer leads through arched columns into great room and dining room with see-through fireplace
- Sunny breakfast room has bay window
- Game room opens up second floor
- 4 bedrooms, 3 baths, 2-car side entry garage
- Basement foundation, drawings also include crawl space and slab foundations

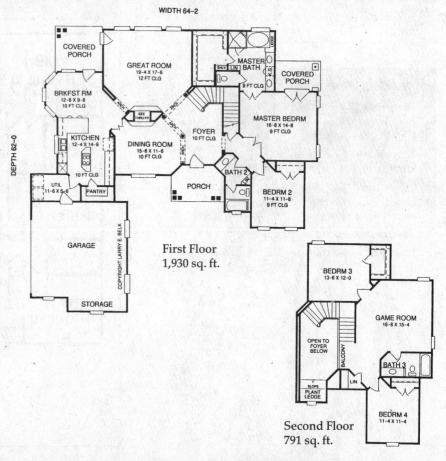

WIDTH 64-2

DEPTH 62-0

COVERED PORCH

GREAT ROOM
19-4 X 17-6
12 FT CLG

MASTER BATH

SHLV LIN

COVERED PORCH

BRKFST RM
12-6 X 9-8
10 FT CLG

BEE THRU FP

9 FT CLG

K S

MASTER BEDRM
16-8 X 14-8
9 FT CLG

KITCHEN
12-4 X 14-6

FOYER
10 FT CLG

10 FT CLG

DINING ROOM
15-6 X 11-6
10 FT CLG

BATH 2

UTIL
11-6 X 5-6

PANTRY

PORCH

BEDRM 2
11-4 X 11-8
9 FT CLG

COPYRIGHT LARRY E. BELK

GARAGE

First Floor
1,930 sq. ft.

STORAGE

BEDRM 3
13-6 X 12-0

GAME ROOM
16-8 X 15-4

OPEN TO FOYER BELOW

BALCONY

BATH 3

SLOPE PLANT LEDGE

LIN

BEDRM 4
11-4 X 11-4

Second Floor
791 sq. ft.

TO ORDER BLUEPRINTS USE THE FORM ON PAGE 15 OR CALL TOLL-FREE 1-877-671-6036
View thousands more home plans online at www.familyhandyman.com/homeplans

209

Interesting Plan For Narrow Lot   Plan #711-007D-0044

1,516 total square feet of living area   **Price Code B**

Special features

- Spacious great room is open to dining area with a bay and unique stair location
- Attractive and well-planned kitchen offers breakfast bar and built-in pantry
- Smartly designed master bedroom enjoys patio views
- 3 bedrooms, 2 baths, 2-car garage
- Basement foundation

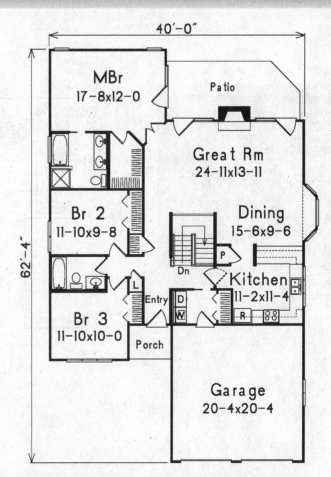

40'-0"

62'-4"

MBr
17-8x12-0

Patio

Great Rm
24-11x13-11

Br 2
11-10x9-8

Dining
15-6x9-6

Dn.

Kitchen
11-2x11-4

Entry

L

Br 3
11-10x10-0

Porch

D
W

R

Garage
20-4x20-4

TO ORDER BLUEPRINTS USE THE FORM ON PAGE 15 OR CALL TOLL-FREE 1-877-671-6036
View thousands more home plans online at www.familyhandyman.com/homeplans

Central Gathering Room

Plan #711-067D-0013

3,272 total square feet of living area

Price Code F

Special features

- Living room with fireplace accesses rear patio and wrap-around front porch
- Large formal dining room
- Master bedroom has a walk-in closet and deluxe bath
- 4 bedrooms, 3 full baths, 2 half baths, 2-car side entry garage
- Basement, crawl space or slab foundation, please specify when ordering

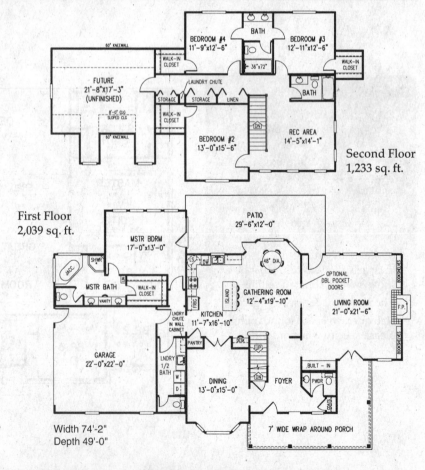

Second Floor
1,233 sq. ft.

First Floor
2,039 sq. ft.

Width 74'-2"
Depth 49'-0"

TO ORDER BLUEPRINTS USE THE FORM ON PAGE 15 OR CALL TOLL-FREE 1-877-671-6036
View thousands more home plans online at www.familyhandyman.com/homeplans

211

Atrium Door Accesses Deck   Plan #711-060D-0007

2,079 total square feet of living area   **Price Code C**

Special features

- Large formal entry foyer with openings to formal dining and great rooms
- Great room has built-in bookshelves, a fireplace, and a coffered ceiling
- Unique angled morning room with bay windows overlooks covered deck
- Master bath with double walk-in closets, step-up tub, separate shower and a coffered ceiling
- 3 bedrooms, 2 baths, 2-car garage
- Slab or crawl space foundation, please specify when ordering

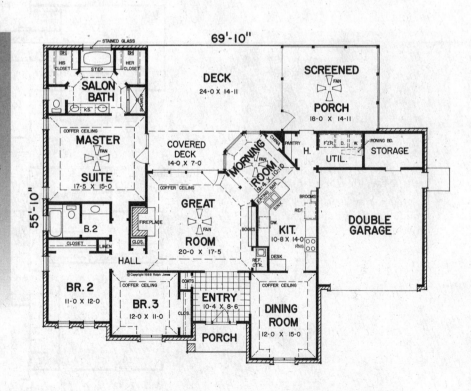

Comfortable Home Has Character   Plan #711-032D-0041

1,482 total square feet of living area   **Price Code A**

Special features

- Energy efficient home with 2" x 6" exterior walls
- Corner fireplace warms living area
- Screened porch is spacious and connects to main living area in the home
- Two bedrooms on second floor share a spacious bath
- 2 bedrooms, 1 1/2 baths
- Basement foundation

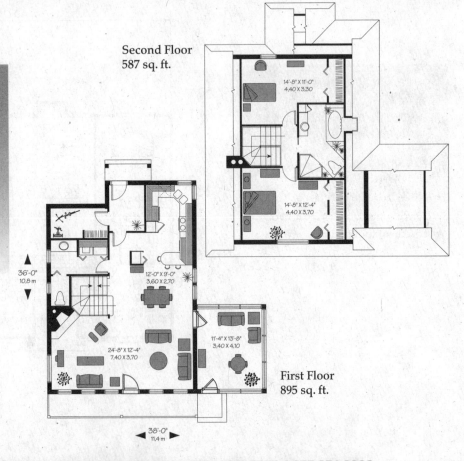

Second Floor
587 sq. ft.

14'-8" X 11'-0"
4.40 X 3.30

14'-8" X 12'-4"
4.40 X 3.70

36'-0"
10,8 m

12'-0" X 9'-0"
3.60 X 2.70

24'-8" X 12'-4"
7.40 X 3.70

11'-4" X 13'-8"
3.40 X 4.10

First Floor
895 sq. ft.

38'-0"
11,4 m

TO ORDER BLUEPRINTS USE THE FORM ON PAGE 15 OR CALL TOLL-FREE 1-877-671-6036
View thousands more home plans online at www.familyhandyman.com/homeplans

213

COMFORTABLE RANCH

Plan #711-051D-0040

1,495 total square feet of living area

Price Code A

Special features

- Dining room has vaulted ceiling creating a large formal gathering area with access to a screened porch
- Cathedral ceiling in great room adds spaciousness
- Nice-sized entry with coat closet
- 3 bedrooms, 2 baths, 2-car garage
- Basement foundation

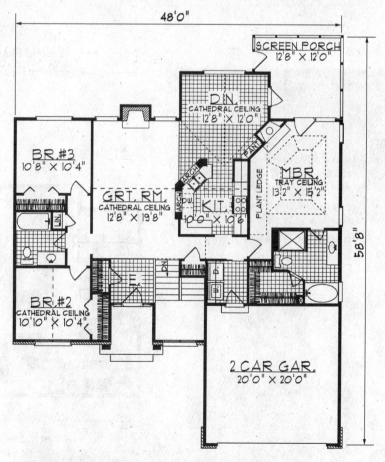

Sunny Garden Tub In Master Bath   Plan #711-043D-0010

2,162 total square feet of living area   **Price Code C**

Special features

- Lovely covered porch
- Appealing double-door two-story entry
- Kitchen has eat-in island bar
- French doors lead to patio from breakfast nook
- Master bedroom has double-door entry, private bath and walk-in closet
- 3 bedrooms, 2 1/2 baths, 2-car garage
- Crawl space foundation

WIDTH 34'-0"
DEPTH 50'-0"

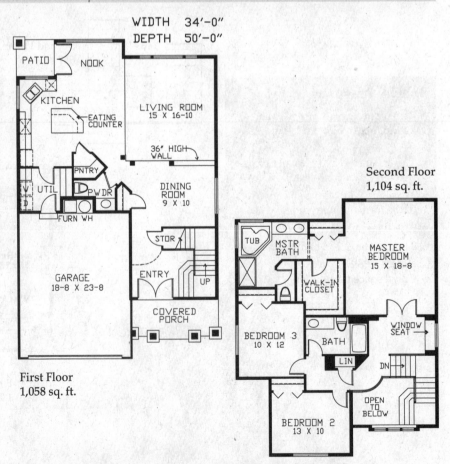

Second Floor
1,104 sq. ft.

First Floor
1,058 sq. ft.

TO ORDER BLUEPRINTS USE THE FORM ON PAGE 15 OR CALL TOLL-FREE 1-877-671-6036
View thousands more home plans online at www.familyhandyman.com/homeplans

215

THE Family Handyman

2,402 total square feet of living area   **Price Code D**

Special features

- Bayed dining area provides an abundance of light and features a bar area
- The expansive living room boasts a vaulted ceiling and fireplace
- 11' ceiling adds to the spacious feel of the formal dining room
- 9' ceilings
- 3 bedrooms, 2 1/2 baths, 2-car side entry garage
- Crawl space foundation

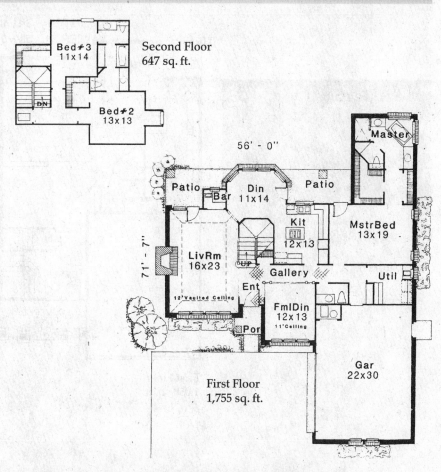

Second Floor
647 sq. ft.

Bed #3
11x14

Bed #2
13x13

First Floor
1,755 sq. ft.

56' - 0"

71' - 7"

Patio   Bar   Din 11x14   Patio   Master

LivRm 16x23   Kit 12x13   MstrBed 13x19

12' Vaulted Ceiling   Gallery   Util

Ent   FmlDin 12x13   11'Ceiling

Por   Gar 22x30

216

TO ORDER BLUEPRINTS USE THE FORM ON PAGE 15 OR CALL TOLL-FREE 1-877-671-6036
View thousands more home plans online at www.familyhandyman.com/homeplans

Double Atrium Embraces The Sun   Plan #711-007D-0056

3,199 total square feet of living area

Price Code E

Special features

- Grand scale kitchen features bay-shaped cabinetry built over atrium that overlooks two-story window wall
- A second atrium dominates the master bedroom which boasts a sitting area with bay window as well as a luxurious bath which has a whirlpool tub open to the garden atrium and lower level study
- 3 bedrooms, 2 1/2 baths, 3-car side entry garage
- Walk-out basement foundation

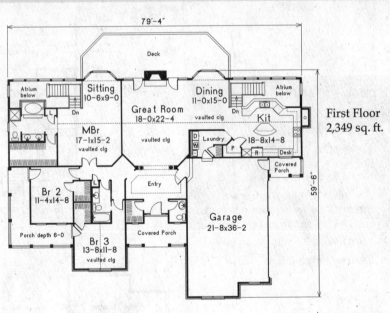

79'-4"

Deck

Atrium below

Sitting 10-6x9-0

Dining 11-0x15-0

Atrium below

Great Room 18-0x22-4 vaulted clg

Kit 18-8x14-8

MBr 17-1x15-2 vaulted clg

vaulted clg

Laundry

Br 2 11-4x14-8

Entry

Covered Porch

Garage 21-8x36-2

Porch depth 6-0

Br 3 13-8x11-8 vaulted clg

Covered Porch

First Floor 2,349 sq. ft.

59'-6"

Up

Up

Study 16-7x21-4

Unfinished Basement

Family Room 18-4x19-4

Lower Level 850 sq. ft.

Rear View

TO ORDER BLUEPRINTS USE THE FORM ON PAGE 15 OR CALL TOLL-FREE 1-877-671-6036
View thousands more home plans online at www.familyhandyman.com/homeplans

217

Functional And Modern Kitchen

Plan #711-038D-0046

4,064 total square feet of living area

Price Code G

Special features

- Sleek lines add a contemporary feel to the front of this home
- Three-sided fireplace creates a cozy feeling to the kitchen, breakfast and hearth rooms
- Decorative columns grace the corner of the formal dining room and help maintain an open feeling
- 4 bedrooms, 3 baths, 3-car garage
- Basement foundation

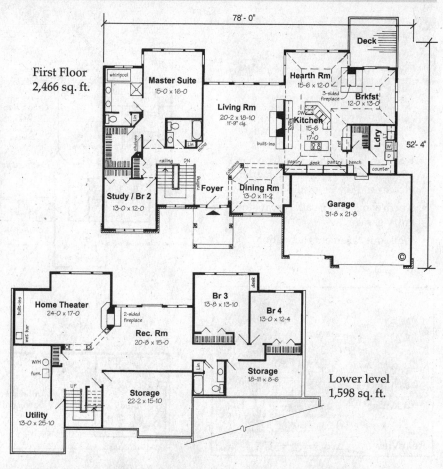

The Family Handyman

Luxury Abounds With Amenities   Plan #711-053D-0027

4,120 total square feet of living area

Price Code G

Special features

- Spacious rooms on both floors include two bedroom suites
- Elaborate master bedroom with a fireplace, double walk-in closets, deluxe tub and two private entrances
- Family room and kitchen form a large living area which includes a fireplace, corner window and vaulted ceiling
- Bonus room above the garage is included in the square footage
- 4 bedrooms, 3 full baths, 2 half baths, 2-car side entry garage
- Partial basement/crawl space foundation

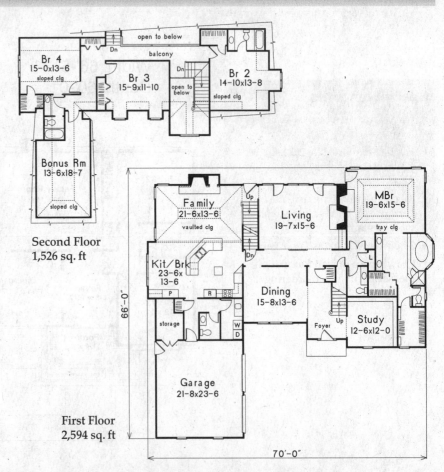

Second Floor
1,526 sq. ft

First Floor
2,594 sq. ft

TO ORDER BLUEPRINTS USE THE FORM ON PAGE 15 OR CALL TOLL-FREE 1-877-671-6036
View thousands more home plans online at www.familyhandyman.com/homeplans

219

Vaulted Rear Porch

Plan #711-039D-0014

1,849 total square feet of living area

Price Code C

Special features

- Open floor plan creates an airy feeling
- Kitchen and breakfast area include center island, pantry and built-in desk
- Master bedroom has private entrance off breakfast area and a view of vaulted porch
- 3 bedrooms, 2 baths, 2-car garage
- Crawl space or slab foundation, please specify when ordering

Width: 66'-5"
Depth: 60'-0"

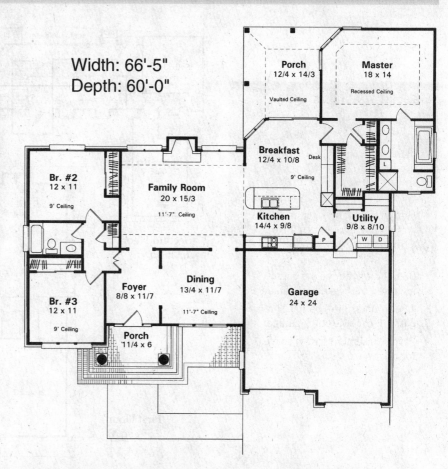

Porch
12/4 x 14/3
Vaulted Ceiling

Master
18 x 14
Recessed Ceiling

Breakfast
12/4 x 10/8
Desk
9' Ceiling

Br. #2
12 x 11
9' Ceiling

Family Room
20 x 15/3
11'-7" Ceiling

Kitchen
14/4 x 9/8

Utility
9/8 x 8/10

Foyer
8/8 x 11/7

Dining
13/4 x 11/7
11'-7" Ceiling

Garage
24 x 24

Br. #3
12 x 11
9' Ceiling

Porch
11/4 x 6

Handyman
The Family

2,104 total square feet of living area   **Price Code C**

Special features

- 9' ceilings on the first floor
- Living room opens onto deck through double French doors
- Second floor includes large storage room
- 3 bedrooms, 2 baths, 2-car garage
- Crawl space foundation

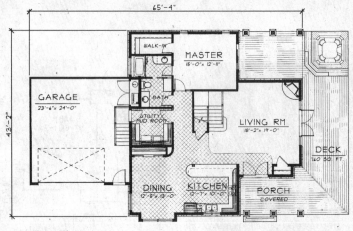

65'-4"

43'-2"

WALK-IN

MASTER
15'-0" x 12'-11"

GARAGE
23'-6" x 24'-0"

BATH

UTILITY/MUD ROOM

LIVING RM
18'-2" x 19'-0"

DECK
±40.50 FT.

DINING
12'-8" x 13'-0"

KITCHEN
12'-7" x 10'-0"

PORCH
COVERED

First Floor
1,435 sq. ft.

BDRM-3
13'-4" x 10'-5"

Second Floor
669 sq. ft.

STORAGE
10'-8" x 13'-2"

LOFT

OPEN TO BELOW

BDRM-2
13'-4" x 10'-5"

TO ORDER BLUEPRINTS USE THE FORM ON PAGE 15 OR CALL TOLL-FREE 1-877-671-6036
View thousands more home plans online at www.familyhandyman.com/homeplans

221

Patio And Pool For Entertaining   Plan #711-048D-0007

3,290 total square feet of living area

Price Code F

Special features

- Patio area surrounds pool with swim-up bar - both pool and spa are great options with this plan
- Formal dining room features dramatic drop down ceiling and easy access to kitchen
- Fireplace provides focal point in the master bedroom which includes a sitting room and elegant master bath
- Observation room and two bedrooms with adjoining bath on the second floor
- Varied ceiling heights throughout
- 4 bedrooms, 3 1/2 baths, 2-car side entry garage
- Slab foundation

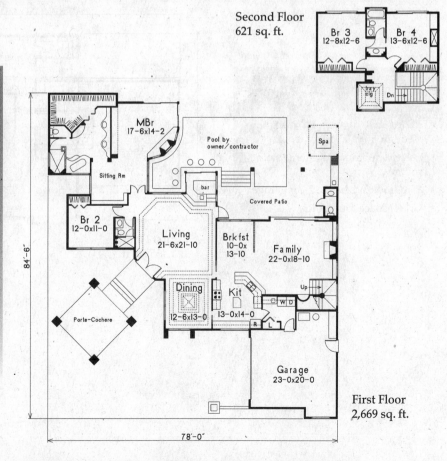

Second Floor
621 sq. ft.

Br 3
12-8x12-6

Br 4
13-6x12-6

First Floor
2,669 sq. ft.

MBr
17-6x14-2

Sitting Rm

Pool by owner/contractor

Spa

bar

Covered Patio

Br 2
12-0x11-0

Living
21-6x21-10

Brk fst
10-0x13-10

Family
22-0x18-10

Porte-Cochere

Dining
12-6x13-0

Kit
13-0x14-0

Garage
23-0x20-0

84'-6"

78'-0"

Classic Atrium Has Room To Spare   Plan #711-007D-0077

1,977 total square feet of living area   **Price Code C**

Special features

- Classic traditional exterior always in style
- Spacious great room boasts a vaulted ceiling, dining area, atrium with elegant staircase and feature windows
- Atrium opens to 1,416 square feet of optional living area below which consists of an optional family room, two bedrooms, two baths and a study
- 4 bedrooms, 2 1/2 baths, 3-car side entry garage
- Walk-out basement foundation

76'-0"

45'-0"

MBr
14-6x15-5

Brk
11-8x13-0

open to below   Dn

Deck

Great Rm
16-4x24-2
vaulted

Kit
11-3x
12-4

Br 2
10-7x
10-0

Dining

Garage
23-4x29-4

P

D W

Br 3
11-4x11x8

Br 4
11-8x12-8
vaulted

Porch

First Floor
1,977 sq. ft.

Up
Atrium

Study
10-9x
13-2

Br 5
15-3x15-6

storage

Family
18-4x23-6

Br 6
11-5x12-7

L

storage

storage

Optional
Lower Level

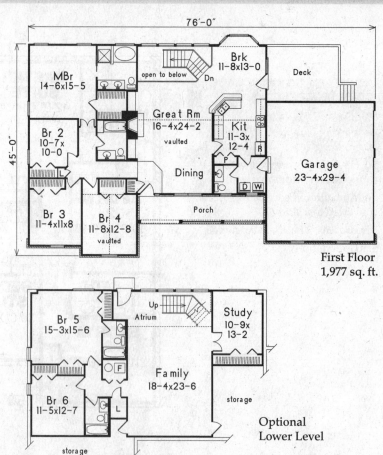

TO ORDER BLUEPRINTS USE THE FORM ON PAGE 15 OR CALL TOLL-FREE 1-877-671-6036
View thousands more home plans online at www.familyhandyman.com/homeplans

223

Appealing Gabled Facade

Plan #711-025D-0009

1,680 total square feet of living area

Price Code B

Special features

- Vaulted great room has a wet bar making it an ideal space for entertaining
- Spacious dining area features an eating bar for additional seating
- Fourth bedroom could easily be converted to a study
- 4 bedrooms, 2 baths, 2-car garage
- Slab foundation

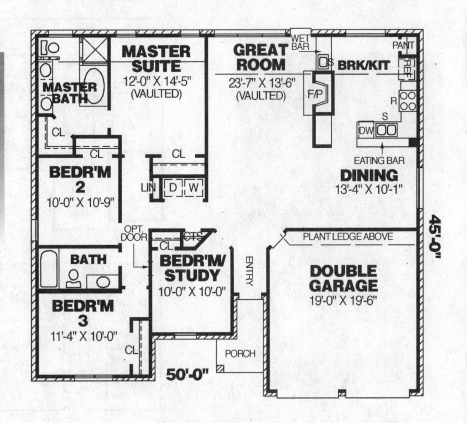

2,455 total square feet of living area

Price Code E

Special features

- Foyer is two stories high and opens to the living room
- 13' ceiling in living room
- Master bedroom includes bayed sitting area ideal for relaxing
- 4 bedrooms, 3 baths, 2-car side entry garage
- Basement, crawl space or slab foundation, please specify when ordering

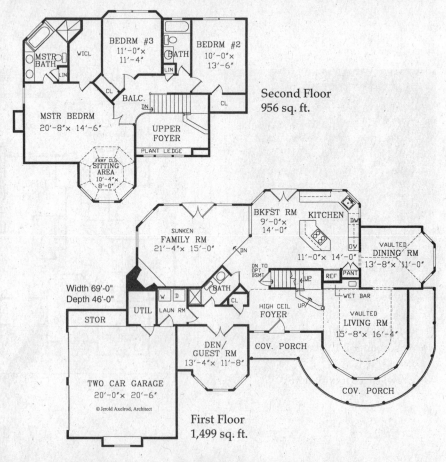

Second Floor
956 sq. ft.

BEDRM #3
11'-0" x
11'-4"

BEDRM #2
10'-0" x
13'-6"

MSTR BATH

WICL

BATH

MSTR BEDRM
20'-8" x 14'-6"

BALC.

UPPER FOYER

PLANT LEDGE

TRAY CLG.
SITTING AREA
10'-4" x 8'-0"

Width 69'-0"
Depth 46'-0"

BKFST RM
9'-0" x
14'-0"

KITCHEN
11'-0" x 14'-0"

SUNKEN
FAMILY RM
21'-4" x 15'-0"

VAULTED
DINING RM
13'-8" x 11'-0"

DN TO OPT. BSMT.

WET BAR

STOR

UTIL

LAUN RM

BATH

CL

HIGH CEIL FOYER

VAULTED
LIVING RM
15'-8" x 16'-4"

DEN/
GUEST RM
13'-4" x 11'-8"

COV. PORCH

COV. PORCH

TWO CAR GARAGE
20'-0" x 20'-6"

© Jerold Axelrod, Architect

First Floor
1,499 sq. ft.

3,003 total square feet of living area

Price Code E

Special features

- Vaulted master bedroom features large walk-in closet, spa, separate shower room and access to rear patio
- Covered entrance opens into foyer with large greeting area
- Formal living room with 12' ceiling and 36" walls on two sides
- Island kitchen features large pantry and nook
- Cozy fireplace accents vaulted family room that opens onto a covered deck
- Utility room with generous space is adjacent to a half bath
- 3 bedrooms, 2 1/2 baths, 3-car garage
- Crawl space foundation

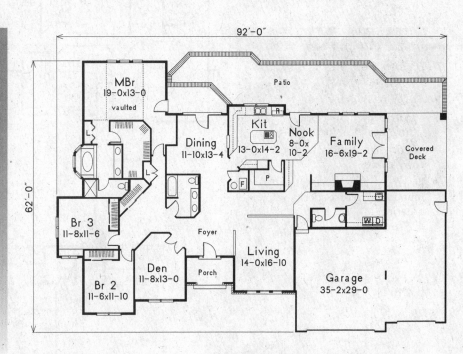

92'-0"

62'-0"

MBr
19-0x13-0
vaulted

Patio

Kit
13-0x14-2

Nook
8-0x
10-2

Family
16-6x19-2

Covered Deck

Dining
11-10x13-4

Br 3
11-8x11-6

Foyer

Living
14-0x16-10

Br 2
11-6x11-10

Den
11-8x13-0

Porch

Garage
35-2x29-0

The Family Handyman

3,485 total square feet of living area   **Price Code F**

© Michael E. Nelson

Special features

- Hearth room adds warmth and light with windows and fireplace
- Study boasts French doors and built-in bookshelves
- Lower level game room has a wet bar which is ideal for entertaining
- 3 bedrooms, 3 1/2 baths, 2-car side entry garage
- Basement, crawl space or slab foundation, please specify when ordering

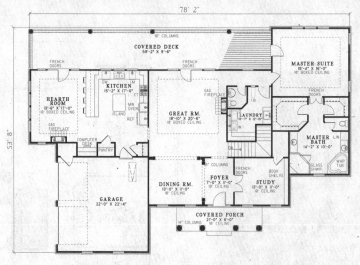

First Floor
2,235 sq. ft.

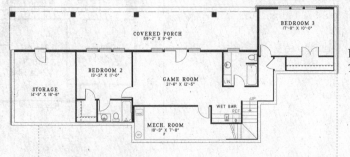

Lower Level
1,250 sq. ft.

TO ORDER BLUEPRINTS USE THE FORM ON PAGE 15 OR CALL TOLL-FREE 1-877-671-6036
View thousands more home plans online at www.familyhandyman.com/homeplans

227

Home Focused On Patio Views   Plan #711-007D-0113

2,547 total square feet of living area   **Price Code D**

Special features

- Grand-sized great room features a 12' volume ceiling, fireplace with built-in wrap-around shelving and patio doors with sidelights and transom windows

- The walk-in pantry, computer desk, large breakfast island for seven and bayed breakfast area are the many features of this outstanding kitchen

- The master bedroom suite enjoys a luxurious bath, large walk-in closets and patio access

- 4 bedrooms, 2 1/2 baths, 3-car side entry garage

- Basement foundation

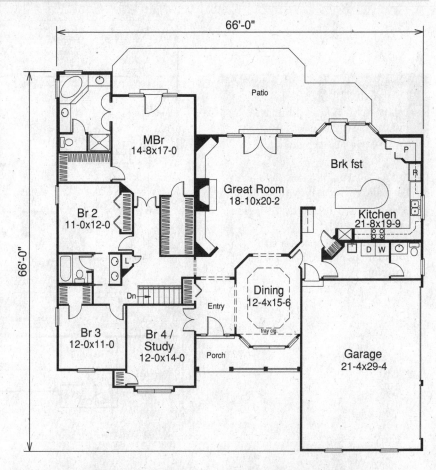

66'-0"

66'-0"

Patio

MBr
14-8x17-0

Great Room
18-10x20-2

Brk fst

Kitchen
21-8x19-9

Br 2
11-0x12-0

Dn

Dining
12-4x15-6

Entry

tray clg.

Br 3
12-0x11-0

Br 4 /
Study
12-0x14-0

Porch

Garage
21-4x29-4

TO ORDER BLUEPRINTS USE THE FORM ON PAGE 15 OR CALL TOLL-FREE 1-877-671-6036
View thousands more home plans online at www.familyhandyman.com/homeplans

2,058 total square feet of living area

Price Code C

Special features

- Energy efficient design with 2"x 6" exterior walls
- Balcony overlooks living room below while easily converting to a bedroom
- Sunny atrium and plenty of windows in eating area brighten kitchen
- 3 bedrooms, 2 1/2 baths, 2-car garage
- Crawl space foundation, drawings also include basement and slab foundations

Second Floor
512 sq. ft.

First Floor
1,546 sq. ft.

3,814 total square feet of living area   **Price Code G**

Special features

- Massive sunken great room with vaulted ceiling includes exciting balcony overlook of towering atrium window wall
- Breakfast bar adjoins open "California" kitchen
- Seven vaulted rooms for drama and four fireplaces for warmth
- Master bath complemented by colonnade and fireplace surrounding sunken tub and deck
- 3 bedrooms, 2 1/2 baths, 3-car side entry garage
- Walk-out basement foundation
- 3,566 square feet on the first floor and 248 square feet on the lower level atrium

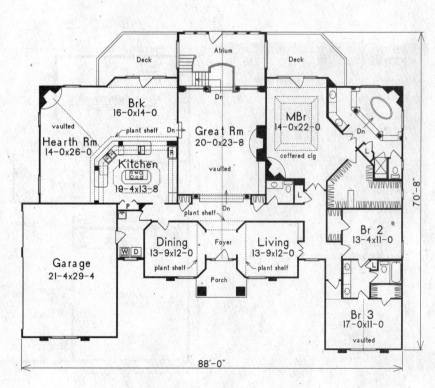

Rear View

A Ranch With Tudor Influence
Plan #711-069D-0019

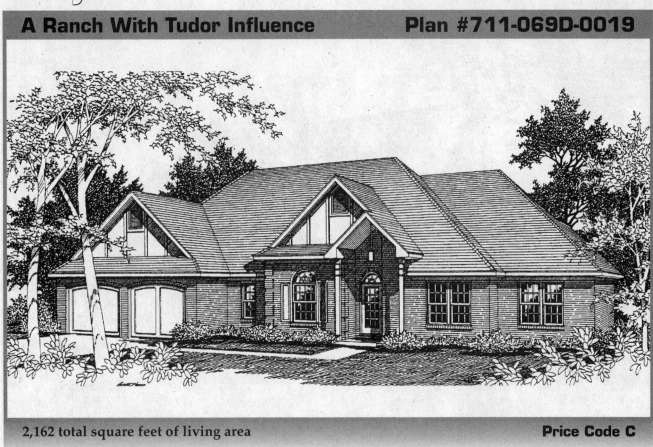

2,162 total square feet of living area

Price Code C

Special features

- 10' ceilings in great room, dining room, master suite and foyer
- Enormous great room overlooks kitchen with oversized snack bar
- Luxurious master bath boasts a triangular whirlpool tub drenched in light from large windows
- 3 bedrooms, 2 baths, 2-car garage
- Crawl space or slab foundation, please specify when ordering

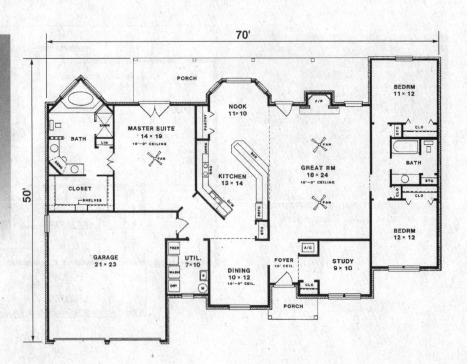

TO ORDER BLUEPRINTS USE THE FORM ON PAGE 15 OR CALL TOLL-FREE 1-877-671-6036
View thousands more home plans online at www.familyhandyman.com/homeplans

231

Open Living

Plan #711-020D-0006

2,665 total square feet of living area

Price Code E

Special features

- Open floor plan makes this home feel spacious
- 12' ceilings in kitchen, living, breakfast and dining areas
- Kitchen is the center of activity with views into all gathering places
- 3 bedrooms, 2 baths, 2-car side entry garage
- Crawl space foundation, drawings also include slab foundation

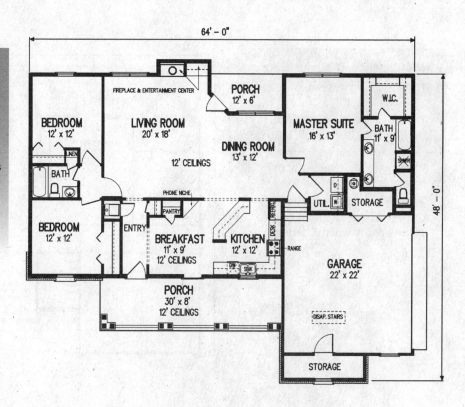

64' – 0"

48' – 0"

BEDROOM
12' x 12'

LIVING ROOM
20' x 18'
12' CEILINGS

FIREPLACE & ENTERTAINMENT CENTER

PORCH
12' x 6'

DINING ROOM
13' x 12'

MASTER SUITE
16' x 13'

W.I.C.

BATH
11' x 9'

BATH

LINEN

PHONE NICHE

PANTRY

UTIL.

STORAGE

BEDROOM
12' x 12'

ENTRY

BREAKFAST
11' x 9'
12' CEILINGS

KITCHEN
12' x 12'

DESK

RANGE

GARAGE
22' x 22'

PORCH
30' x 8'
12' CEILINGS

DISAP. STAIRS

STORAGE

The Family Handyman

Enormous Majestic Two-Story Plan #711-011D-0034

©Alan Mascord Design Assoc

4,211 total square feet of living area

Price Code H

Special features

- Master suite has every luxury including an enormous bath with a see-through fireplace from master bath near spa tub into the bedroom and a huge walk-in closet
- A convenient butler's pantry connects the kitchen to the formal dining room
- A grand foyer is highlighted with an oversized curved staircase
- 9' ceilings on the first floor
- Bonus room on the second floor has an additional 567 square feet of living area
- 4 bedrooms, 3 full baths, 2 half baths, 3-car garage
- Crawl space foundation

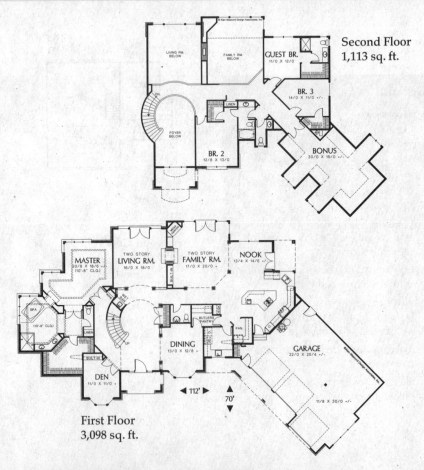

Second Floor
1,113 sq. ft.

First Floor
3,098 sq. ft.

Classic American Styling

Plan #711-060D-0031

© COPYRIGHT MCMXCV Ralph Jones

2,566 total square feet of living area

Price Code D

Special features

- Two-story great room has a fireplace plus first and second floor windows
- Hearth room with bayed walls includes another fireplace for coziness
- Master suite with raised ceiling has bath with huge walk-in closet, stained glass over corner tub and separate shower
- Loft retreat on second floor can be converted into bedroom #4
- Future play room on the second floor includes an additional 315 square feet of living area
- 3 bedrooms, 3 baths, 2-car side entry garage
- Slab or crawl space foundation, please specify when ordering

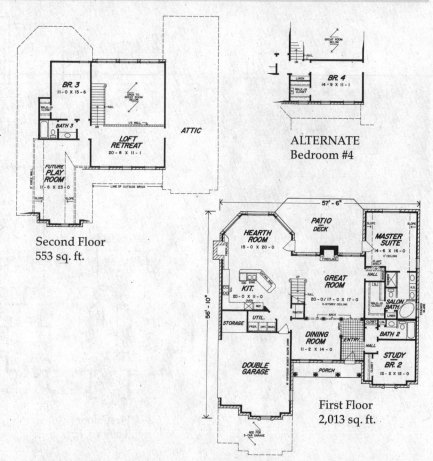

Second Floor
553 sq. ft.

ALTERNATE
Bedroom #4

First Floor
2,013 sq. ft.

234

TO ORDER BLUEPRINTS USE THE FORM ON PAGE 15 OR CALL TOLL-FREE 1-877-671-6036
View thousands more home plans online at www.familyhandyman.com/homeplans

Office With Separate Entrance

Plan #711-039D-0024

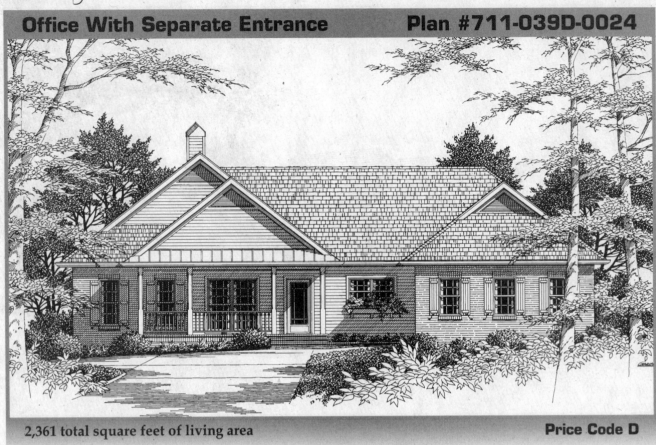

2,361 total square feet of living area

Price Code D

Special features

- Enormous breakfast area and kitchen create a perfect gathering place
- Family room enhanced with wall of windows and a large fireplace
- Office/gameroom is easily accessible through separate side entrance
- 4 bedrooms, 3 baths, 2-car side entry garage
- Basement foundation

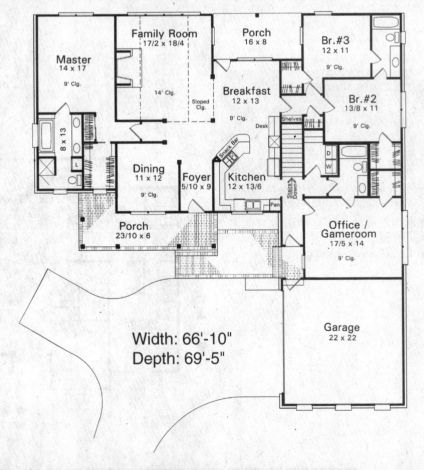

Master
14 x 17
9' Clg.

Family Room
17/2 x 18/4
14' Clg.

Sloped Clg.

Porch
16 x 8

Br.#3
12 x 11
9' Clg.

Breakfast
12 x 13
9' Clg.

Br.#2
13/8 x 11
9' Clg.

8 x 13

Dining
11 x 12
9' Clg.

Foyer
5/10 x 9

Kitchen
12 x 13/6

Stairs Down

Office /
Gameroom
17/5 x 14
9' Clg.

Porch
23/10 x 6

Width: 66'-10"
Depth: 69'-5"

Garage
22 x 22

TO ORDER BLUEPRINTS USE THE FORM ON PAGE 15 OR CALL TOLL-FREE 1-877-671-6036
View thousands more home plans online at www.familyhandyman.com/HOMEPLANS

235

Great Views At Rear Of Home
Plan #711-011D-0010

2,197 total square feet of living area

Price Code C

Special features

- Centrally located great room opens to kitchen, breakfast nook and private backyard
- Den located off entry ideal for home office
- Vaulted master bath has spa tub, shower and double vanity
- 3 bedrooms, 2 1/2 baths, 3-car garage
- Crawl space foundation

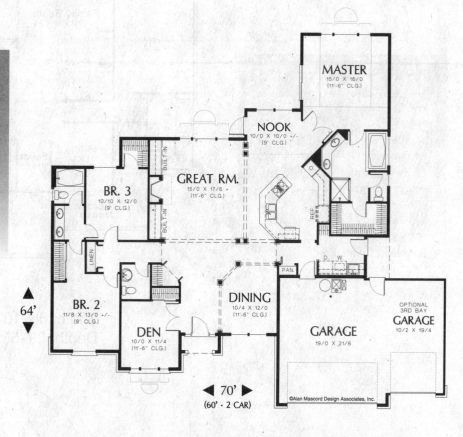

MASTER
15/0 X 16/0
(11'-6" CLG.)

NOOK
10/0 X 10/0 +/-
(9' CLG.)

GREAT RM.
15/0 X 17/6
(11'-6" CLG.)

BR. 3
10/10 X 12/0
(9' CLG.)

BUILT-IN

LINEN

BR. 2
11/8 X 13/0 +/-
(9' CLG.)

DEN
10/0 X 11/4
(11'-6" CLG.)

DINING
10/4 X 12/0
(11'-6" CLG.)

PAN.

D. W.

REF.

GARAGE
19/0 X 21/6

OPTIONAL
3RD BAY
GARAGE
10/2 X 19/4

64'

70'
(60' - 2 CAR)

©Alan Mascord Design Associates, Inc.

1,734 total square feet of living area   **Price Code B**

Special features

- Bayed dining room is cheerful and convenient to kitchen
- Large breakfast room is tucked between the kitchen and the family room
- Master bedroom has its own bath and two closets
- 3 bedrooms, 2 1/2 baths, 2-car garage
- Basement foundation

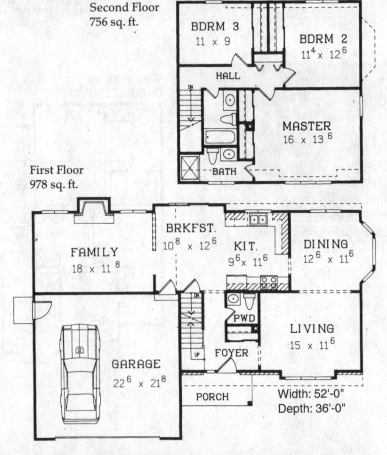

Second Floor
756 sq. ft.

BDRM 3
11 x 9

BDRM 2
11^4 x 12^6

HALL

MASTER
16 x 13^6

BATH

First Floor
978 sq. ft.

BRKFST.
10^8 x 12^6

FAMILY
18 x 11^8

KIT.
9^6 x 11^6

DINING
12^6 x 11^6

PWD

LIVING
15 x 11^6

GARAGE
22^6 x 21^8

FOYER

PORCH

Width: 52'-0"
Depth: 36'-0"

Decorative Touches Throughout   Plan #711-043D-0007

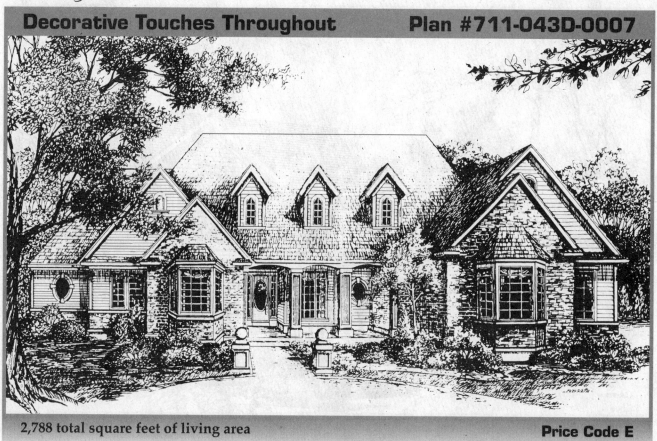

2,788 total square feet of living area

Price Code E

Special features

- Breakfast nook flooded with sunlight from skylights
- Fireplace in great room framed by media center and shelving
- Large game room is secluded for active children
- 3 bedrooms, 2 1/2 baths, 3-car side entry garage
- Crawl space foundation

Width: 76'-6"
Depth: 72'-0"

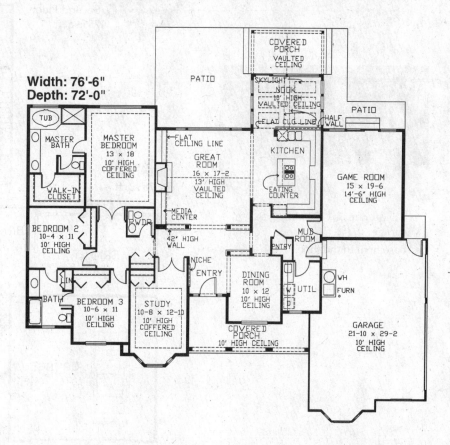

3,013 total square feet of living area

Price Code E

Special features

- Oversized rooms throughout
- Kitchen features island sink, large pantry and opens into breakfast room with a sunroom feel
- Large family room with fireplace accesses rear deck and front porch
- Master bedroom includes large walk-in closet and private deluxe bath
- 4 bedrooms, 3 1/2 baths, 2-car side entry garage
- Basement foundation

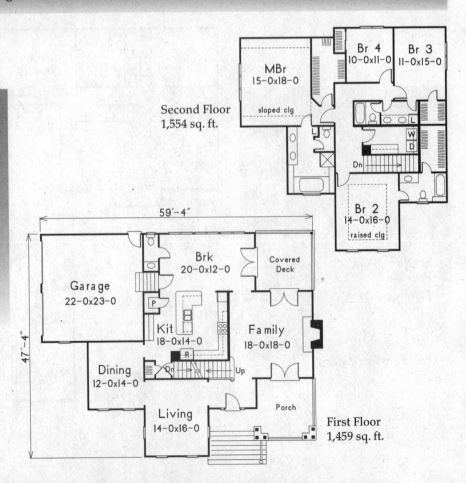

Second Floor
1,554 sq. ft.

MBr
15-0x18-0
sloped clg

Br 4
10-0x11-0

Br 3
11-0x15-0

L

W
D

Dn

Br 2
14-0x16-0
raised clg

59'-4"

47'-4"

Garage
22-0x23-0

Brk
20-0x12-0

Covered Deck

P

Kit
18-0x14-0

Family
18-0x18-0

Dining
12-0x14-0

Dn   R   Up

Living
14-0x16-0

Porch

First Floor
1,459 sq. ft.

TO ORDER BLUEPRINTS USE THE FORM ON PAGE 15 OR CALL TOLL-FREE 1-877-671-6036
View thousands more home plans online at www.familyhandyman.com/homeplans

239

Grandscale Elegance

Plan #711-007D-0059

3,169 total square feet of living area

Price Code F

Special features

- Formal areas include an enormous entry with handcrafted stairway and powder room, French doors to living room and open dining area with tray ceiling

- Informal areas consist of a large family room with bay window, fireplace, walk-in wet bar and kitchen open to breakfast room

- Stylish master bedroom is located on second floor for privacy

- Front secondary bedroom includes a private study

- 4 bedrooms, 2 1/2 baths, 3-car side entry garage

- Basement foundation

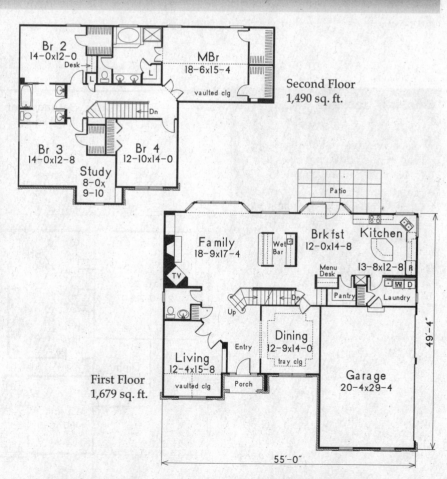

Br 2
14-0x12-0
Desk

MBr
18-6x15-4
vaulted clg

Second Floor
1,490 sq. ft.

Br 3
14-0x12-8

Br 4
12-10x14-0

Study
8-0x
9-10

Patio

Family
18-9x17-4

Wet Bar

Brk fst
12-0x14-8

Kitchen
13-8x12-8

TV

Menu Desk

Pantry

Laundry
W D

Up

Dn

Dining
12-9x14-0
tray clg

Living
12-4x15-8
vaulted clg

Entry

Porch

Garage
20-4x29-4

First Floor
1,679 sq. ft.

49'-4"

55'-0"

2,228 total square feet of living area

Price Code D

Special features

- Dining area is cheerful and bright
- Kitchen with eat-in breakfast bar overlooks family room with fireplace
- Unique box bay window in bedroom #2
- 3 bedrooms, 2 baths, 2-car garage
- Basement foundation

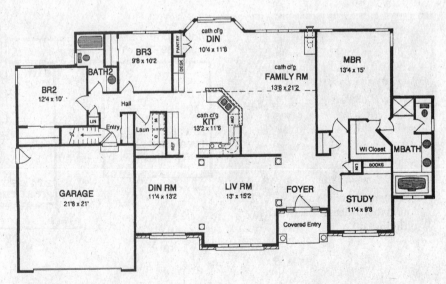

Width: 77'-0"
Depth: 41'-8"

TO ORDER BLUEPRINTS USE THE FORM ON PAGE 15 OR CALL TOLL-FREE 1-877-671-6036
View thousands more home plans online at www.familyhandyman.com/homeplans

241

Spacious Wrap-Around Porch

Plan #711-062D-0041

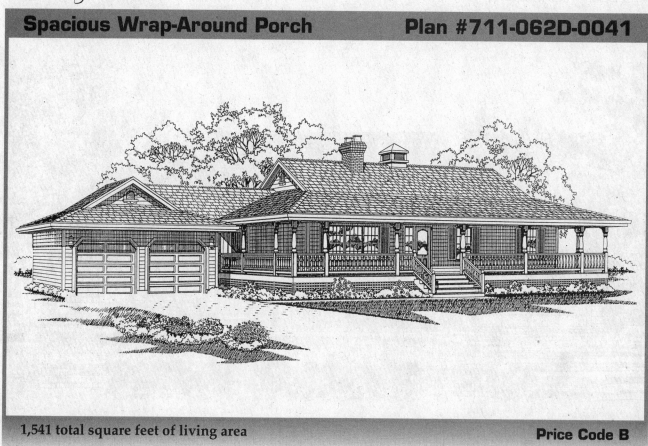

1,541 total square feet of living area

Price Code B

Special features

- Dining area offers access to a screened porch for outdoor dining and entertaining
- Country kitchen features a center island and a breakfast bay for casual meals
- Great room is warmed by a woodstove
- 3 bedrooms, 2 baths, 2-car garage
- Basement or crawl space foundation, please specify when ordering

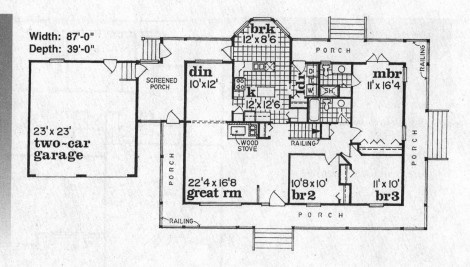

Width: 87'-0"
Depth: 39'-0"

SCREENED PORCH

23' x 23'
two-car garage

PORCH

22'4 x 16'8
great rm

RAILING

brk
12' x 8'6

din
10' x 12'

k
12' x 12'6

WOOD STOVE

PORCH

RAILING

10'8 x 10'
br 2

PORCH

mbr
11' x 16'4

RAILING

PORCH

11' x 10'
br3

PORCH

Optional Living Quarters   Plan #711-035D-0026

1,845 total square feet of living area   Price Code C

Special features

- Vaulted living room has cozy fireplace
- Breakfast area and kitchen are lovely gathering places
- Dining room overlooks living room
- Optional second floor with bath has additional 354 square feet of living area
- 3 bedrooms, 2 1/2 baths, 2-car side entry garage
- Walk-out basement or crawl space foundation, please specify when ordering

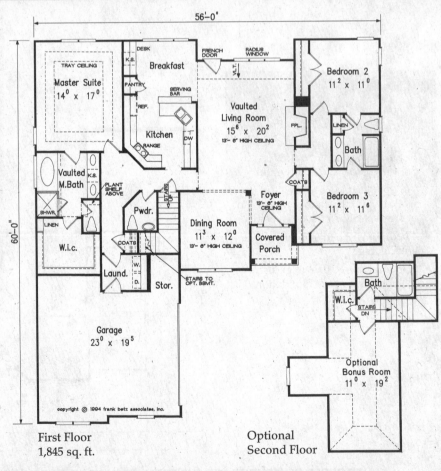

First Floor
1,845 sq. ft.

Optional
Second Floor

TO ORDER BLUEPRINTS USE THE FORM ON PAGE 15 OR CALL TOLL-FREE 1-877-671-6036
View thousands more home plans online at www.familyhandyman.com/homeplans

243

Exterior Finishes Enrich Facade

Plan #711-018D-0007

2,696 total square feet of living area

Price Code E

Special features

- Magnificent master bedroom with private covered porch and luxurious bath
- Second floor game room with balcony access and adjacent loft
- Well-planned kitchen includes walk-in pantry, island cooktop and nearby spacious breakfast room
- 4 bedrooms, 3 baths, 2-car side entry garage
- Slab foundation, drawings also include crawl space foundation

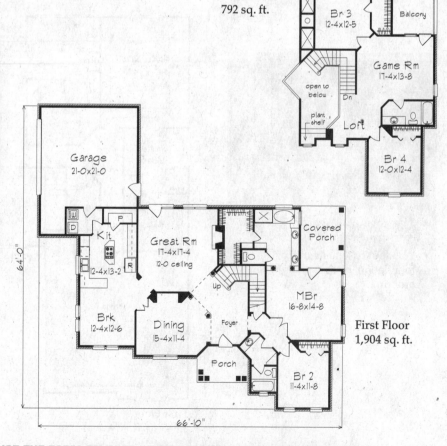

Second Floor
792 sq. ft.

Br 3
12-4x12-5

Balcony

Game Rm
17-4x13-8

open to below

Dn

plant shelf

Loft

Br 4
12-0x12-4

Garage
21-0x21-0

Kit
12-4x13-2

Great Rm
17-4x17-4
12-0 ceiling

Covered Porch

Brk
12-4x12-6

Dining
15-4x11-4

Foyer

Up

MBr
16-8x14-8

First Floor
1,904 sq. ft.

Porch

Br 2
11-4x11-8

64'-0"

66'-10"

Handyman

Elegant Touches Grace Home

Plan #711-051D-0076

3,376 total square feet of living area

Price Code G

Special features

- The two-story family room boasts a grand fireplace flanked by built-in shelves
- The sunroom creates a warm and cheerful atmosphere and connects with the bayed nook and kitchen
- The elegant master bedroom features a bayed sitting area and double-door entry to the deluxe bath with vaulted ceiling
- All secondary bedrooms enjoy walk-in closets
- 4 bedrooms, 3 1/2 baths, 4-car side entry garage
- Basement foundation

Second Floor
1,000 sq. ft.

First Floor
2,376 sq. ft.

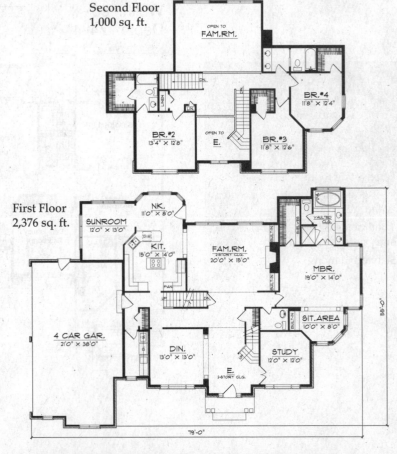

TO ORDER BLUEPRINTS USE THE FORM ON PAGE 15 OR CALL TOLL-FREE 1-877-671-6036
View thousands more home plans online at www.familyhandyman.com/homeplans

Elegant Master Suite

Plan #711-047D-0048

2,660 total square feet of living area

Price Code E

Special features

- Enormous family room with fireplace is situated near breakfast nook and kitchen
- Spacious master bedroom has floor-to-ceiling windows and a large sitting room
- Well-designed kitchen has a center island
- 4 bedrooms, 3 baths, 2-car side entry garage
- Slab foundation

Width: 66'-4"
Depth: 74'-4"

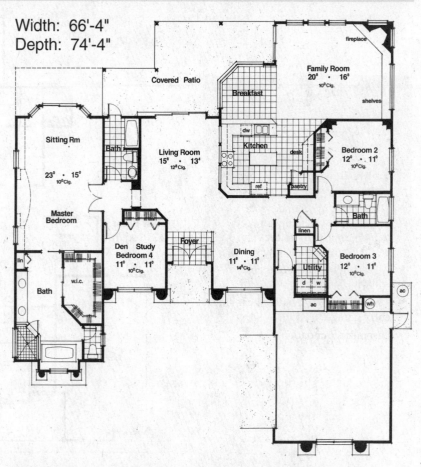

Victorian Home Has A Custom Feel   Plan #711-071D-0006

3,746 total square feet of living area

Price Code G

Special features

- Upon entering a large foyer guests are greeted by a beautiful central two-story rotunda with circular staircase
- An oval tray ceiling in the formal dining room creates a Victorian feel
- Two-story family room is sunny and bright with windows on two floors
- Bonus room on the second floor has an additional 314 square feet of living area
- 4 bedrooms, 3 1/2 baths, 3-car garage
- Crawl space foundation

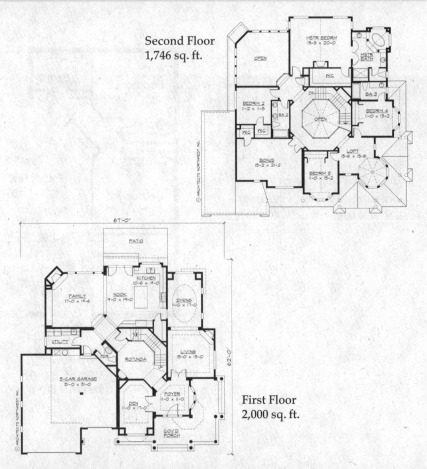

Second Floor
1,746 sq. ft.

First Floor
2,000 sq. ft.

TO ORDER BLUEPRINTS USE THE FORM ON PAGE 15 OR CALL TOLL-FREE 1-877-671-6036
View thousands more home plans online at www.familyhandyman.com/homeplans

247

Trio Of Dormers Adds Curb Appeal   Plan #711-047D-0025

1,806 total square feet of living area   **Price Code C**

Special features

- Covered porch in the rear of the home adds an outdoor living area
- Private and formal living room
- Kitchen has snack counter that extends into family room
- 3 bedrooms, 2 baths, 2-car garage
- Slab foundation

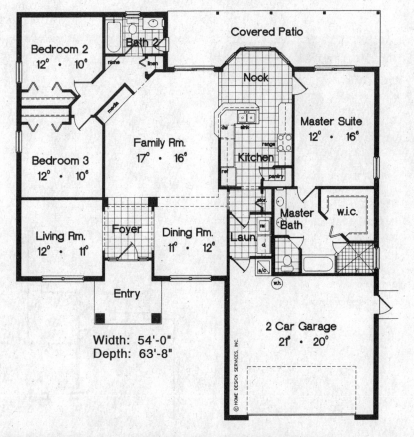

Bedroom 2
12⁰ • 10⁰

Bath 2

Covered Patio

Nook

Master Suite
12⁰ • 16⁰

Family Rm.
17⁰ • 16⁰

Kitchen

Bedroom 3
12⁰ • 10⁰

Master Bath

w.i.c.

Living Rm.
12⁰ • 11⁰

Foyer

Dining Rm.
11⁰ • 12⁰

Laun.

Entry

Width: 54'-0"
Depth: 63'-8"

2 Car Garage
21⁰ • 20⁰

© HOME DESIGN SERVICES, INC.

1,318 total square feet of living area

Price Code A

Special features

- Vaulted kitchen, dining and family rooms create an open and dramatic feel
- Luxurious master suite with all the amenities
- Two secondary bedrooms share a hall bath
- 3 bedrooms, 2 baths, 2-car drive under garage
- Walk-out basement foundation

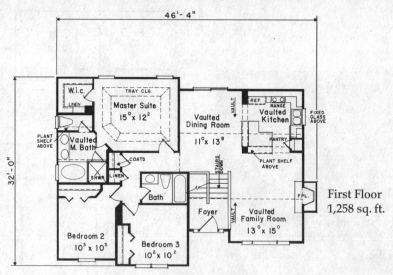

46'- 4"

32'- 0"

W.i.c.
LINEN

TRAY CLG.

Master Suite
15⁰ x 12²

Vaulted Dining Room
11⁰ x 13⁸

REF.
RANGE

Vaulted Kitchen

FIXED GLASS ABOVE

PLANT SHELF ABOVE

Vaulted M. Bath

COATS

PANTRY

PLANT SHELF ABOVE

SHWR LINEN

Bath

STAIRS DOWN

VAULT

First Floor
1,258 sq. ft.

Bedroom 2
10³ x 10⁵

Bedroom 3
10² x 10²

Foyer

VAULT

Vaulted Family Room
13⁰ x 15⁰

FPL.

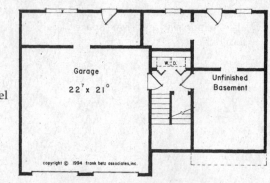

Lower Level
60 sq. ft.

Garage
22⁷ x 21⁰

W. D.

Unfinished Basement

copyright © 1994 frank betz associates, inc.

TO ORDER BLUEPRINTS USE THE FORM ON PAGE 15 OR CALL TOLL-FREE 1-877-671-6036
View thousands more home plans online at www.familyhandyman.com/homeplans

249

Compact Design Offers Privacy — Plan #711-001D-0016

2,847 total square feet of living area

Price Code E

Special features

- Secluded first floor master bedroom includes an oversized window and a large walk-in closet
- Extensive attic storage and closet space
- Spacious second floor bedrooms, two of which share a private bath
- Great starter home with option to finish the second floor as needed
- 4 bedrooms, 3 1/2 baths, 2-car garage
- Basement foundation, drawings also include slab and crawl space foundations

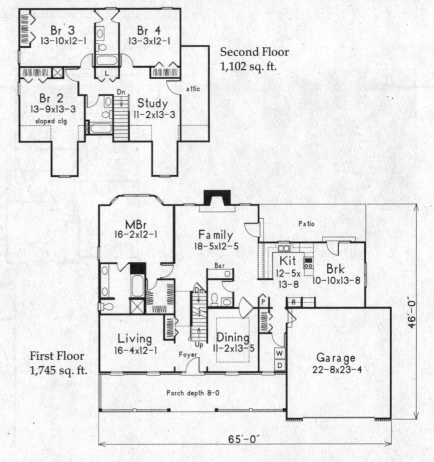

Second Floor 1,102 sq. ft.

Br 3 13-10x12-1
Br 4 13-3x12-1
Br 2 13-9x13-3 sloped clg
Study 11-2x13-3
attic

First Floor 1,745 sq. ft.

MBr 16-2x12-1
Family 18-5x12-5
Patio
Kit 12-5x 13-8
Brk 10-10x13-8
Bar
Living 16-4x12-1
Foyer
Dining 11-2x13-5
Garage 22-8x23-4
Porch depth 8-0

46'-0"
65'-0"

Columned Breakfast Room

Plan #711-033D-0005

1,954 total square feet of living area

Price Code D

Special features

- Living and dining areas include vaulted ceilings and combine for added openness
- Convenient access to laundry room from garage
- Appealing bay window in family room attracts light
- Raised jacuzzi tub featured in master bath
- 3 bedrooms, 2 1/2 baths, 2-car garage
- Basement foundation

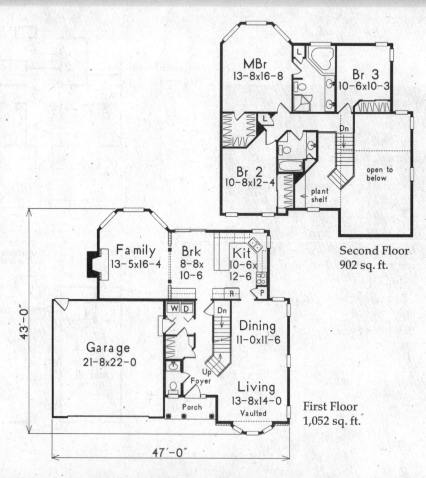

MBr
13-8x16-8

Br 3
10-6x10-3

Br 2
10-8x12-4

open to below

plant shelf

Second Floor
902 sq. ft.

Family
13-5x16-4

Brk
8-8x
10-6

Kit
10-6x
12-6

Garage
21-8x22-0

Dining
11-0x11-6

Living
13-8x14-0
Vaulted

Foyer

Porch

43'-0"

47'-0"

First Floor
1,052 sq. ft.

TO ORDER BLUEPRINTS USE THE FORM ON PAGE 15 OR CALL TOLL-FREE 1-877-671-6036
View thousands more home plans online at www.familyhandyman.com/homeplans

251

CHARMING COUNTRY HOME

Plan #711-052D-0052

1,936 total square feet of living area

Price Code C

Special features

- Covered porch creates an inviting entrance
- Kitchen, breakfast and great rooms combine for an open area and include double doors to the rear sundeck
- Second floor includes an abundance of storage area
- Bonus room on the second floor has an additional 528 square feet of living area
- 3 bedrooms, 2 1/2 baths, 2-car side entry garage
- Basement foundation

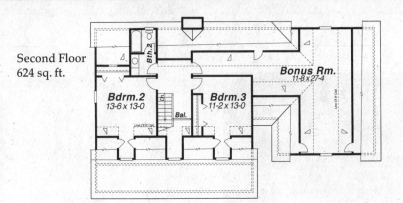

Second Floor
624 sq. ft.

Bonus Rm.
11-8 x 27-4

Bdrm.2
13-6 x 13-0

Bdrm.3
11-2 x 13-0

Bth.2

Bal.

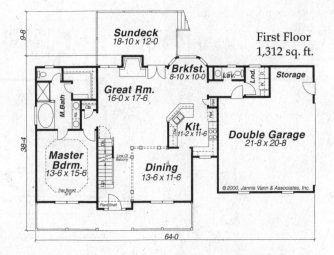

First Floor
1,312 sq. ft.

Sundeck
18-10 x 12-0

Brkfst.
8-10 x 10-0

Great Rm.
16-0 x 17-6

Lav.

Lnd.

Storage

W.D.

M.Bath

Kit.
11-2 x 11-6

Double Garage
21-8 x 20-8

Master Bdrm.
13-6 x 15-6

Dining
13-6 x 11-6

© 2000, Jannis Vann & Associates, Inc.

64-0

3,017 total square feet of living area

Price Code E

Special features

- Impressive two-story entry has curved staircase
- Family room has unique elliptical vault above window
- Master bedroom includes a private covered patio and bath with walk-in closet
- Breakfast area overlooks great room
- Bonus room on the second floor has an additional 234 square feet of living area
- 4 bedrooms, 3 1/2 baths, 3-car side entry garage
- Slab foundation

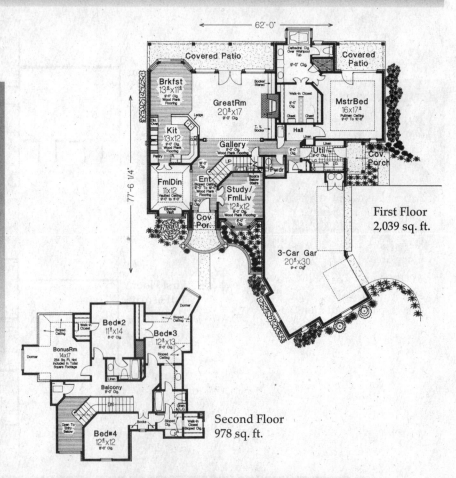

First Floor
2,039 sq. ft.

Second Floor
978 sq. ft.

TO ORDER BLUEPRINTS USE THE FORM ON PAGE 15 OR CALL TOLL-FREE 1-877-671-6036
View thousands more home plans online at www.familyhandyman.com/homeplans

253

Perfect Two-Story Traditional

Plan #711-013D-0018

1,998 total square feet of living area

Price Code C

Special features

- Large open living areas have enough space for gathering
- All bedrooms on the second floor for peace and quiet from living areas
- Formal dining space has direct access to the kitchen
- Bonus room on the second floor has an additional 320 square feet of living area
- 4 bedrooms, 2 1/2 baths, 2-car garage
- Crawl space foundation

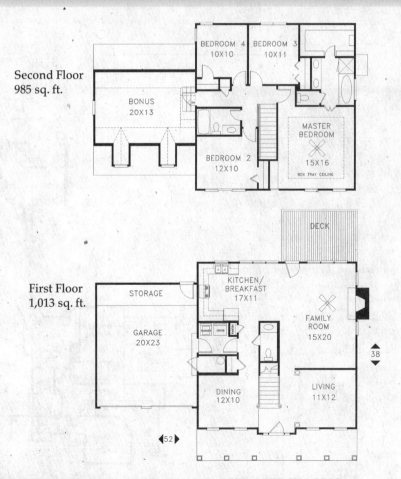

Second Floor
985 sq. ft.

First Floor
1,013 sq. ft.

254

TO ORDER BLUEPRINTS USE THE FORM ON PAGE 15 OR CALL TOLL-FREE 1-877-671-6036
View thousands more home plans online at www.familyhandyman.com/homeplans

Traditional Style, Farmhouse Flavor   Plan #711-038D-0055

1,763 total square feet of living area

Price Code C

Special features

- Dining room has a large box bay window and a recessed ceiling
- Living room includes a large fireplace
- Kitchen has plenty of workspace, a pantry and a double sink overlooking the deck
- Master bedroom features a large bath with walk-in closet
- 3 bedrooms, 2 1/2 baths, 2-car garage
- Basement foundation

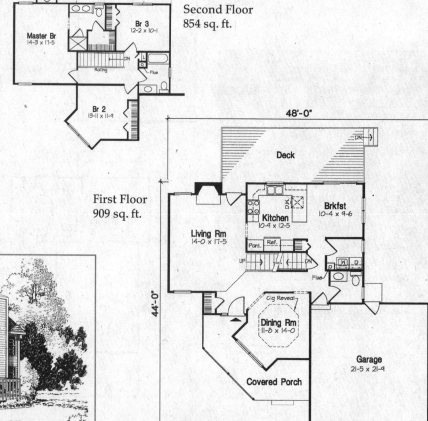

Line of Floor Below

Master Br
14-3 x 17-5

Br 3
12-2 x 10-1

Second Floor
854 sq. ft.

DN

Railing

Flue

Br 2
13-11 x 11-9

First Floor
909 sq. ft.

48'-0"

DN

Deck

Kitchen
10-4 x 12-5

Brkfst
10-4 x 9-6

Living Rm
14-0 x 17-5

Pant.   Ref.

UP

DN

Flue

44'-0"

Clg Reveal

Dining Rm
11-8 x 14-0

Garage
21-5 x 21-4

Covered Porch

Rear View

TO ORDER BLUEPRINTS USE THE FORM ON PAGE 15 OR CALL TOLL-FREE 1-877-671-6036
View thousands more home plans online at www.familyhandyman.com/homeplans

255

Spacious Two-Story Foyer

Plan #711-040D-0001

1,814 total square feet of living area

Price Code D

Special features

- Large master bedroom includes a spacious bath with garden tub, separate shower and large walk-in closet
- Spacious kitchen and dining area brightened by large windows and patio access
- Detached two-car garage with walkway leading to house adds charm to this country home
- Large front porch
- 3 bedrooms, 2 1/2 baths, 2-car detached side entry garage
- Crawl space foundation, drawings also include slab foundation

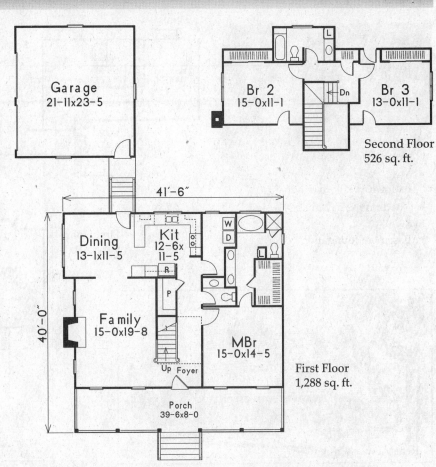

Garage
21-11x23-5

Br 2
15-0x11-1

Br 3
13-0x11-1

Dn

Second Floor
526 sq. ft.

41'-6"

Dining
13-1x11-5

Kit
12-6x
11-5

40'-0"

Family
15-0x19-8

MBr
15-0x14-5

Up Foyer

First Floor
1,288 sq. ft.

Porch
39-6x8-0

Outdoor Living Indoors

Plan #711-36D-0054

2,793 total square feet of living area

Price Code E

Special features

- Beautiful curved staircase invites guests into home
- Large great room stretches from the front to the back of the first floor
- Master bedroom has many amenities
- Future play room above the garage has an additional 285 square feet of living area
- 4 bedrooms, 3 1/2 baths, 3-car rear entry garage
- Crawl space or slab foundation, please specify when ordering

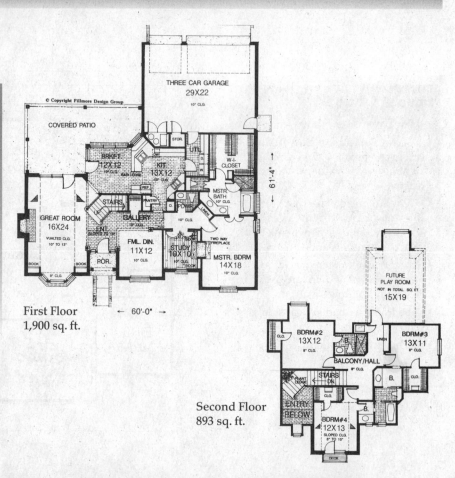

First Floor
1,900 sq. ft.

Second Floor
893 sq. ft.

TO ORDER BLUEPRINTS USE THE FORM ON PAGE 15 OR CALL TOLL-FREE 1-877-671-6036
View thousands more home plans online at www.familyhandyman.com/homeplans

257

KITCHEN Is Center Of Activity · Plan #711-007D-0017

1,882 total square feet of living area

Price Code C

Special features

- Handsome brick facade
- Spacious great room and dining room combination brightened by unique corner windows and patio access
- Well-designed kitchen incorporates breakfast bar peninsula, sweeping casement window above sink and walk-in pantry island
- Master bedroom features large walk-in closet and private bath with bay window
- 4 bedrooms, 2 baths, 2-car side entry garage
- Basement foundation

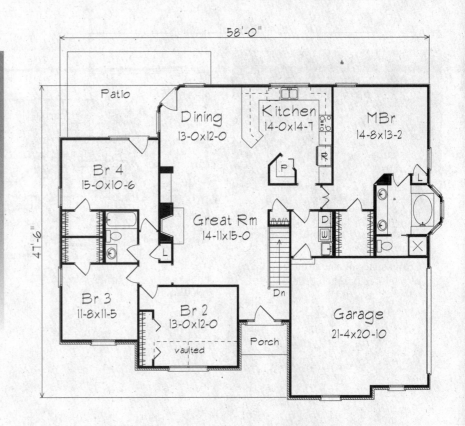

TO ORDER BLUEPRINTS USE THE FORM ON PAGE 15 OR CALL TOLL-FREE 1-877-671-6036
View thousands more home plans online at www.familyhandyman.com/homeplans

THE Family Handyman

3,274 total square feet of living area

Price Code F

Special features

- Second floor game room makes a great casual family room
- Eating bar in kitchen overlooks into hearth room with fireplace flanked by bookshelves
- 3 bedrooms, 3 baths, 2-car side entry garage
- Slab foundation

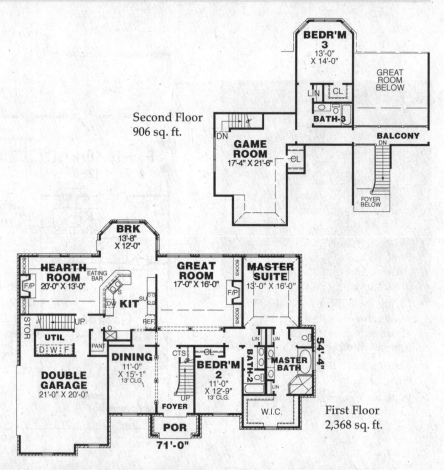

Second Floor
906 sq. ft.

BEDR'M 3
13'-0" X 14'-0"

GREAT ROOM BELOW

LIN   CL

BATH-3

BALCONY
DN

DN

GAME ROOM
17'-4" X 21'-6"

CL

FOYER BELOW

First Floor
2,368 sq. ft.

BRK
13'-8" X 12'-0"

HEARTH ROOM
20'-0" X 13'-0"

EATING BAR

F/P

BOOKS

STOR

UTIL

D W F

DOUBLE GARAGE
21'-0" X 20'-0"

KIT

DW

SU

PANT

DINING
11'-0" X 15'-1"
13' CLG.

FOYER

UP

POR

71'-0"

GREAT ROOM
17'-0" X 16'-0"

BOOKS

F/P

BOOKS

REF

CTS

CL

BEDR'M 2
11'-0" X 12'-9"
13' CLG.

BATH-2

W.I.C.

MASTER SUITE
13'-0" X 16'-0"

LIN   LIN

MASTER BATH

LIN

54'-4"

TO ORDER BLUEPRINTS USE THE FORM ON PAGE 15 OR CALL TOLL-FREE 1-877-671-6036
View thousands more home plans online at www.familyhandyman.com/homeplans

259

Spacious Plan With Many Features   Plan #711-058D-0015

2,308 total square feet of living area   **Price Code D**

Special features

- Efficient kitchen designed with many cabinets and large walk-in pantry adjoins family/breakfast area featuring a beautiful fireplace
- Dining area has architectural colonnades that separate it from living area while maintaining spaciousness
- Enter master bedroom through double-doors and find double walk-in closets and a beautiful luxurious bath
- Living room includes vaulted ceiling, fireplace and a sunny atrium window wall creating a dramatic atmosphere
- 3 bedrooms, 2 baths, 2-car side entry garage
- Walk-out basement foundation

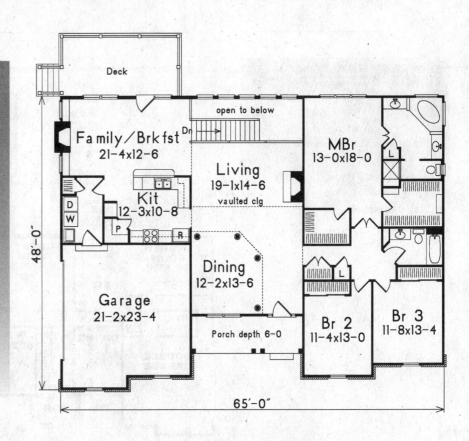

Deck

Family/Brkfst Dr
21-4x12-6

open to below

MBr
13-0x18-0

Living
19-1x14-6
vaulted clg

Kit
12-3x10-8

48'-0"

Dining
12-2x13-6

Garage
21-2x23-4

Porch depth 6-0

Br 2
11-4x13-0

Br 3
11-8x13-4

65'-0"

2,995 total square feet of living area

Price Code E

Special features

- Large island kitchen is complete with a generous walk-in pantry
- Dining room has built-in china cabinet
- First floor master bedroom offers alternate handicap accessible version
- 4 bedrooms, 2 1/2 baths, 2-car side entry garage
- Crawl space or slab foundation, please specify when ordering

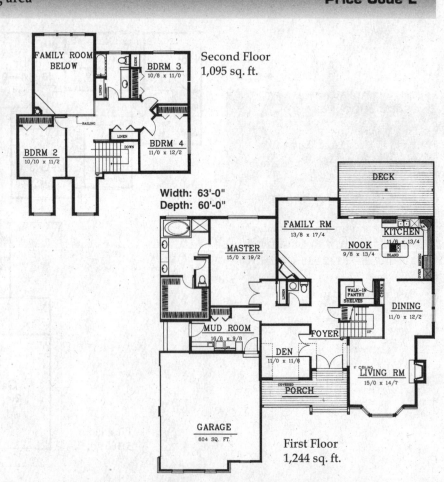

FAMILY ROOM BELOW

BDRM 3
10/8 x 11/0

Second Floor
1,095 sq. ft.

BDRM 2
10/10 x 11/2

LINEN

DOWN

BDRM 4
11/0 x 12/2

RAILING

Width: 63'-0"
Depth: 60'-0"

DECK

FAMILY RM
13/8 x 17/4

KITCHEN
11/8 x 13/4

NOOK
9/8 x 13/4

ISLAND

MASTER
15/0 x 19/2

WALK-IN PANTRY SHELVES

DINING
11/0 x 12/2

MUD ROOM
16/8 x 9/8

DEN
11/0 x 11/6

FOYER

UP

LIVING RM
15/0 x 14/7

COVERED PORCH

GARAGE
604 SQ. FT.

First Floor
1,244 sq. ft.

Centralized Living Area

Plan #711-045D-0002

2,186 total square feet of living area

Price Code C

Special features

- See-through fireplace is a focal point in family and living areas
- Columns grace the entrance into the living room
- Large laundry room with adjoining half bath
- Ideal second floor bath includes separate vanity with double sinks
- 3 bedrooms, 2 1/2 baths, 2-car garage
- Basement foundation

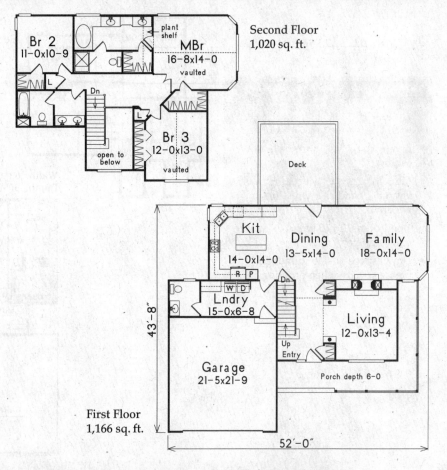

Second Floor
1,020 sq. ft.

Br 2
11-0x10-9

plant shelf

MBr
16-8x14-0
vaulted

Dn

open to below

Br 3
12-0x13-0
vaulted

Deck

Kit
14-0x14-0

Dining
13-5x14-0

Family
18-0x14-0

Lndry
15-0x6-8

Dn

Living
12-0x13-4

Up
Entry

Garage
21-5x21-9

Porch depth 6-0

43'-8"

52'-0"

First Floor
1,166 sq. ft.

CHARMING Covered Porch

Plan #711-055D-0093

1,965 total square feet of living area

Price Code C

Special features

- Master bedroom has cozy fireplace and luxurious bath featuring whirlpool tub, double vanities and a large walk-in closet
- Breakfast room has sunny bay windows
- Great room with fireplace has access to rear grilling porch
- Optional second floor has an additional 251 square feet of living area
- 4 bedrooms, 2 baths, 2-car garage
- Slab or crawl space foundation, please specify when ordering

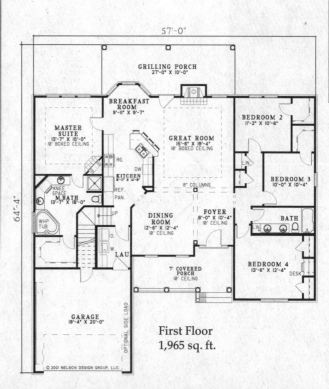

First Floor
1,965 sq. ft.

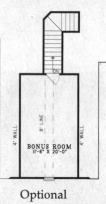

Optional
Second Floor

TO ORDER BLUEPRINTS USE THE FORM ON PAGE 15 OR CALL TOLL-FREE 1-877-671-6036
View thousands more home plans online at www.familyhandyman.com/homeplans

263

2,243 total square feet of living area   Price Code E

Special features

- An angled floor plan allows for flexible placement on any lot
- Great room has a 16' high tray ceiling, a fireplace and an entertainment center
- The luxurious master bedroom is separated for privacy
- The secondary bedrooms are in a private wing and share a common bath
- 3 bedrooms, 2 1/2 baths, 2-car side entry garage
- Basement, crawl space or slab foundation, please specify when ordering

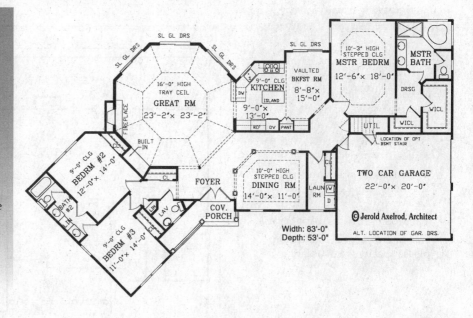

Stately Ranch

Plan #711-013D-0034

2,499 total square feet of living area

Price Code D

Special features

- Dramatic iiving area with tray ceiling, fireplace, and French doors leading onto the deck
- Spacious kitchen and breakfast room, emphasized by vaulted ceiling
- Large laundry room with a wash tub and a nearby half bath
- Sumptuous master bedroom offers a tray ceiling and two walk-in closets
- 4 bedrooms, 2 1/2 baths, 2-car side entry garage
- Basement, crawl space or slab foundation, please specify when ordering

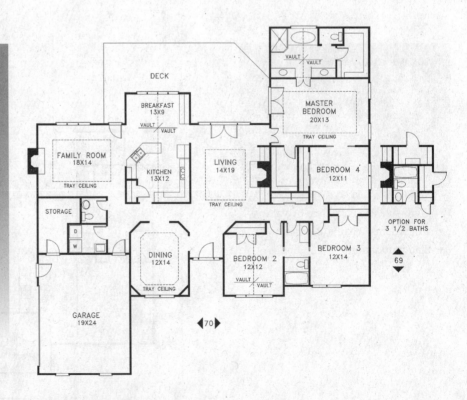

TO ORDER BLUEPRINTS USE THE FORM ON PAGE 15 OR CALL TOLL-FREE 1-877-671-6036
View thousands more home plans online at www.familyhandyman.com/homeplans

265

Fully Columned Front Entrance
Plan #711-023D-0012

2,365 total square feet of living area

Price Code D

Special features

- 9' ceilings throughout home
- Expansive central living room complemented by corner fireplace
- Breakfast bay overlooks rear porch
- Master bedroom features bath with double walk-in closets and vanities, separate tub and shower and handy linen closet
- Peninsula keeps kitchen private
- 4 bedrooms, 2 baths, 2-car carport
- Slab foundation

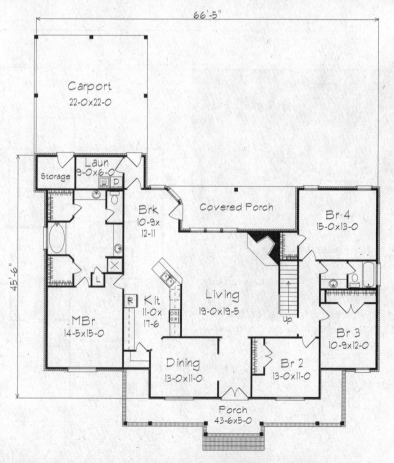

TO ORDER BLUEPRINTS USE THE FORM ON PAGE 15 OR CALL TOLL-FREE 1-877-671-6036
View thousands more home plans online at www.familyhandyman.com/homeplans

Handyman

Double Wrap-Around Porch   Plan #711-024D-0033

3,366 total square feet of living area   **Price Code G**

Special features

- Cozy den connects to bayed breakfast area creating the feel of a hearth room
- Spacious master bedroom has access onto its own covered porch and includes a luxurious bath with whirlpool tub in a sunny bay window
- Living area accesses both a front and rear covered porch for added outdoor living area
- 4 bedrooms, 3 baths, 2-car detached garage
- Crawl space foundation

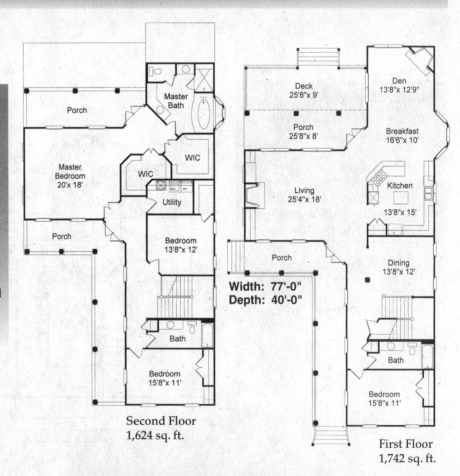

Porch

Master Bath

Master Bedroom
20'x 18'

WIC

WIC

Utility

Porch

Porch

Bedroom
13'8"x 12'

Bath

Bedroom
15'8"x 11'

Second Floor
1,624 sq. ft.

Deck
25'8"x 9'

Porch
25'8"x 8'

Den
13'8"x 12'9'

Breakfast
16'6"x 10'

Living
25'4"x 18'

Kitchen
13'8"x 15'

Porch

Width: 77'-0"
Depth: 40'-0"

Dining
13'8"x 12'

Bath

Bedroom
15'8"x 11'

First Floor
1,742 sq. ft.

TO ORDER BLUEPRINTS USE THE FORM ON PAGE 15 OR CALL TOLL-FREE 1-877-671-6036
View thousands more home plans online at www.familyhandyman.com/homeplans

267

Arched Windows Decorate Exterior   Plan #711-026D-0100

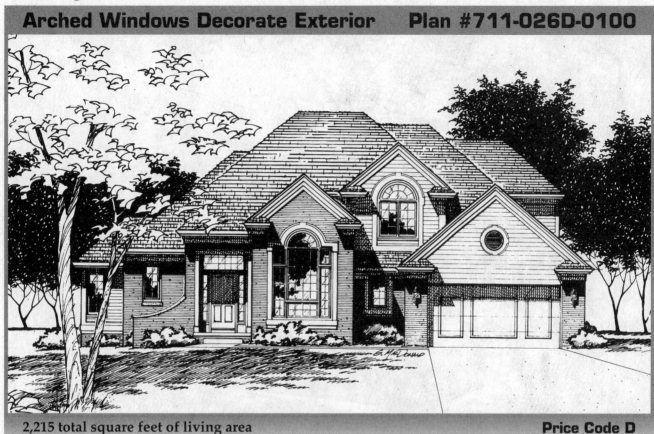

2,215 total square feet of living area   **Price Code D**

Special features

- Breakfast area features snack bar, bookshelves, curio cabinet and access to the outdoors
- The dining room is an elegant entertaining space with a 13' ceiling and transom window
- The master bedroom is a brilliant escape with a double-door entry, 9' ceiling, massive walk-in closet and whirlpool tub
- 4 bedrooms, 2 1/2 baths, 3-car garage
- Basement foundation

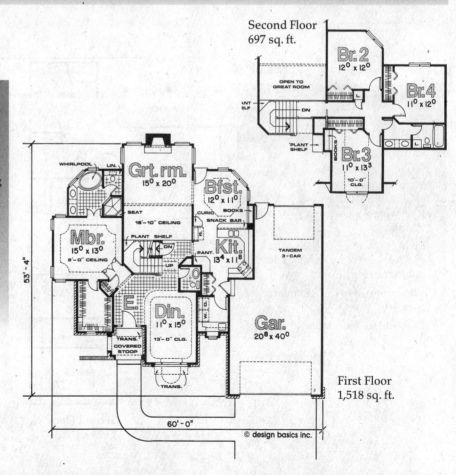

Second Floor
697 sq. ft.

First Floor
1,518 sq. ft.

© design basics inc.

268

TO ORDER BLUEPRINTS USE THE FORM ON PAGE 15 OR CALL TOLL-FREE 1-877-671-6036
View thousands more home plans online at www.familyhandyman.com/homeplans

Ranch With Traditional Feel

Plan #711-056D-0007

© 2003, Garrell Associates, Inc.

1,985 total square feet of living area

Price Code G

Special features

- 9' ceilings throughout home
- Master suite has direct access into sunroom
- Sunny breakfast room features bay window
- Bonus room on the second floor has an additional 191 square feet of living area
- 3 bedrooms, 3 baths, 2-car side entry garage
- Slab foundation

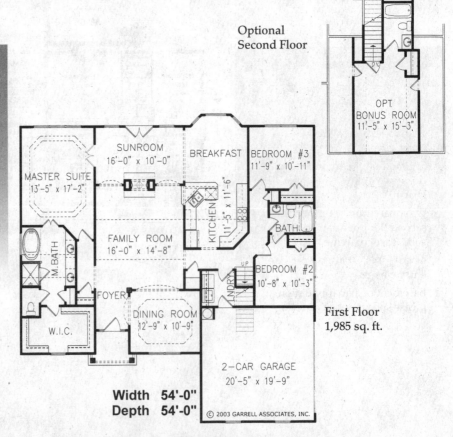

Optional Second Floor

OPT. BONUS ROOM
11'-5" x 15'-3"

SUNROOM
16'-0" x 10'-0"

BREAKFAST

BEDROOM #3
11'-9" x 10'-11"

MASTER SUITE
13'-5" x 17'-2"

KITCHEN
11'-5" x 11'-6"

BATH

FAMILY ROOM
16'-0" x 14'-8"

M. BATH

BEDROOM #2
10'-8" x 10'-3"

W.I.C.

FOYER

LNDRY

DINING ROOM
12'-9" x 10'-9"

UP

First Floor
1,985 sq. ft.

2-CAR GARAGE
20'-5" x 19'-9"

Width 54'-0"
Depth 54'-0"

© 2003 GARRELL ASSOCIATES, INC.

TO ORDER BLUEPRINTS USE THE FORM ON PAGE 15 OR CALL TOLL-FREE 1-877-671-6036
View thousands more home plans online at www.familyhandyman.com/homeplans

269

Impressive Gallery

Plan #711-036D-0059

2,674 total square feet of living area

Price Code E

Special features

- First floor master bedroom has convenient location
- Kitchen and breakfast area have island and access to covered front porch
- Second floor bedrooms have dormer window seats for added charm
- Optional future rooms on the second floor have an additional 520 square feet of living area
- 4 bedrooms, 3 baths, 3-car side entry garage
- Basement or slab foundation, please specify when ordering

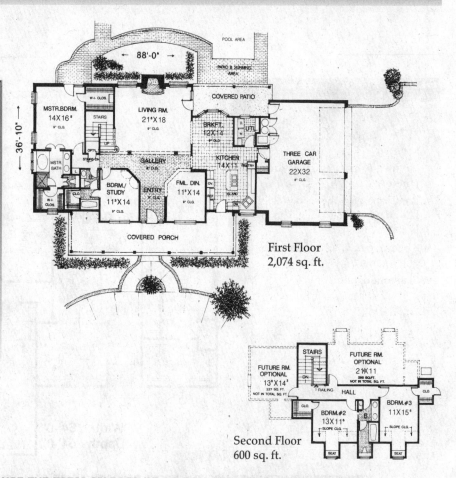

First Floor
2,074 sq. ft.

Second Floor
600 sq. ft.

TO ORDER BLUEPRINTS USE THE FORM ON PAGE 15 OR CALL TOLL-FREE 1-877-671-6036
View thousands more home plans online at www.familyhandyman.com/homeplans

2,050 total square feet of living area

Price Code C

Special features

- Angled dining area has lots of windows and opens into family room and kitchen
- All bedrooms located on second floor for privacy from living areas
- Master bedroom has private bath and a walk-in closet
- 4 bedrooms, 2 1/2 baths, 2-car garage
- Basement foundation

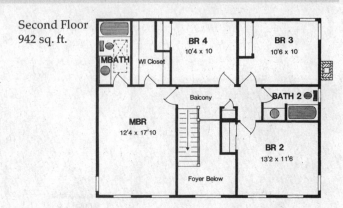

Second Floor
942 sq. ft.

BR 4
10'4 x 10

BR 3
10'6 x 10

MBATH

WI Closet

BATH 2

Balcony

MBR
12'4 x 17'10

BR 2
13'2 x 11'6

Foyer Below

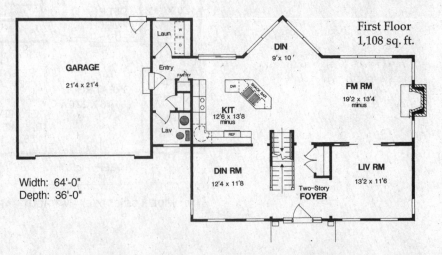

First Floor
1,108 sq. ft.

GARAGE
21'4 x 21'4

Laun

Entry

DIN
9' x 10'

PANTRY

KIT
12'6 x 13'8
minus

DW

SNACK BAR

FM RM
19'2 x 13'4
minus

Lav

REF

DIN RM
12'4 x 11'8

Two-Story
FOYER

LIV RM
13'2 x 11'6

Width: 64'-0"
Depth: 36'-0"

TO ORDER BLUEPRINTS USE THE FORM ON PAGE 15 OR CALL TOLL-FREE 1-877-671-6036
View thousands more home plans online at www.familyhandyman.com/homeplans

271

Extra Large Porches

Plan #711-028D-0003

1,716 total square feet of living area

Price Code B

Special features

- Great room boasts a fireplace and access to the kitchen/breakfast area through a large arched opening
- Master bedroom includes a huge walk-in closet and French doors that lead onto an L-shaped porch
- Bedrooms #2 and #3 share a bath and linen closet
- 3 bedrooms, 2 baths, 2-car detached garage
- Crawl space or slab foundation, please specify when ordering

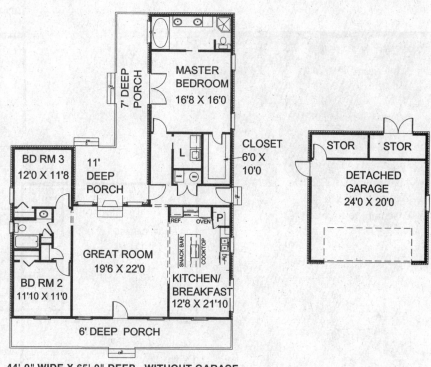

7' DEEP PORCH

MASTER BEDROOM
16'8 X 16'0

CLOSET
6'0 X 10'0

BD RM 3
12'0 X 11'8

11' DEEP PORCH

L

REF. OVEN P

BD RM 2
11'10 X 11'0

GREAT ROOM
19'6 X 22'0

SNACK BAR

COOKTOP

KITCHEN/
BREAKFAST
12'8 X 21'10

6' DEEP PORCH

STOR STOR

DETACHED GARAGE
24'0 X 20'0

44'-0" WIDE X 65'-0" DEEP - WITHOUT GARAGE

The Family Handyman

1,997 total square feet of living area   **Price Code C**

Special features

- Screened porch leads to a rear terrace with access to the breakfast room
- Living and dining rooms combine adding spaciousness to the floor plan
- Other welcome amenities include boxed windows in breakfast and dining rooms, a fireplace in living room and a pass-through snack bar in the kitchen
- 3 bedrooms, 2 1/2 baths
- Basement foundation

Second Floor
886 sq. ft.

ROOF   ROOF

WALL BELOW

RECESSED ROOF

UPPER BREAKFAST RM

BEDROOM
11^{10} x 11^4

BEDROOM
11^4 x 11^4

WALK-IN CLOSET

LINEN   CL

BATH

WHIRLPOOL

DN   RAILING

OPEN BELOW

BATH

DRESS. RM

UPPER FOYER

MASTER BEDROOM
12^4 x 16^0

WALK-IN CLOSET

RECESSED ROOF

ROOF   ROOF

First Floor
1,111 sq. ft.

32'8"

TERRACE

UP   UP

BREAKFAST RM.
16^8 x 10^6

SCREENED PORCH
11^{10} x 11^2

SNACK BAR

RANGE

DESK

BC

DINING RM
12^0 x 12^8

FLOWER BOX

KITCHEN
16^8 x 11^2

DW

REF'G

PANTRY

PDR RM

50'0"

DN   DN

OPEN ABOVE

UP

FOYER

CURIO

CURIO

LIVING RM
18^4 x 14^0

VERANDA

RAILING   RAILING

UP

Rear View

TO ORDER BLUEPRINTS USE THE FORM ON PAGE 15 OR CALL TOLL-FREE 1-877-671-6036
View thousands more home plans online at www.familyhandyman.com/homeplans

273

Impressive Foyer

Plan #711-016D-0020

1,994 total square feet of living area

Price Code E

Special features

- Office/parlor/bedroom #4 has a double-door entry and is a very versatile space
- Sliding glass doors and many windows create a cheerful great room and breakfast room
- Double walk-in closets and vanity grace the master bath
- 3 bedrooms, 2 baths, optional 2-car side entry garage
- Basement, crawl space or slab foundation, please specify when ordering

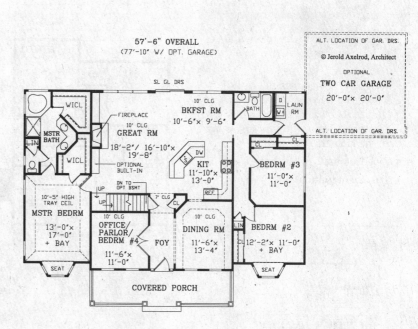

Two-Story Sunken Family Room   Plan #711-053D-0054

3,315 total square feet of living area

Price Code F

Special features

- Island kitchen, breakfast room and two-story sunken family room combine for convenient family dining or entertaining
- Two-story foyer opens into bayed formal dining and living rooms
- Master bedroom features sitting area, large walk-in closet and deluxe bath
- 4 bedrooms, 3 1/2 baths, 2-car side entry garage
- Basement foundation

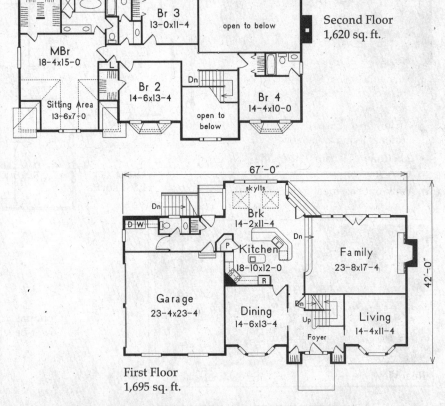

MBr
18-4x15-0

Sitting Area
13-6x7-0

Br 3
13-0x11-4

open to below

Br 2
14-6x13-4

Dn

Br 4
14-4x10-0

open to below

Second Floor
1,620 sq. ft.

67'-0"

Dn

skylts

Brk
14-2x11-4

Dn

Family
23-8x17-4

Kitchen
18-10x12-0

R

Garage
23-4x23-4

Dining
14-6x13-4

Dn

Up

Living
14-4x11-4

Foyer

42'-0"

First Floor
1,695 sq. ft.

TO ORDER BLUEPRINTS USE THE FORM ON PAGE 15 OR CALL TOLL-FREE 1-877-671-6036
View thousands more home plans online at www.familyhandyman.com/homeplans

275

1,384 total square feet of living area

Price Code B

Special features

- Wrap-around country porch for peaceful evenings
- Vaulted great room enjoys a large bay window, stone fireplace, pass-through kitchen and awesome rear views through atrium window wall
- Master bedroom features double entry doors, walk-in closet and a fabulous bath
- Atrium opens to 611 square feet of optional living area below
- 2 bedrooms, 2 baths, 1-car side entry garage
- Walk-out basement foundation

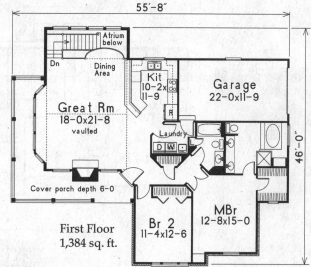

55'-8"

Dn

Atrium below

Dining Area

Kit
10-2x
11-9

Garage
22-0x11-9

Great Rm
18-0x21-8
vaulted

Laundry

D W

R

46'-0"

Cover porch depth 6-0

MBr
12-8x15-0

Br 2
11-4x12-6

First Floor
1,384 sq. ft.

Rear View

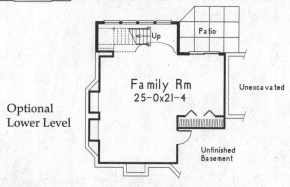

Up

Patio

Family Rm
25-0x21-4

Unexcavated

Optional
Lower Level

Unfinished
Basement

TO ORDER BLUEPRINTS USE THE FORM ON PAGE 15 OR CALL TOLL-FREE 1-877-671-6036
View thousands more home plans online at www.familyhandyman.com/homeplans

Bookshelves Flank Fireplace   Plan #711-043D-0012

2,407 total square feet of living area   Price Code D

Special features

- Enjoyable covered porch
- Two-story entry with balcony above
- Vaulted living room
- Display niches and arch accents throughout design add interest
- Coffered ceiling in dining room
- Useful second floor study alcove
- 4 bedrooms, 2 1/2 baths, 3-car garage
- Crawl space foundation

Second Floor
1,107 sq. ft.

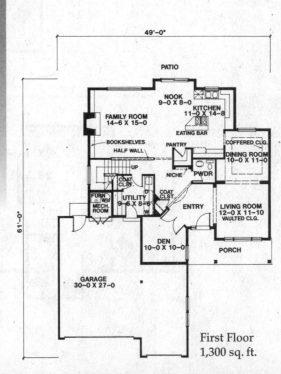

First Floor
1,300 sq. ft.

TO ORDER BLUEPRINTS USE THE FORM ON PAGE 15 OR CALL TOLL-FREE 1-877-671-6036
View thousands more home plans online at www.familyhandyman.com/homeplans

277

Perfect For Family Living

Plan #711-032D-0047

2,129 total square feet of living area

Price Code C

Special features

- Energy efficient home with 2" x 6" exterior walls
- Home office has a double-door entry and is secluded from other living areas
- Corner fireplace in living area is a nice focal point
- Bonus room above the garage has an additional 407 square feet of living area
- 3 bedrooms, 2 1/2 baths, 2-car side entry garage
- Basement foundation

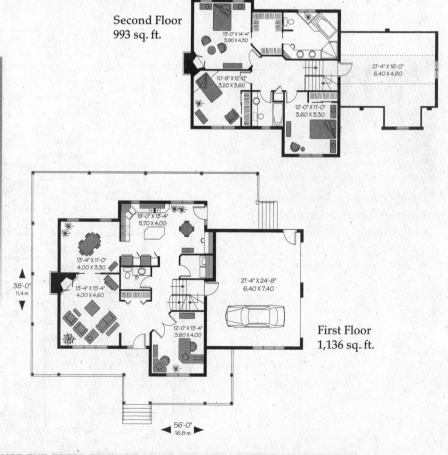

Second Floor 993 sq. ft.

13'-0" X 14'-4"
3,90 X 4,30

10'-8" X 12'-0"
3,20 X 3,60

12'-0" X 11'-0"
3,60 X 3,30

21'-4" X 16'-0"
6,40 X 4,80

First Floor 1,136 sq. ft.

19'-0" X 13'-4"
5,70 X 4,00

13'-4" X 11'-0"
4,00 X 3,30

13'-4" X 15'-4"
4,00 X 4,60

12'-0" X 13'-4"
3,60 X 4,00

21'-4" X 24'-8"
6,40 X 7,40

38'-0"
11,4 m

56'-0"
16,8 m

Charming Dormers And Porch   Plan #711-069D-0016

1,925 total square feet of living area

Price Code C

Special features

- Angled snack bar in kitchen provides extra dining space overlooking into the great room and dining area
- Wonderful master bath includes sunny whirlpool tub, corner oversized shower and a makeup counter
- Dining area has sliding glass doors leading to the outdoors
- 3 bedrooms, 2 1/2 baths, 2-car garage
- Slab or crawl space foundation, please specify when ordering

Second Floor
596 sq. ft.

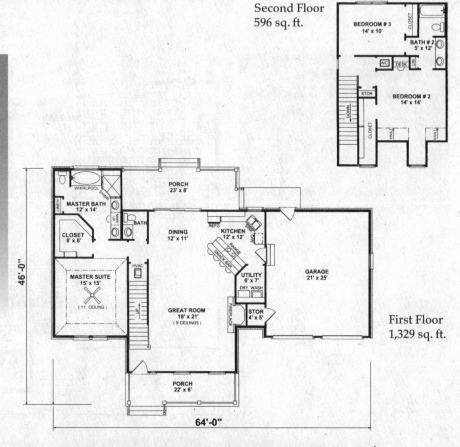

First Floor
1,329 sq. ft.

TO ORDER BLUEPRINTS USE THE FORM ON PAGE 15 OR CALL TOLL-FREE 1-877-671-6036
View thousands more home plans online at www.familyhandyman.com/homeplans

279

Narrow Lot Charmer

Plan #711-051D-0052

1,600 total square feet of living area

Price Code B

Special features

- Optional den with cathedral ceiling
- Kitchen has a large island for additional counterspace
- Master bedroom has a large walk-in closet and a full bath with double vanity
- 3 bedrooms, 2 baths, 2-car garage
- Basement foundation

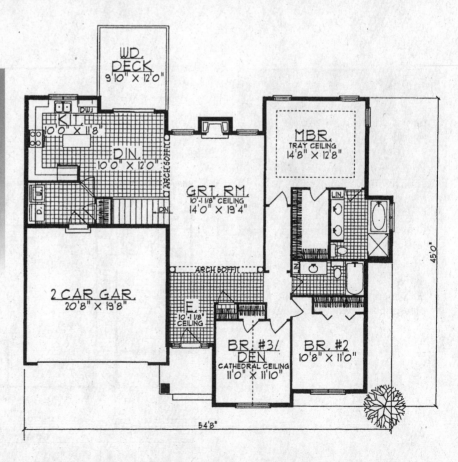

280

TO ORDER BLUEPRINTS USE THE FORM ON PAGE 15 OR CALL TOLL-FREE 1-877-671-6036
View thousands more home plans online at www.familyhandyman.com/HOMEPLANS

Handyman

2,726 total square feet of living area

Price Code E

Special features

- Angled sink area with snack bar defines the kitchen
- First floor guest bedroom has its own bath
- Great room features a fireplace flanked by bookshelves and has French doors leading to the covered rear porch
- 4 bedrooms, 3 1/2 baths, 2-car side entry garage
- Basement, crawl space or slab foundation, please specify when ordering

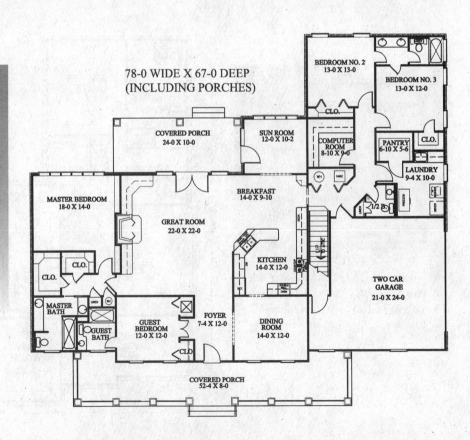

78-0 WIDE X 67-0 DEEP
(INCLUDING PORCHES)

BEDROOM NO. 2
13-0 X 13-0

BEDROOM NO. 3
13-0 X 12-0

COVERED PORCH
24-0 X 10-0

SUN ROOM
12-0 X 10-2

COMPUTER ROOM
8-10 X 9-0

PANTRY
6-10 X 5-6

CLO.

LAUNDRY
9-4 X 10-0

MASTER BEDROOM
18-0 X 14-0

BREAKFAST
14-0 X 9-10

GREAT ROOM
22-0 X 22-0

CLO.

CLO.

KITCHEN
14-0 X 12-0

TWO CAR GARAGE
21-0 X 24-0

MASTER BATH

GUEST BATH

GUEST BEDROOM
12-0 X 12-0

FOYER
7-4 X 12-0

DINING ROOM
14-0 X 12-0

CLO.

COVERED PORCH
52-4 X 8-0

TO ORDER BLUEPRINTS USE THE FORM ON PAGE 15 OR CALL TOLL-FREE 1-877-671-6036
View thousands more home plans online at www.familyhandyman.com/homeplans

281

Elegant European Styling   Plan #711-060D-0010

2,600 total square feet of living area   **Price Code E**

Special features

- Formal entry has large openings to dining and great rooms both with coffered ceilings
- Great room has corner fireplace and atrium doors leading to rear covered porch
- Morning room with rear view and an angled eating bar is sunny and bright
- Exercise room could easily serve as an office or computer room
- 4 bedrooms, 2 1/2 baths, 3-car side entry garage
- Slab or crawl space foundation, please specify when ordering

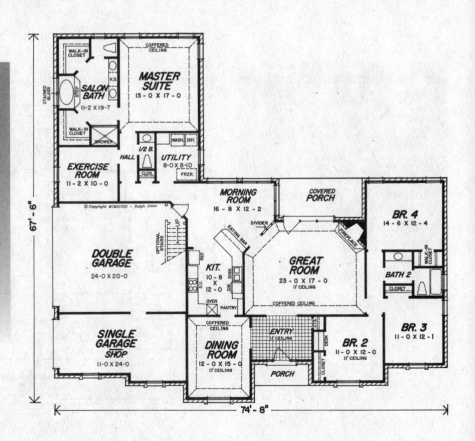

282

TO ORDER BLUEPRINTS USE THE FORM ON PAGE 15 OR CALL TOLL-FREE 1-877-671-6036
View thousands more home plans online at www.familyhandyman.com/homeplans

Inviting Double French Doors   Plan #711-040D-0022

2,327 total square feet of living area

Price Code D

Special features

- 9' ceilings throughout
- Covered porches on both floors create outdoor living space
- Secondary bedrooms share full bath
- L-shaped kitchen features island cooktop and convenient laundry room
- 3 bedrooms, 2 1/2 baths, 2-car side entry garage
- Basement foundation

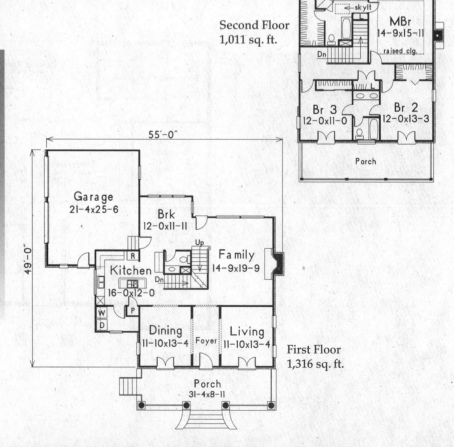

Second Floor
1,011 sq. ft.

First Floor
1,316 sq. ft.

TO ORDER BLUEPRINTS USE THE FORM ON PAGE 15 OR CALL TOLL-FREE 1-877-671-6036
View thousands more home plans online at www.familyhandyman.com/homeplans

283

RAISED FOYER And LIVING ROOM   Plan #711-047D-0038

2,221 total square feet of living area

Price Code D

Special features

- Master bedroom is open, airy and well-located
- Family room has 12' wall of sliding glass doors bringing the outdoors in
- Separate secondary bedrooms for privacy
- 4 bedrooms, 3 baths, 2-car garage
- Slab foundation

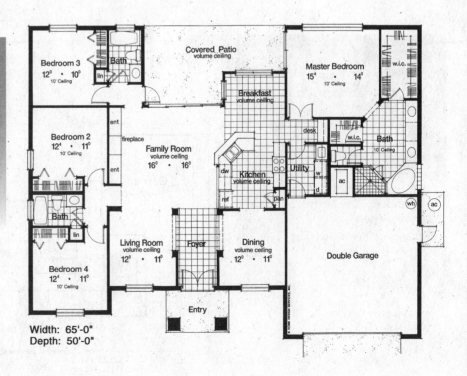

Width: 65'-0"
Depth: 50'-0"

1,945 total square feet of living area

Price Code C

Special features

- Master suite separated from other bedrooms for privacy
- Vaulted breakfast room is directly off great room
- Kitchen includes a built-in desk area
- Elegant dining room has an arched window
- 4 bedrooms, 2 baths, 2-car side entry garage
- Walk-out basement, crawl space or slab foundation, please specify when ordering

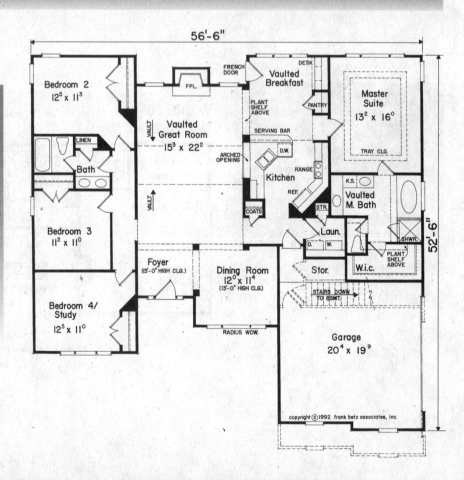

TO ORDER BLUEPRINTS USE THE FORM ON PAGE 15 OR CALL TOLL-FREE 1-877-671-6036
View thousands more home plans online at www.familyhandyman.com/homeplans

285

Vaults Add Spaciousness

Plan #711-062D-0050

1,408 total square feet of living area

Price Code A

Special features

- A bright country kitchen boasts an abundance of counterspace and cupboards
- The front entry is sheltered by a broad verandah
- A spa tub is brightened by a box bay window in the master bath
- 3 bedrooms, 2 baths, 2-car side entry garage
- Basement or crawl space foundation, please specify when ordering

Width: 70'-0"
Depth: 28'-0"

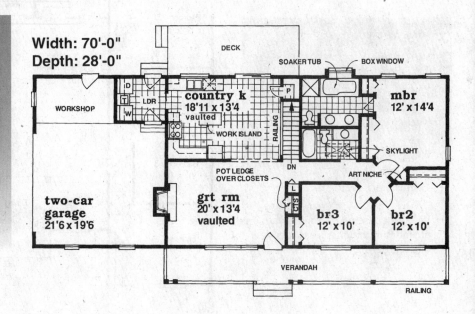

TO ORDER BLUEPRINTS USE THE FORM ON PAGE 15 OR CALL TOLL-FREE 1-877-671-6036
View thousands more home plans online at www.familyhandyman.com/homeplans

The Family Handyman

Impressive Breakfast Room

Plan #711-070D-0013

2,525 total square feet of living area

Price Code D

Special features

- A sunny great room has an entire wall of windows creating an open, airy feel
- Unique spa tub is the focal point of the private master bath
- A spacious kitchen is surely a gathering place
- Bonus room on the second floor has an additional 296 square feet of living area
- 3 bedrooms, 2 1/2 baths, 2-car side entry garage
- Basement foundation

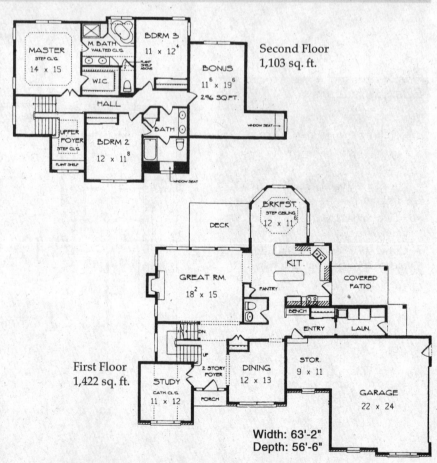

Second Floor
1,103 sq. ft.

First Floor
1,422 sq. ft.

Width: 63'-2"
Depth: 56'-6"

TO ORDER BLUEPRINTS USE THE FORM ON PAGE 15 OR CALL TOLL-FREE 1-877-671-6036
View thousands more home plans online at www.familyhandyman.com/homeplans

287

2,061 total square feet of living area   **Price Code C**

Special features

- Charming stone facade entry
- Centrally located great room
- Private study in the front of the home is ideal as a home office
- Varied ceiling heights throughout this home
- 3 bedrooms, 2 1/2 baths, 2-car garage
- Crawl space or slab foundation, please specify when ordering

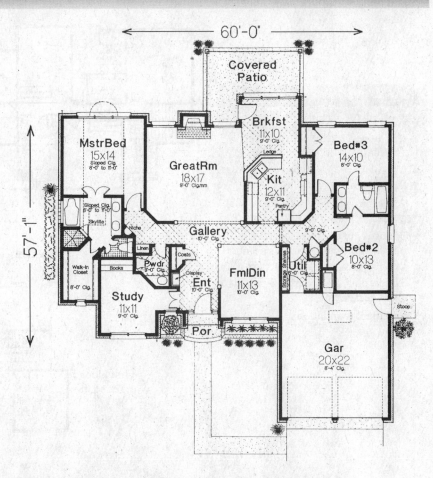

Fireplaces Add Warm Cozy Feeling   Plan #711-037D-0014

2,932 total square feet of living area   **Price Code F**

Special features

- 9' ceilings throughout home
- Rear stairs create convenient access to second floor from living area
- Spacious kitchen has pass-through to the family room, a convenient island and pantry
- Cozy built-in table in breakfast area
- Secluded master bedroom has a luxurious bath and patio access
- 4 bedrooms, 3 1/2 baths, 2-car side entry garage
- Slab foundation

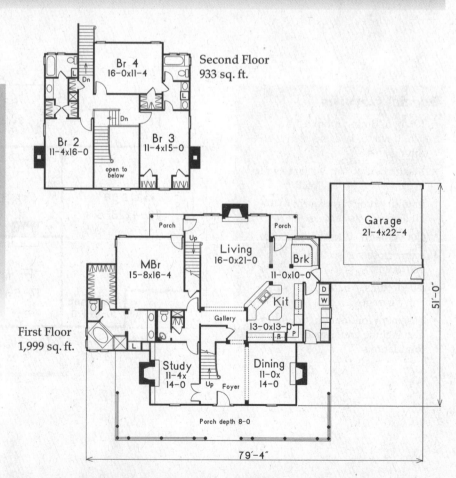

Second Floor
933 sq. ft.

Br 4
16-0x11-4

Br 2
11-4x16-0

Br 3
11-4x15-0

open to below

First Floor
1,999 sq. ft.

Garage
21-4x22-4

Porch

Porch

MBr
15-8x16-4

Living
16-0x21-0

Brk
11-0x10-0

Kit
13-0x13-0

Gallery

Up

Up

Study
11-4x 14-0

Foyer

Dining
11-0x 14-0

51'-0"

Porch depth 8-0

79'-4"

TO ORDER BLUEPRINTS USE THE FORM ON PAGE 15 OR CALL TOLL-FREE 1-877-671-6036
View thousands more home plans online at www.familyhandyman.com/homeplans

289

LAYOUT For Comfortable Living   Plan #711-001D-0024

1,360 total square feet of living area   **Price Code A**

Special features

- Kitchen/dining room features island workspace and plenty of dining area
- Master bedroom has a large walk-in closet and private bath
- Laundry room is adjacent to the kitchen for easy access
- Convenient workshop in garage
- Large closets in secondary bedrooms
- 3 bedrooms, 2 baths, 2-car side entry garage
- Basement foundation, drawings also include crawl space and slab foundations

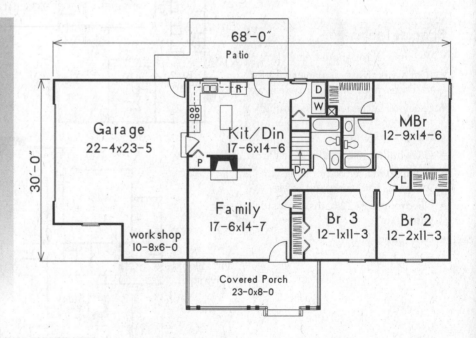

68'-0"

Patio

30'-0"

Garage
22-4x23-5

Kit/Din
17-6x14-6

MBr
12-9x14-6

P

Family
17-6x14-7

Br 3
12-1x11-3

Br 2
12-2x11-3

workshop
10-8x6-0

Dn

L

Covered Porch
23-0x8-0

Spacious Country Home

Plan #711-028D-0011

2,123 total square feet of living area

Price Code C

Special features

- L-shaped porch extends the entire length of this home creating lots of extra space for outdoor living
- Master bedroom is secluded for privacy and has two closets, double vanity in bath and a double-door entry onto covered porch
- Efficiently designed kitchen
- 3 bedrooms, 2 1/2 baths
- Crawl space foundation

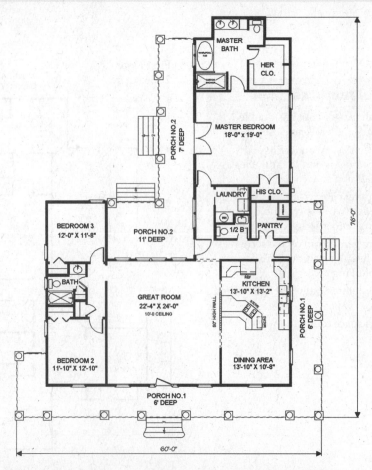

TO ORDER BLUEPRINTS USE THE FORM ON PAGE 15 OR CALL TOLL-FREE 1-877-671-6036
View thousands more home plans online at www.familyhandyman.com/homeplans

291

Two-Story Has A Farmhouse Feel

Plan #711-024D-0032

3,444 total square feet of living area

Price Code G

Special features

- Lavish master bath has double vanities and walk-in closets
- Kitchen has a wonderful food preparation island that doubles as extra dining space
- Computer/library area on second floor has two sets of double-doors leading onto a second floor balcony
- Future gameroom on the second floor has an additional 318 square feet of living area
- 5 bedrooms, 4 baths, 2-car detached garage
- Crawl space foundation

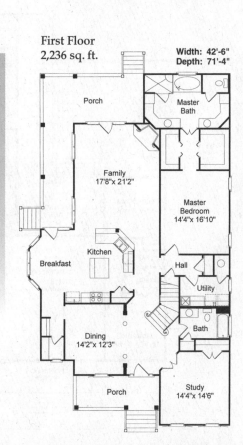

First Floor
2,236 sq. ft.

Width: 42'-6"
Depth: 71'-4"

Porch

Master Bath

Family
17'8"x 21'2"

Master Bedroom
14'4"x 16'10"

Kitchen

Breakfast

Hall

Utility

Bath

Dining
14'2"x 12'3"

Porch

Study
14'4"x 14'6"

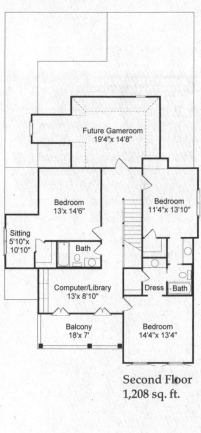

Future Gameroom
19'4"x 14'8"

Bedroom
13'x 14'6"

Bedroom
11'4"x 13'10"

Sitting
5'10"x
10'10"

Bath

Computer/Library
13'x 8'10"

Dress

Bath

Balcony
18'x 7'

Bedroom
14'4"x 13'4"

Second Floor
1,208 sq. ft.

292

TO ORDER BLUEPRINTS USE THE FORM ON PAGE 15 OR CALL TOLL-FREE 1-877-671-6036
View thousands more home plans online at www.familyhandyman.com/homeplans

Atrium's Dramatic Ambiance

Plan #711-007D-0010

1,721 total square feet of living area

Price Code C

Special features

- Roof dormers add great curb appeal
- Vaulted dining and great rooms immersed in light from atrium window wall
- Breakfast room opens onto covered porch
- Functionally designed kitchen
- 3 bedrooms, 2 baths, 3-car garage
- Walk-out basement foundation, drawings also include crawl space and slab foundations
- 1,604 square feet on the first floor and 117 square feet on the lower level

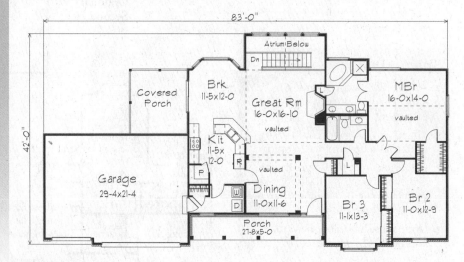

Rear View

TO ORDER BLUEPRINTS USE THE FORM ON PAGE 15 OR CALL TOLL-FREE 1-877-671-6036
View thousands more home plans online at www.familyhandyman.com/homeplans

293

Beautiful Master Bedroom

Plan #711-016D-0005

2,347 total square feet of living area

Price Code E

Special features

- Angled floor plan provides enhanced flexibility in site placement
- The fourth bedroom could easily double as a home office or study
- A spacious rear facing great room is the focal point of the living area with high stepped ceiling, fireplace and space for built-ins
- Optional second floor has an additional 823 square feet of living area
- 4 bedrooms, 2 1/2 baths, 2-car side entry garage
- Basement, crawl space or slab foundation, please specify when ordering

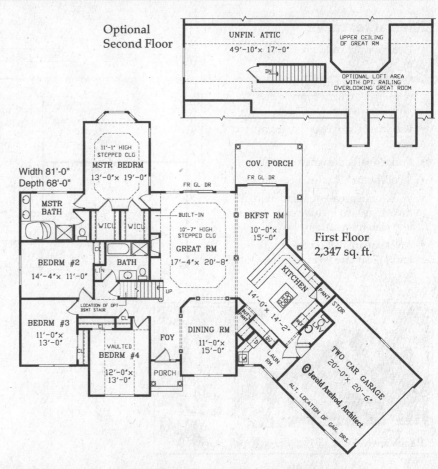

Optional Second Floor

UNFIN. ATTIC
49'-10" x 17'-0"

UPPER CEILING OF GREAT RM

DN

OPTIONAL LOFT AREA WITH OPT. RAILING OVERLOOKING GREAT ROOM

Width 81'-0"
Depth 68'-0"

11'-1" HIGH STEPPED CLG
MSTR BEDRM
13'-0" x 19'-0"

COV. PORCH

FR GL DR

FR GL DR

MSTR BATH

WICL WICL

BUILT-IN
10'-7" HIGH STEPPED CLG
GREAT RM
17'-4" x 20'-8"

BKFST RM
10'-0" x 15'-0"

First Floor
2,347 sq. ft.

BEDRM #2
14'-4" x 11'-0"

BATH

KITCHEN
14'-0" x 14'-2"

PANT

STOR

BEDRM #3
11'-0" x 13'-0"

LOCATION OF OPT. BSMT STAIR

CL

UP

LAV

LAUN RM

DINING RM
11'-0" x 15'-0"

TWO CAR GARAGE
20'-0" x 20'-6"

VAULTED
BEDRM #4
12'-0" x 13'-0"

FOY

PORCH

© Jerold Axelrod, Architect

ALT. LOCATION OF GAR. DRS.

Vaulted Ceiling Adds Spaciousness   Plan #711-033D-0003

2,838 total square feet of living area   **Price Code F**

Special features

- 10' ceilings throughout first floor
- Dining room enhanced with large corner bay windows
- Master bath boasts double sink and an oversized tub
- Kitchen features an island and double sink which overlooks dinette and family room
- 4 bedrooms, 2 1/2 baths, 3-car garage
- Basement foundation

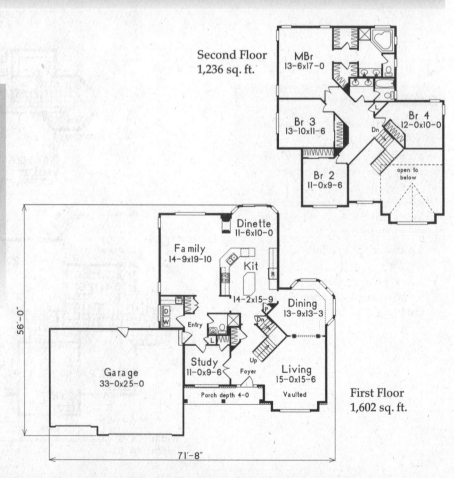

Second Floor
1,236 sq. ft.

MBr
13-6x17-0

Br 3
13-10x11-6

Br 4
12-0x10-0

Dn

open to below

Br 2
11-0x9-6

Dinette
11-6x10-0

Family
14-9x19-10

Kit
14-2x15-9

Dining
13-9x13-3

R

P

Dn

Entry

D W

L

Study
11-0x9-6

Up

Foyer

Living
15-0x15-6

Garage
33-0x25-0

Porch depth 4-0

Vaulted

56'-0"

71'-8"

First Floor
1,602 sq. ft.

TO ORDER BLUEPRINTS USE THE FORM ON PAGE 15 OR CALL TOLL-FREE 1-877-671-6036
View thousands more home plans online at www.familyhandyman.com/homeplans

295

RICH WITH VICTORIAN DETAILS

Plan #711-062D-0046

2,632 total square feet of living area

Price Code E

Special features

- Energy efficient home with 2" x 6" exterior walls
- Master bedroom has a cheerful octagon-shaped sitting area
- Arched entrances create a distinctive living room with a lovely tray ceiling and help define the dining room
- 4 bedrooms, 2 1/2 baths, 2-car garage
- Basement or crawl space foundation, please specify when ordering

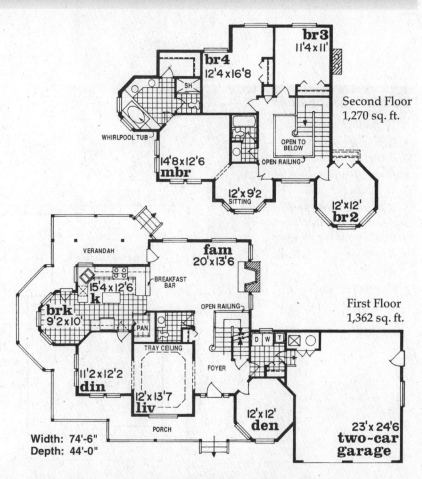

Second Floor 1,270 sq. ft.

First Floor 1,362 sq. ft.

Width: 74'-6"
Depth: 44'-0"

TO ORDER BLUEPRINTS USE THE FORM ON PAGE 15 OR CALL TOLL-FREE 1-877-671-6036
View thousands more home plans online at www.familyhandyman.com/homeplans

3,060 total square feet of living area   **Price Code E**

Special features

- Double-doors in hearth room lead into a private study with built-in shelves
- Kitchen includes a large wrap-around style eating counter capable of serving five
- Breakfast area has access onto a large covered grilling porch
- 3 bedrooms, 2 1/2 baths, 2-car side entry garage
- Crawl space or slab foundation, please specify when ordering

Second Floor
856 sq. ft.

First Floor
2,204 sq. ft.

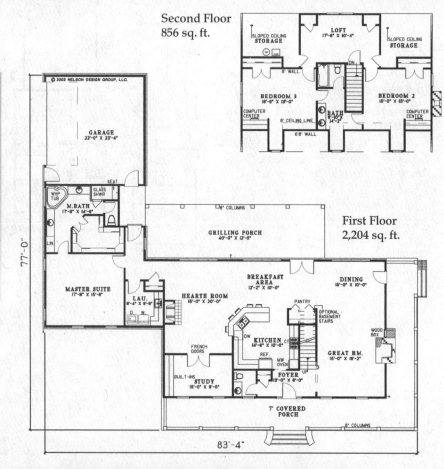

Front Gables Add Curb Appeal Plan #711-011D-0024

2,820 total square feet of living area

Price Code E

Special features

- Curved staircase in central foyer demands attention
- Master suite located on the second floor for privacy has a glorious oversized tub with feature window above
- Butler's pantry connects the kitchen to the formal dining room
- 4 bedrooms, 3 1/2 baths, 2-car garage
- Crawl space foundation

Second Floor
1,437 sq. ft.

First Floor
1,383 sq. ft.

© Alan Mascord Design Associates, Inc.

Wrap-Around Porch Adds Charm   Plan #711-029D-0002

1,619 total square feet of living area

Price Code B

Special features

- Private second floor bedroom and bath
- Kitchen features a snack bar and adjacent dining area
- Master bedroom has a private bath
- Centrally located washer and dryer
- 3 bedrooms, 3 baths
- Basement foundation, drawings also include crawl space and slab foundations

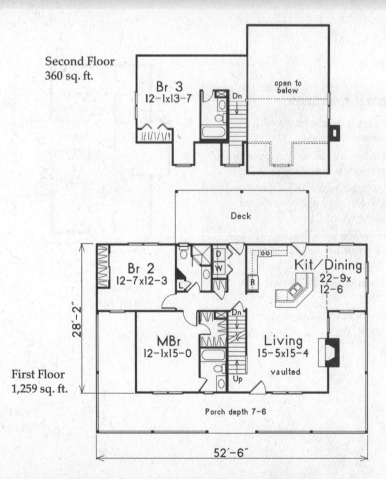

Second Floor
360 sq. ft.

Br 3
12-1x13-7

open to
below

Dn

Deck

Br 2
12-7x12-3

Kit/Dining
22-9x
12-6

28'-2"

MBr
12-1x15-0

Living
15-5x15-4

vaulted

Up

Dn

First Floor
1,259 sq. ft.

Porch depth 7-6

52'-6"

TO ORDER BLUEPRINTS USE THE FORM ON PAGE 15 OR CALL TOLL-FREE 1-877-671-6036
View thousands more home plans online at www.familyhandyman.com/homeplans

299

Two-Sided Fireplace

Plan #711-032D-0046

1,754 total square feet of living area

Price Code B

Special features

- Energy efficient home with 2" x 6" exterior walls
- Utilities are located conveniently in first floor powder room
- U-shaped island in kitchen has stovetop as well as additional dining space
- Bonus room on the second floor has an additional 421 square feet of living area
- 3 bedrooms, 2 1/2 baths, 2-car garage
- Basement foundation

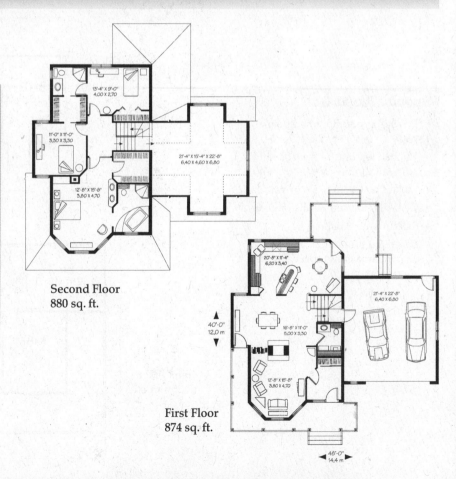

Second Floor
880 sq. ft.

First Floor
874 sq. ft.

Home Has A Contemporary Feel   Plan #711-047D-0052

3,098 total square feet of living area   **Price Code F**

Special features

- Master bedroom is ultra luxurious with private bath, enormous walk-in closet and sitting area leading to the lanai
- Vaulted family room has lots of windows and a corner fireplace
- Secluded study has double closets and built-ins
- Optional second floor has an additional 849 square feet of living area
- Framing - only concrete block available
- 4 bedrooms, 4 baths, 3-car side entry garage
- Slab foundation

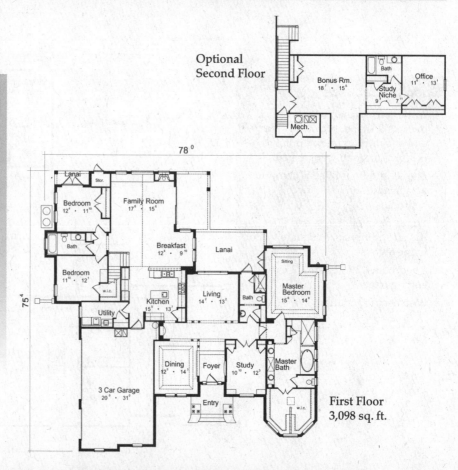

Optional Second Floor

First Floor
3,098 sq. ft.

TO ORDER BLUEPRINTS USE THE FORM ON PAGE 15 OR CALL TOLL-FREE 1-877-671-6036
View thousands more home plans online at www.familyhandyman.com/homeplans

301

Front Porch Is Inviting

Plan #711-065D-0042

2,362 total square feet of living area

Price Code D

Special features

- A spacious kitchen with an oversized island, breakfast area and delightful screened porch combine for family enjoyment
- The second floor offers a computer area in addition to the two bedrooms
- Bonus room on the second floor has an additional 271 square feet of living area
- 3 bedrooms, 2 1/2 baths, 2-car side entry garage
- Basement foundation

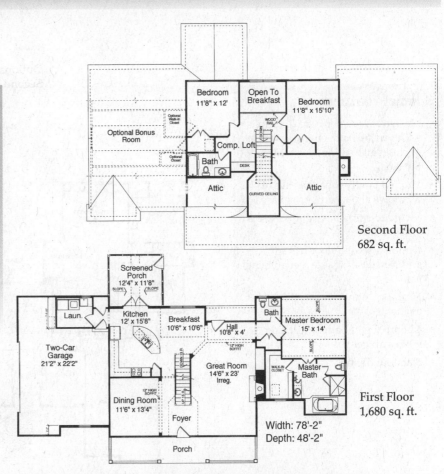

Second Floor
682 sq. ft.

First Floor
1,680 sq. ft.

Width: 78'-2"
Depth: 48'-2"

Well-Organized Living Area

Plan #711-070D-0008

2,083 total square feet of living area

Price Code C

Special features

- A handy server counter located between the kitchen and formal dining room is ideal for entertaining
- Decorative columns grace the entrance into the great room
- A large island in the kitchen aids in food preparation
- 3 bedrooms, 2 1/2 baths, 2-car garage
- Basement foundation

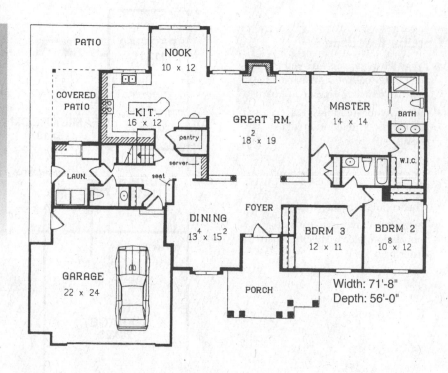

TO ORDER BLUEPRINTS USE THE FORM ON PAGE 15 OR CALL TOLL-FREE 1-877-671-6036
View thousands more home plans online at www.familyhandyman.com/homeplans

303

COVERED REAR PORCH

Plan #711-013D-0010

1,593 total square feet of living area

Price Code C

Special features

- Large sitting area is enjoyed by the master bedroom which also features a walk-in closet and bath
- Centrally located kitchen accesses the family dining and breakast rooms with ease
- Storage/mechanical area is ideal for seasonal storage or hobby supplies
- 3 bedrooms, 2 baths, 2-car garage
- Basement, crawl space or slab foundation, please specify when ordering

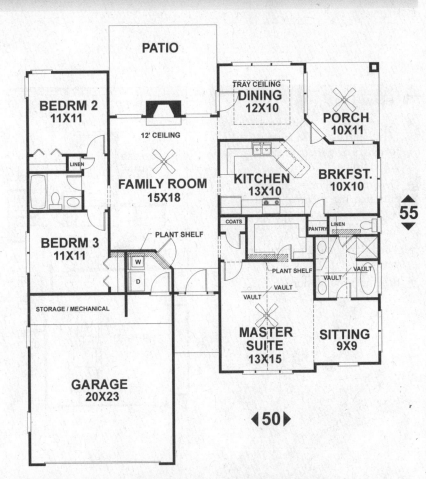

304

TO ORDER BLUEPRINTS USE THE FORM ON PAGE 15 OR CALL TOLL-FREE 1-877-671-6036
View thousands more home plans online at www.familyhandyman.com/homeplans

Home With Much To Offer

Plan #711-055D-0109

2,217 total square feet of living area

Price Code C

Special features

- Great room features a fireplace and is open to the foyer, breakfast and dining rooms
- Laundry room and storage closet are located off the garage
- Secluded master suite includes a bath with a corner whirlpool tub, split vanities, corner shower and a large walk-in closet
- 4 bedrooms, 2 baths, 2-car garage
- Crawl space or slab foundation, please specify when ordering

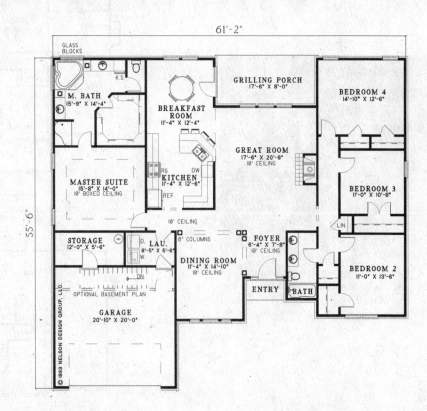

TO ORDER BLUEPRINTS USE THE FORM ON PAGE 15 OR CALL TOLL-FREE 1-877-671-6036
View thousands more home plans online at www.familyhandyman.com/homeplans

305

Handyman

Impressive Front Balcony   Plan #711-001D-0017

2,411 total square feet of living area

Price Code D

Special features

- Elegant entrance features a two-story vaulted foyer
- Large family room enhanced by masonry fireplace and wet bar
- Master bath includes walk-in closet, oversized tub and separate shower
- Second floor study could easily convert to a fourth bedroom
- 3 bedrooms, 2 1/2 baths, 2-car garage
- Basement foundation, drawings also include slab and crawl space foundations

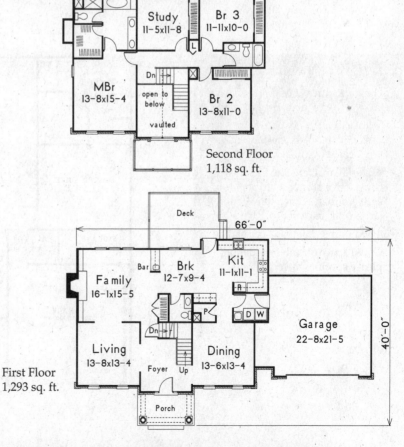

Study 11-5x11-8

Br 3 11-11x10-0

MBr 13-8x15-4

Dn
open to below
vaulted

Br 2 13-8x11-0

Second Floor
1,118 sq. ft.

Deck

66'-0"

Bar

Brk 12-7x9-4

Kit 11-1x11-1

Family 16-1x15-5

R

P

D W

Garage 22-8x21-5

Living 13-8x13-4

Dn

Foyer

Up

Dining 13-6x13-4

40'-0"

First Floor
1,293 sq. ft.

Porch

Outdoor Living Areas

Plan #711-071D-0002

2,770 total square feet of living area

Price Code E

Special features

- Formal living and dining areas combine for optimal entertaining possibilities including access outdoors and a fireplace
- The cheerful family and breakfast rooms connect for added spaciousness
- Enter the master bedroom through double-doors to find a private covered deck, a sitting area and a luxurious bath
- 4 bedrooms, 2 1/2 baths, 3-car side entry garage
- Crawl space foundation

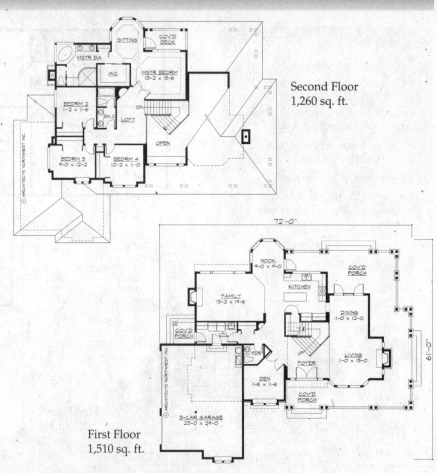

Second Floor
1,260 sq. ft.

First Floor
1,510 sq. ft.

TO ORDER BLUEPRINTS USE THE FORM ON PAGE 15 OR CALL TOLL-FREE 1-877-671-6036
View thousands more home plans online at www.familyhandyman.com/homeplans

307

Lattice Detail And Brickwork   Plan #711-038D-0054

1,560 total square feet of living area   **Price Code B**

Special features

- Two-story master bedroom has sunny dormer above, large walk-in closet and private bath
- Great room has unique two-story ceiling with dormers
- Spacious kitchen has large center island creating an ideal workspace
- 3 bedrooms, 2 1/2 baths
- Basement, crawl space or slab foundation, please specify when ordering

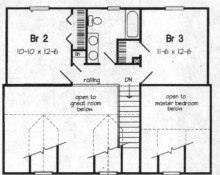

Second Floor
499 sq. ft.

Br 2
10-10 x 12-6

Br 3
11-6 x 12-6

railing

DN

open to great room below

open to master bedroom below

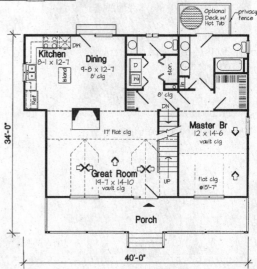

First Floor
1,061 sq. ft.

Optional Deck w/ Hot Tub

privacy fence

Kitchen
8-1 x 12-7

Dining
9-8 x 12-7
8' clg

8' clg

17' flat clg

Master Br
12 x 14-6
vault clg

Great Room
19-7 x 14-10
vault clg

flat clg @15'-7"

UP

Porch

34'-0"

40'-0"

Rear View

A Special Home For Views   Plan #711-007D-0075

1,684 total square feet of living area   **Price Code B**

Special features

- Delightful wrap-around porch anchored by full masonry fireplace
- The vaulted great room includes a large bay window, fireplace, dining balcony and atrium window wall
- Double walk-in closets, large luxury bath and sliding doors to exterior balcony are a few fantastic features of the master bedroom
- Atrium opens to 611 square feet of optional living area on the lower level
- 3 bedrooms, 2 baths, 2-car drive under garage
- Walk-out basement foundation

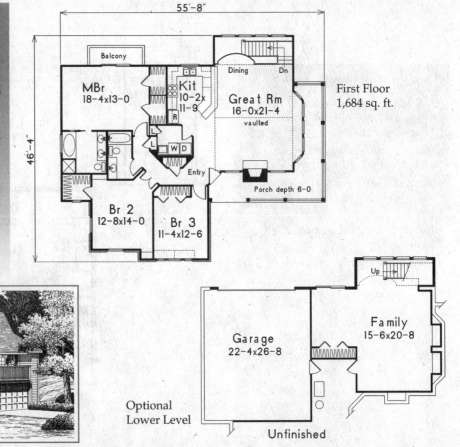

55'-8"

46'-4"

Balcony

MBr
18-4x13-0

Kit
10-2x
11-9

Dining   Dn

Great Rm
16-0x21-4
vaulted

First Floor
1,684 sq. ft.

Entry

Porch depth 6-0

Br 2
12-8x14-0

Br 3
11-4x12-6

Up

Garage
22-4x26-8

Family
15-6x20-8

Optional
Lower Level

Unfinished

Rear View

TO ORDER BLUEPRINTS USE THE FORM ON PAGE 15 OR CALL TOLL-FREE 1-877-671-6036
View thousands more home plans online at www.familyhandyman.com/homeplans

309

Distinctive Stone And Stucco

Plan #711-025D-0010

1,677 total square feet of living area

Price Code B

Special features

- Master suite has a secluded feel with a private and remote location from other bedrooms
- Great room is complete with fireplace and beautiful windows
- Optional second floor has an additional 350 square feet of living area
- 3 bedrooms, 2 baths, 2-car side entry garage
- Slab foundation

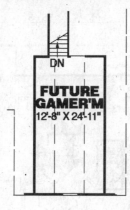

Optional
Second Floor

FUTURE GAMER'M
12'-8" X 24'-11"

DN

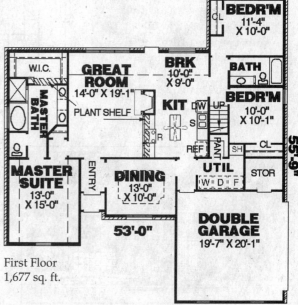

First Floor
1,677 sq. ft.

310

TO ORDER BLUEPRINTS USE THE FORM ON PAGE 15 OR CALL TOLL-FREE 1-877-671-6036
View thousands more home plans online at www.familyhandyman.com/homeplans

Large Master Suite

Plan #711-035D-0014

2,236 total square feet of living area

Price Code D

Special features

- Luxurious master suite has enormous sitting room with fireplace and vaulted private bath
- Cozy family room off kitchen/breakfast area
- Two secondary bedrooms share a bath
- 3 bedrooms, 2 1/2 baths, 2-car side entry garage
- Walk-out basement or crawl space foundation, please specify when ordering

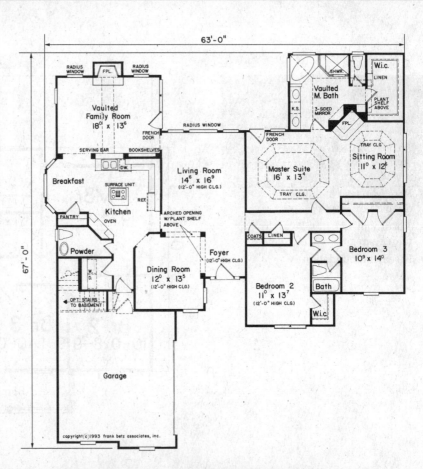

TO ORDER BLUEPRINTS USE THE FORM ON PAGE 15 OR CALL TOLL-FREE 1-877-671-6036
View thousands more home plans online at www.familyhandyman.com/homeplans

311

Enchanting Country Cottage — Plan #711-007D-0030

1,140 total square feet of living area

Price Code AA

Special features

- Open and spacious living and dining areas for family gatherings
- Well-organized kitchen with an abundance of cabinetry and a built-in pantry
- Roomy master bath features double-bowl vanity
- 3 bedrooms, 2 baths, 2-car drive under garage
- Basement foundation

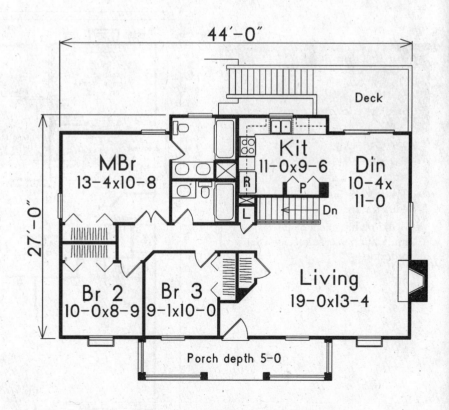

44'-0"

27'-0"

Deck

MBr 13-4x10-8

Kit 11-0x9-6

Din 10-4x 11-0

R P Dn L

Br 2 10-0x8-9

Br 3 9-1x10-0

Living 19-0x13-4

Porch depth 5-0

2,158 total square feet of living area   **Price Code C**

Special features

- Private master suite has walk-in closet and bath
- Sloped ceiling in family room adds drama
- Secondary bedrooms include 9' ceilings and walk-in closets
- Covered porch adds a charming touch
- 4 bedrooms, 3 baths, 2-car side entry garage
- Crawl space or slab foundation, please specify when ordering

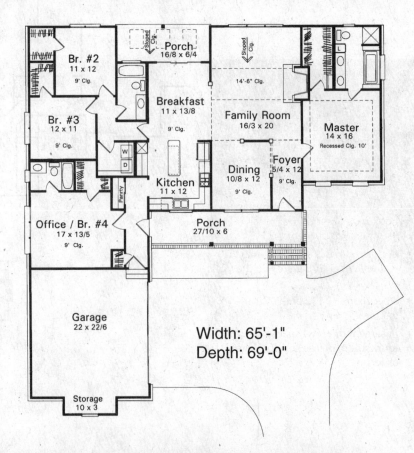

Br. #2
11 x 12
9' Clg.

Porch
16/8 x 6/4

Sloped Clg.

Sloped Clg.

14'-6" Clg.

Br. #3
12 x 11
9' Clg.

Breakfast
11 x 13/8
9' Clg.

Family Room
16/3 x 20

Master
14 x 16
Recessed Clg. 10'

W D

Kitchen
11 x 12

Dining
10/8 x 12
9' Clg.

Foyer
5/4 x 12
9' Clg.

Office / Br. #4
17 x 13/5
9' Clg.

Porch
27/10 x 6

Garage
22 x 22/6

Width: 65'-1"
Depth: 69'-0"

Storage
10 x 3

Irresistible Farmhouse

Plan #711-013D-0035

2,484 total square feet of living areaa

Price Code D

Special features

- Convenient first floor master bedroom features two walk-in closets and a dramatic bath with whirlpool tub and separate vanities
- Living room has 18' ceiling with a radius top window, decorative columns and a plant shelf
- Family room includes built-in bookcases and double French doors leading to an outdoor deck
- Bonus room has an additional 262 square feet of living area on the second floor
- 3 bedrooms, 2 1/2 baths, 2-car garage
- Basement or crawl space foundation, please specify when ordering

Second Floor
598 sq. ft.

First Floor
1,886 sq. ft.

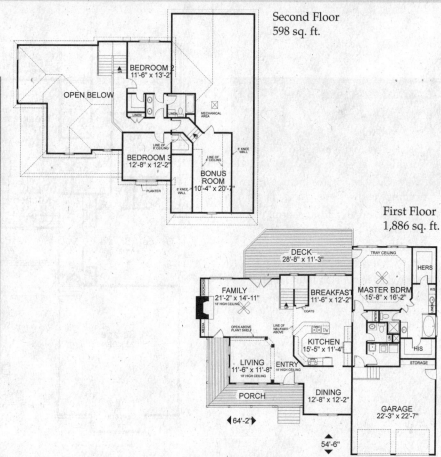

314

TO ORDER BLUEPRINTS USE THE FORM ON PAGE 15 OR CALL TOLL-FREE 1-877-671-6036
View thousands more home plans online at www.familyhandyman.com/homeplans

2,578 total square feet of living area   **Price Code D**

Special features

- Enormous entry has an airy feel with gallery area nearby
- Living room with bay window is tucked away from traffic areas
- Large kitchen and breakfast area both access covered patio
- Great room has an entertainment center, fireplace and cathedral ceiling
- 4 bedrooms, 3 1/2 baths, 3-car side entry garage
- Slab foundation

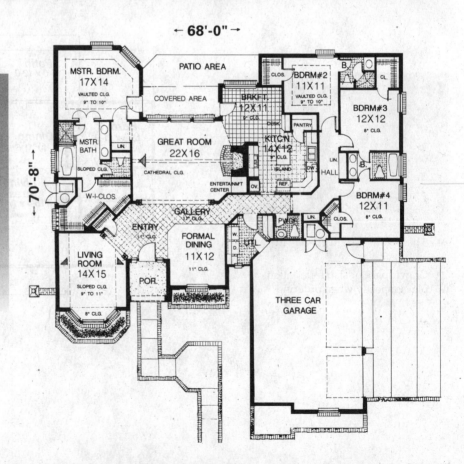

TO ORDER BLUEPRINTS USE THE FORM ON PAGE 15 OR CALL TOLL-FREE 1-877-671-6036
View thousands more home plans online at www.familyhandyman.com/homeplans

315

1,675 total square feet of living area

Price Code B

Special features

- Country accents give this home curb appeal
- Spacious laundry room is located off master bedroom
- Cathedral ceiling in living area
- Alternate floor plan design includes handicap accessibility that is 100% ADA compliant
- 3 bedrooms, 2 baths, 2-car side entry garage
- Crawl space or slab foundation, please specify when ordering

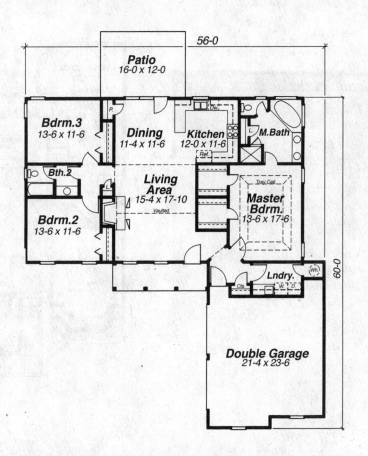

1,546 total square feet of living area

Price Code C

Special features

- Spacious, open rooms create a casual atmosphere
- Master bedroom is secluded for privacy
- Dining room features large bay window
- Kitchen and dinette combine for added space and include access to the outdoors
- Large laundry room includes convenient sink
- 3 bedrooms, 2 baths, 2-car garage
- Basement foundation

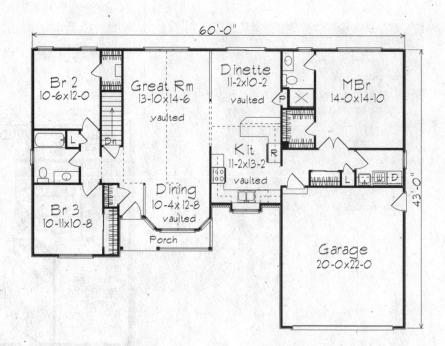

60'-0"

Br 2
10-6x12-0

Great Rm
13-10x14-6
vaulted

Dinette
11-2x10-2
vaulted

MBr
14-0x14-10

Kit
11-2x13-2
vaulted

Dining
10-4x12-8
vaulted

Br 3
10-11x10-8

Porch

Garage
20-0x22-0

43'-0"

TO ORDER BLUEPRINTS USE THE FORM ON PAGE 15 OR CALL TOLL-FREE 1-877-671-6036
View thousands more home plans online at www.familyhandyman.com/HOMEPLANS

317

1,191 total square feet of living area

Price Code AA

Special features

- Energy efficient home with 2" x 6" exterior walls
- Master bedroom located near living areas for maximum convenience
- Living room has cathedral ceiling and stone fireplace
- 3 bedrooms, 2 baths, 2-car side entry garage
- Crawl space foundation, drawings also include slab foundation

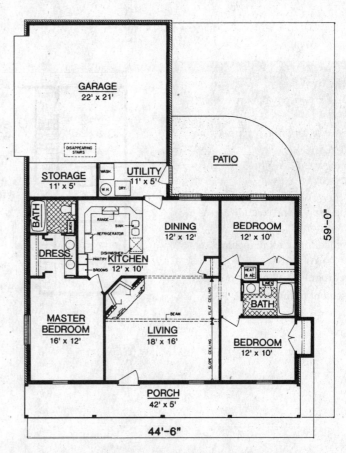

GARAGE
22' x 21'

DISAPPEARING STAIRS

STORAGE
11' x 5'

UTILITY
11' x 5'

PATIO

WASH.
DRY.

BATH

DINING
12' x 12'

BEDROOM
12' x 10'

DRESS.

KITCHEN
12' x 10'

RANGE
SINK
REFRIGERATOR
DISHWASHER
PANTRY
BROOMS

HEAT & AC

BATH

MASTER BEDROOM
16' x 12'

BEAM

LIVING
18' x 16'

BEDROOM
12' x 10'

PORCH
42' x 5'

44'-6"

59'-0"

Convenient Pool Bath

Plan #711-047D-0046

2,597 total square feet of living area

Price Code D

Special features

- Angled design creates unlimited views and spaces that appear larger
- Den/bedroom #4 makes a perfect home office or guest suite
- Island kitchen with view to nook and family room includes a walk-in pantry
- Pool bath is shared by outdoor and indoor areas
- 4 bedrooms, 3 baths, 3-car rear entry garage
- Slab foundation

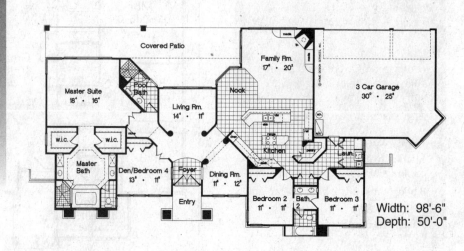

TO ORDER BLUEPRINTS USE THE FORM ON PAGE 15 OR CALL TOLL-FREE 1-877-671-6036
View thousands more home plans online at www.familyhandyman.com/homeplans

319

The Family Handyman

2,723 total square feet of living area

Price Code E

Special features

- Large porch invites you into an elegant foyer which accesses a vaulted study with private hall and coat closet
- Great room is second to none, comprised of fireplace, built-in shelves, vaulted ceiling and a 1 1/2 story window wall
- A spectacular hearth room with vaulted ceiling and masonry fireplace opens to an elaborate kitchen featuring two snack bars, cooking island and walk-in pantry
- 3 bedrooms, 2 1/2 baths, 3-car side entry garage
- Basement foundation

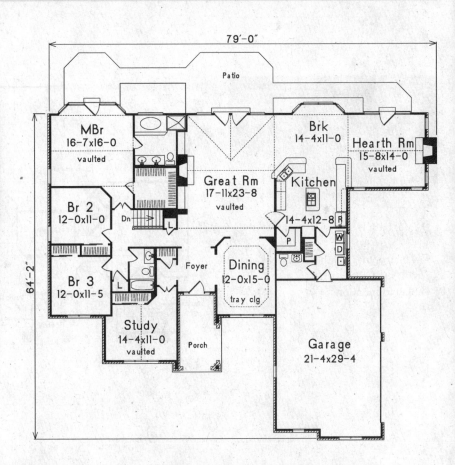

79'-0"

Patio

MBr
16-7x16-0
vaulted

Brk
14-4x11-0

Hearth Rm
15-8x14-0
vaulted

Br 2
12-0x11-0

Great Rm
17-11x23-8
vaulted

Kitchen
14-4x12-8

Dn

64'-2"

Br 3
12-0x11-5

Foyer

Dining
12-0x15-0
tray clg

Study
14-4x11-0
vaulted

Porch

Garage
21-4x29-4

TO ORDER BLUEPRINTS USE THE FORM ON PAGE 15 OR CALL TOLL-FREE 1-877-671-6036
View thousands more home plans online at www.familyhandyman.com/homeplans

320